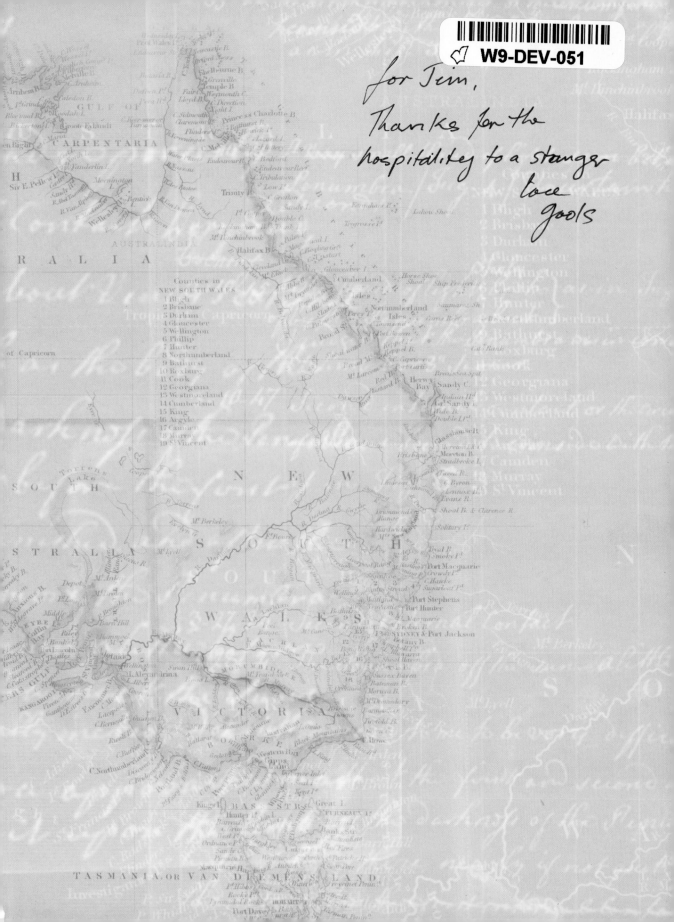

for Jim,

Thanks for the

hospitality to a stranger

love

gools

TONY ROBINSON'S
History of Australia

from New Holland to Neighbours

TONY ROBINSON'S
HISTORY OF Australia

from New Holland to Neighbours

VIKING
an imprint of
PENGUIN BOOKS

For my wonderful wife, Louise,
my companion on our Australian adventure and through life

Contents

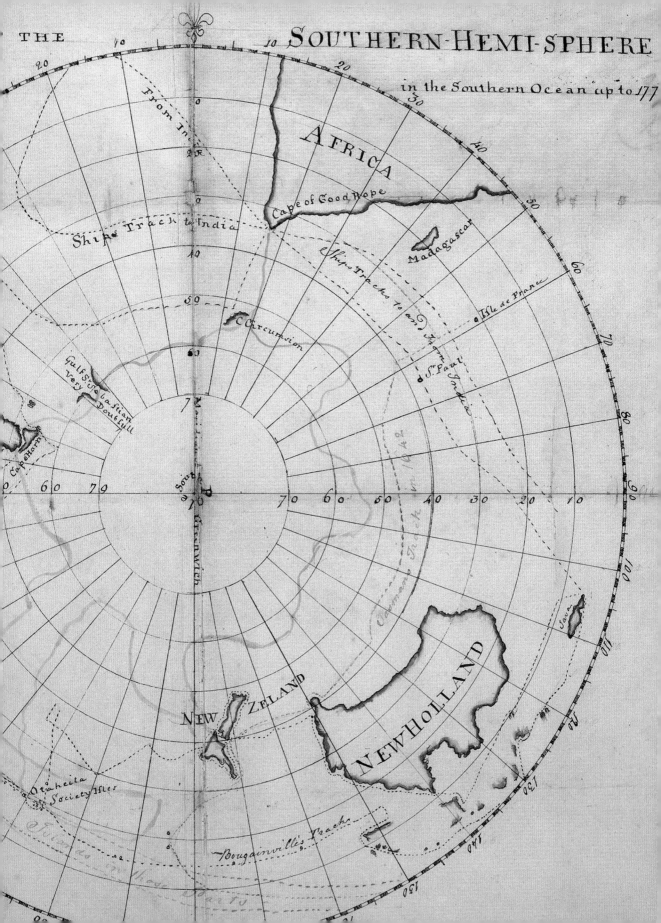

THE SOUTHERN-HEMI-SPHERE

in the Southern Ocean up to 177

AFRICA

Cape of Good Hope

Madagascar

Ships Track to India

From India

Ships Tracks to and from China

Isle de France

St Paul India

C. Circumcision

Gulf St. Sebastian Very Doubtfull

Cape Horn

South Pole

Meridian of Greenwich

Tasmans Track in 1642

Java

NEW ZELAND

NEWHOLLAND

Otaheita Society Isles

Bougainville's Track

Introduction

When I was a little boy I learnt about the heroes of the British Empire from a procession of monumental coloured prints stapled to the walls of the upstairs corridor of my primary school. Every day I was confronted by Gordon of Khartoum being butchered at dawn by Sudanese fanatics, Clive of India relieving the siege of Trichinopoly, and Stanley presuming that the sickly man he had just bumped into on the shores of Lake Tanganyika was indeed Dr Livingstone.

But the print which stuck in my mind most indelibly (and it's a tough call because they were all pretty awesome), was 'Captain Cook Discovers Australia'. It showed a whey-faced man in a white wig and old-fashioned sailor's uniform standing nobly at the prow of his ship as it approached a deserted, sandy beach that swept majestically from the top right of the picture to the bottom left.

For a child whose only experiences of beaches were the sharp stones of Clacton-on-Sea, and the estuary mud of Southend, I was in awe of Cook's bravery. To sail for thousands of miles through unchartered waters on behalf of my nation, in order to discover a totally empty piece of seaside of such inestimable quality, ranked him in my eyes alongside Biggles, Dan Dare and The Lone Ranger. But it was only after several terms-worth of traipsing up and down that corridor that I realised the beach in question wasn't as empty as I'd originally thought. Tucked away in the shadows of the dense stands of trees which fringed this paradise were several

LEFT: Map of the Southern Hemisphere showing the discoveries made in the Southern Ocean up to 1770, by Captain James Cook

pairs of eyes, attached to which were squat, dusky bodies drawn in scribbled cross-hatching, looking like aliens knitted out of dark brown wool.

This then was my introduction to Australia and its people – a land of unsurpassable beauty, a gift freely given to the people of Great Britain, but with some rather indistinguishable and slightly scary-looking figures hidden in the shadows.

Fifty years later when I was asked to visit Australia to write a book and make a television programme about its history I, like Cook, jumped at the opportunity. I knew it would be absurd for me to attempt a comprehensive tome on the scale of Robert Hughes' *The Fatal Shore* or Frank Welsh's *Great Southern Land*. Like the redoubtable Captain I would have to approach my subject in ignorance rather than with wisdom, and in a way I was even more disadvantaged than Captain Cook: his ignorance was total whereas mine was illuminated by Skippy the kangaroo, Baz Luhrmann's *Australia*, and the exploits of Madge and Harold in *Neighbours*.

I was convinced that the best strategy would be for me to approach this awesome island continent with an open heart and an open mind, to divest myself of any clichéd visions and prejudices which might cloud my eyes, to read voraciously, to make copious notes in my battered and dusty journal, to listen closely to the people I met, and then to knit together a narrative history while trying to recreate some of the sense of wonder and discovery I experienced on my journey. This is what I have tried to do, and it is in that spirit that I offer you, the reader, this book.

Tony Robinson

Before 1770

The Inhabitants of this Country are the Miserablest People in the World

Hook, Not Cook

My first ever visit to the theatre was to see *Peter Pan*, J M Barrie's cloying tale of middle-class Edwardian children, tinkly fairies and unreconstructed Red Indians. The play was pottering along in its own rather tedious fashion, when suddenly onto the stage burst a fearsome, loquacious and hilariously funny pirate. My evening was completely

BELOW: *The Landing of Dampier,* by Norman Lindsay, c 1925

transformed. 'How,' I remember asking myself, 'could this terrifying captain, with his even more terrifying hook, possibly occupy the same universe as Wendy, Tinker Bell and a large cuddly dog called Nana?'

I had a similar feeling of disjuncture when I discovered that the first Englishman to land in Australia was not the austere and highly respectable Captain Cook, but a free-wheeling adventurer in the Captain Hook mould, who nearly a hundred years previously had set foot on Australia's northern coast and declared it to be absolutely ghastly. 'If it were not for that sort of pleasure which results from the discovery of the barrenest spot upon the globe, this coast would not have charmed me much,' he avowed. His name was William Dampier, and like Hook he was bewigged, dysfunctional and more than a little ridiculous.

The Bullshit Artist

Dampier's life was the stuff of boys' adventure yarns. He was born in Somerset and orphaned at an early age, was sent to sea, and by his early twenties was a battle-hardened sea-salt with Dutch blood on his hands. He left the navy to manage a large estate in Jamaica but developed a loathing for the slave trade, and so in a magnificent gesture of Christian high-mindedness became a pirate instead.

He spent his next fifteen years living a life of derring-do, stopping off in Mexico, Peru, Chile, Virginia, California and the Galapagos Islands like a stoned young backpacker

endlessly drifting from one bunch of mates to the next.

Then in 1686 he crossed the Pacific for the first time, as a crew member of the *Cygnet*. After six months of drunkenness, debauchery and violence in the Philippines, he and the majority of the crew mutinied, abandoned the ship's captain in Mindanao and took the *Cygnet* on to China and from there to the Spice Islands (which we now call the Malukus, or the Moluccas).

They then set course for a vaguely known land to the south called New Holland, partly to investigate it but also to patch the leaks in the ship's rotting hull. There the *Cygnet* stayed for the next few weeks, with the crew living on the rice they'd brought with them, supplemented by local turtle, barramundi and sea cow.

Unfortunately, Dampier couldn't stand the locals. The Aboriginal men threatened the crew with spears, and the women cried and kept their children hidden. Dampier's opinion was that 'the inhabitants of this country are the miserablest people in the world. The Hodmadods of Monomatapa, though a nasty people, yet for wealth are gentlemen to these.'

Had the map that Dampier drew of the north Australian coast survived, it would have become an icon of world cartography, a profound aid to generations of navigators who negotiated its difficult waters, but predictably he lost it when he jumped ship in the Nicobar Islands, leaving the 'mad crew' of the *Cygnet* behind him. After several more adventures worthy of the great Baron Münchausen, he returned to England in 1691, and it

was then that his life was completely transformed. Like so many of these early trans-global adventurers, he got himself a book deal.

His skills as a sailor and leader of men may have left something to be desired, but he was a great bullshit artist and a superb storyteller. His rollicking tales of near-death experiences captured the public's attention and he became not only a best-selling author but a celebrity. Within two years of its publication, *A New Voyage Round the World* was republished four times and sparked a vogue for travel writing. As for the phrase 'the Hodmadods of Monomatapa', if it has the ring of familiarity that may be because Jonathan Swift loved the book so much that it inspired him to write *Gulliver's Travels*, in which the fictional voyager Lemuel Gulliver

discovers exotic races like the Lilliputians, the Brobdingnagians and the Glubbdubdribians.

One of the aspects of Dampier's book that particularly enthralled the public was his use of language. He was a great collector, not only of exotic bits and bobs, but also of vocabulary. He peppered his book with exotic local words that described his discoveries, and more than a thousand of them have since found their way into common English usage. For instance, if you and your *posse* wanted to pick up your *chopsticks*, knock up a *cashew* and *avocado tortilla*, and throw an *albatross* on the *barbeque*, you'd be hard-pressed to describe what you were doing without Dampier's contributions to our language.

Dampier's reputation had been miraculously transformed from that of a pirate to a respectable authority on the South Seas. The admiralty not only sought his advice on exploring the region, but also bestowed on him the rank of captain and gave him his own ship to command, HMS *Roebuck*.

In January 1699 he set off once more to explore the seven seas – and where did he go this time? Well, he may have been less than impressed by 'New Holland' first time round, but despite hideous privations he headed there again and made detailed observations of the local wildlife and plants. But he remained unenthusiastic. He described Australia's coast as low and sandy, with no fresh water and scarcely any animals, except one which looked like a racoon and jumped about on its hind legs.

He had also planned a major exploration of the continent's eastern seaboard, but by this time the *Roebuck* was leaking so badly he was forced to turn back towards England. This was a typical Dampier voyage: his men were suffering from the heat and began to display symptoms of scurvy, his ship was rotting around him, and the garbage in the bilges was fermenting in the tropical air. The *Roebuck* finally ran aground near Ascension Island and he and his crew, like drunks queuing for the last bus, had to wait over a month for a ship to come along and rescue them. It was an ignominious end to what might have been a glorious post-piracy career.

On Dampier's return home, things fared even worse. He was court-martialled for cruelty to a crew member and found guilty, for which his pay for the voyage was docked and he was declared unfit to command any of His Majesty's ships ever again.

But his writing career went from strength to strength, and his book *Capt. Dampier's Vindication of his Voyage to the South Seas* became another big hit. And finally he had the success at sea he must always have craved, not as a captain but as sailing master under the privateer Captain Woodes Rogers. The expedition amassed a staggering £170000 in plunder – nearly $30 million in today's money! But typically, Dampier's triumph was marred by the fact that he died before he was able to collect his share of the cash.

William Dampier's exploits don't make him a revered figure in the story of Australia – indeed, it could be argued that he was so negative about New Holland's potential that other explorers were deterred from investigating it. But his enduringly popular writing surely contributed to a continuing European fascination with the Great Southern Land, and it was only a matter of time before such curiosity would be satisfied.

Horror in New Holland

The fact that Dampier already knew of the existence of this vast swathe of land, and also knew it was called New Holland, undermines the wholly British notion that Cook was the great discoverer who brought Australia into Europe's consciousness, and thus, as far as the Europeans were concerned, into being.

The reality is that for three centuries the European powers had jostled for supremacy just north of Australia in the seas of South-East Asia. The prize for which they were prepared to invest so much money and so many ships was control of the lucrative spice trade between Asia and Europe.

In the seventeenth century it had been the Spanish and the Dutch who were prepared to risk their lives for the lure of cinnamon, nutmeg and all those other little coloured powders that grace our spice racks. Great seamen like the Dutchman Abel Tasman had made unbelievably dangerous voyages of discovery with only rudimentary navigational equipment. But not all of these journeys ended happily; indeed, one culminated in a grizzly tragedy of epic proportions.

The story of the Dutch ship *Batavia* begins, like that of the *Titanic*, with

high expectations, a state-of-the-art ship on its maiden voyage, opulence, excitement and crowded decks full of excited faces. But there the similarity ends. Whereas the *Titanic* is a tale of natural disaster, the *Batavia* is an essay in human evil.

In 1629, fifty years before Dampier first landed in Australia, the *Batavia* set off from North Holland loaded with gold and silver to buy spices in the East Indies. Onboard were merchants, settlers and a bankrupt pharmacist called Jeronimus Cornelisz, who was fleeing the Netherlands to avoid arrest as a heretic.

During the voyage, Jeronimus cooked up a plan to hijack the ship, steal the loot and sail away to start a new life. But before his mutiny could come to fruition, a storm blew

RIGHT: A Dutch engraving of the massacre after the wreck of the *Batavia*, 1647

up and smashed the ship onto a reef off western Australia. Thirty-two of those onboard were drowned, but 268 passengers and crew survived and were taken to nearby islands in the ship's longboats. Their troubles were only just beginning: they couldn't find any fresh water, and the only food available was the unappetising flesh of sea lions and seagulls.

The ship's commander felt he had no alternative other than to set out with some of his men in the longboats in order to try to find help, leaving the other survivors praying that they hadn't been abandoned. Miraculously, after a terrifying thirty-three-day journey through hostile seas, they made it to present-day Jakarta without serious mishap.

A rescue ship was organised and two months later it arrived in New Holland. But the rescuers weren't greeted by happy, smiling castaways – instead they found themselves in the middle of a bloody massacre.

In a plot twist worthy of a 1970s horror movie, the fanatical potential-mutineer Jeronimus Cornelisz had assumed charge of the survivors. Fearing reprisals for his part in the threatened mutiny, he sent the ship's soldiers off to explore a nearby isle they named 'High Island', in order to look for water. He then marooned them there, expecting them to die of thirst.

Now he was able to exercise complete control over the other castaways, assisted by a gang of murderous followers, young men who he kitted up in red and gold uniforms plundered from the ship's stores. He ordered all available water

and weapons to be placed under his command, then began to execute those who he thought might stand in the way of his plans to hijack any rescue boat and sail off in it with the gold.

The killing spree was soon so out of control that his men found any flimsy excuse to murder men, women and children, adding drowning and strangulation to their gruesome repertoire of death. Ultimately, they even abandoned the pretence of having to think up a reason, and killed simply for pleasure or to relieve their boredom.

Meanwhile, Jeronimus looked on, never actually taking part in the killing (apart from one horrifically botched incident when he attempted but failed to murder a baby) but, like despots throughout history, demonstrating that he felt absolutely justified in unleashing this terror. As far as he was concerned, his actions were a virtuous necessity – he only had enough supplies for forty-five people, so the rest had to be sacrificed for the greater good.

But Jeronimus's plan had one fatal flaw. The marooned soldiers hadn't perished. Instead, they had found a plentiful supply of water and fresh food, and when they learnt from fleeing survivors about the carnage on the mainland, they quickly collected wood from the wrecked boat and erected a fort.

Once Jeronimus became aware that they were alive and had water, he mounted a series of attacks on them.

The soldiers only had rudimentary weapons, which they had made from timber and the metal hoops off barrels that had washed up onto the island. But they managed to fend off the attacks until the rescue ship arrived, whereupon both sides immediately became embroiled in a desperate race to be the first onboard it to tell their side of the story. The soldiers won, joined forces with the rescuers and, after a brief battle, all the mutineers were captured.

It wasn't considered necessary to wait for their return to Jakarta before holding a trial. It took place there and then. The worst offenders were executed, and Jeronimus and several of the most culpable mutineers were hanged after having their hands hacked off with a chisel and a hammer. Two hundred and ten people had died before the last survivors finally made it to the safety of the Dutch East Indies.

Two lesser offenders, a seaman and a cabin boy, were pardoned execution but instead were left marooned on the mainland. Their ultimate fate is unknown, although later British settlers told tales of unusually light-skinned Aboriginals in the area, whom they believed were descendants of the two abandoned mutineers.

The Eunuch Admiral

The Dutch aren't the only candidates for the title of being the first Europeans to land in Australia. That honour may well belong to the Portuguese. They were based in the Spice Islands, and hence were relatively close by. In the sixteenth century they were the world's foremost sailors and navigators, so it seems improbable that they wouldn't have bumped into the Australian coast, even if only by accident. Unfortunately for Portuguese national pride, though, most of their early records were destroyed in the Great Lisbon Earthquake of 1755, so a Portuguese discovery of Australia doesn't feature very large in the history books. But tantalising clues do exist, including Aboriginal rock paintings of what appear to be early Portuguese ships, and a silver coin dated 1597 that was found in a snake-infested swamp on Queensland's Stradbroke Island.

But of course, all this is a shamelessly Eurocentric view of the various adventurers who have landed in Australia over the millennia. Traders from New Guinea and the Torres Strait Islands have left evidence of their presence. It's even possible that the Maori made it across from New Zealand. And there was one incentive for which plucky sailors from Indonesia were only too happy to risk their lives – not territorial advantage or fertile pastures, but sex aids! For centuries, traders crossed the open sea to harvest sea cucumbers on Australia's coast for their aphrodisiac qualities, so they could sell them at a high price to wealthy detumescent Chinese men.

TOP: Chinese admiral eunuch Zheng He, possibly an early visitor in 1421
ABOVE: Sadly, even a barrel full of sea cucumbers wouldn't have solved the admiral's problem

Early Arrivals

1606 – First authenticated arrival of Europeans in Australian territory. Dutch ship Duyfken *skippered by Willem Janszoon gets lost in the Torres Strait Islands. Janszoon maps coastline of Cape York and lands in the Gulf of Carpentaria. Nine crew murdered by natives.*

1607 – Spaniard Pedro Fernandez de Queirós petitions the Spanish King for three ships to search for the southern continent. His men see the mountains on Cape York Peninsula but believe them to be islands. Comes within a few miles of Australia but doesn't land – duh!

1616 – Dirk Hartog lands on an island just off western Australia – leaves a pewter plate behind!

1629 – The wreck of the Batavia.

1642 – Dutch explorer Abel Tasman claims Van Diemen's Land (present-day Tasmania) for Holland.

1644 – Tasman explores northern Australia from Cape York to North West Cape, hence the name New Holland. N.B. By this stage the Dutch have effectively mapped all of Australia except its east coast – but virtually ignore it as they don't see any financial gain in doing so.

1688 – Dampier's first Australian landing.

1696 – Willem de Vlamingh commands rescue mission to find survivors from the Ridderschap van Holland, *lost two years previously. Sails up the Swan River. Visits Dirk Hartog's Island and replaces Hartog's plate with one that records both visits.*

1699 – Dampier's second Australia landing.

1768 – Louis Antoine de Bougainville hopes to claim the east coast of Australia for France, but hits heavy breakers off the Great Barrier Reef and sails away again.

1770 – Captain Cook arrives in Botany Bay.

And there may well have been early visitors from even further afield. Ancient Chinese texts referred to a 'Great Ocean Continent' in the 'Southern Seas' and describe animals that appear to be the kangaroo and the koala. The Chinese were certainly capable of sailing that far from their homeland. During the Ming Dynasty in the early 1400s, the Ming navy had a well-established trading post at one of the southernmost islands of Indonesia, as close to Australia as the sea-cucumber traders' base. It's thought that in 1421 the emperor's admiral, a eunuch called Zheng who had command of the emperor's mighty ocean-going ships, landed in northern Australia.

You've probably noticed, though, that I've begun using qualifying terms like 'it's thought', 'may well', 'apparently' and 'it's possible', which are a sure sign that the writer is on shaky ground. The reality that is what we know about these early discoveries is clouded, tempered and dwarfed by what we *don't* know. But there is one theory about an early visitor that blows all other competitors clear out of the water . . .

Australia and the Pharaoh's Son

Around four thousand years ago, sailors from Ancient Egypt landed in Australia. An expedition led by the Pharaoh's son, Lord Djes-eb, became shipwrecked off the coast of what's now New South Wales. The survivors headed west, battered by wind, rain, desert and flies, until the prince was bitten by a poisonous snake, died and was buried in a tomb.

How do we know this? Jake Cassar, youth worker, former pub bouncer and wildlife guide, took me for a walk through the bush he's known all his life, an hour's drive from Sydney, and showed me something I certainly wasn't expecting to see in Australia – Egyptian hieroglyphics hidden away among the dense thickets of eucalyptus. And they weren't just the occasional few scribbles of graffiti, like the random prehistoric scratches archaeologists get so excited about in England. This was a complete Egyptian novel etched in to the rocks – bird-headed priests, vipers, quails, even phalluses. All of which, according to at least one now-dead Australian Egyptologist, tell the story of Djes-eb's fatal journey.

'He was killed while carrying the Golden Falcon standard up front in a foreign land,' the writing apparently says. (See, I used that word 'apparently' again.) 'He who died is here laid to rest. He will never again stand beside the waters of Sacred Love.'

I like Jake – he's got that traditional Australian 'can-do' optimism about him and is fiercely protective of his little bit of bush. And he's not daft. He's well aware that if these carvings are authentic, the history of the ancient world will have to be completely rewritten. So I had to challenge him.

'It's not very likely that the Ancient Egyptians would have had the technology to build a ship that could sail across the Pacific, is it?'

'Well, if the Maori could sail from Polynesia to New Zealand, and

ABOVE: Jake Cassar and his bush tour of 'ancient' Egyptian carvings

the Aboriginals could get across to Darwin from Asia, why shouldn't the Egyptians be capable of something similar?' he replied.

'Yes, but the carvings look really fresh, and they're obviously not all the work of the same person.'

'I know it looks like that,' admitted Jake. 'But they were probably re-carved a few years ago by a couple of blokes who were stopped by the national park rangers with chisels in their hands.'

'What! What!' I went. 'There have been blokes here with chisels? Come on, Jake!'

'Look,' he said. 'They couldn't have carved them from scratch, could they? What's the chances that a couple of ordinary Aussie blokes out in the bush would have known how to write all this stuff? Pretty slim, mate.'

Jake, and a lot of people like him, are determined to believe this story is true. But I'm an old English sceptic. The idea that an ancient Egyptian civilisation could have discovered Australia four thousand years ago is just very, very daft. Except, of course, it reveals what I think is an important point – we all yearn to have exotic and magical ancestors. The irony is that the Australians don't have to look to Ancient Egypt for a long-ago cultural fix. Thousands of years before Cook, Dampier, the Indonesian sea-cucumber harvesters and the Chinese eunuch admiral were around, a truly glorious manifestation of early human life blossomed in Australia, and we can prove it with absolute certainty because it's still there today.

Just minutes away from the Egyptian carvings, on the walls of a little cave, are a series of ancient handprints – the mark of the Aboriginals who have occupied this landscape for tens of thousands of years. Like their owners, these prints are largely hidden from view, but they tell the real magical story of early Australia.

The Very First Arrivals

Some sixty thousand years ago, during one of those periods of dramatic climate change with which we've all recently become so familiar, sea levels in Australasia plunged by more than 100 metres, and Australia and New Guinea became joined together. If your Pleistocene ancestors had wanted to get from Jakarta to Darwin, they would have had to take a succession of hazardous journeys on bamboo rafts, wade through a few rivers, and do a hell of a lot of walking.

It was along this so-called 'land bridge' that the ancestors of the present-day Australian Aboriginals came to the continent, and they quickly spread all over it until they'd inhabited even its most inhospitable corners. Forty-thousand-year-old tools and fossils have been found in south-west Australia; five thousand years later there were Aboriginals in the south-east and (having crossed another land bridge) in Tasmania too.

Then, ten thousand years ago, when the earth entered a period of global warming, the seas rose and separated the giant landmass from New Guinea again. Australia was virtually cut off from the rest of the world.

These early Aboriginal travellers

RIGHT: Aboriginal rock painting with hand prints, at a protected location in NSW

ABOVE: Ancient
Aboriginal rock art
in a remote area of
the Northern Territory

lived in an *Avatar*-like world of giant kangaroos, marsupial lions, huge lizards and enormous sloths. They made maps of the land they inhabited, not like a *UBD Road Atlas* of New South Wales, but from the songlines they sang, painted, danced and talked about, which not only described the location of hills, waterholes and other landmarks but also explained their creation and purpose. Their whole land was a mythical, ceremonial landscape, and the songlines they navigated to criss-cross it also told of their 'dreaming', their eternal stories of the natural world around them and the life within it.

Am I falling into the European trap of idolising the lives of ancient people? Maybe. It was certainly no Garden of Eden; life could be unbelievably hard. There were disputes, vendettas, sexual transgressions and jealousies that caused mayhem, as they do in any society. But by and large, until the white sails of the European ships began to flutter in the bays of Australia, Aboriginal society had, by any measure, been a remarkably long-lasting and stable culture. Is it any wonder that the first words spoken to Captain Cook by the inhabitants of Botany Bay were 'Go away!'?

1769–1770

The Most Humane Men
Will Censure My Conduct

Secret Orders

1769 was going to be a big year for the scientists of Europe. On 3rd June, Venus was due to pass between the Earth and the sun, an event that wouldn't be repeated for a hundred years. And if this phenomenon could be scrutinised from enough different places, it would be possible to work out the precise distance from the Earth to Venus and from the Earth to the sun. This information may seem a little arcane to us, however not only were the scientists at the British Royal Society – those standard-bearers of eighteenth-century enlightenment and reason – eager to learn more about the mysteries of the universe, but

BELOW: *The Bark, Earl of Pembroke, later Endeavour, leaving Whitby Harbour in 1768*, by Thomas Luny, c 1790

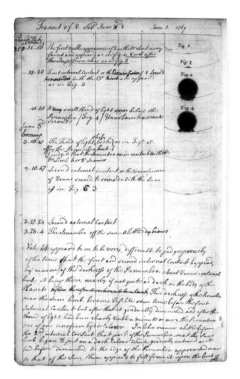

the knowledge gained would be of enormous value to long-distance seafarers. It would assist navigators in the complicated calculations they had to make when they were far out at sea without a glimpse of land.

In order to observe this celestial event properly, a vantage point was needed in the furthest extremities of the Southern Hemisphere. But the scientific community wasn't alone in their desire for information from below the equator. The British Admiralty was particularly interested in supporting this quest for celestial data for reasons of defence, national security and, not to put too fine a point on it, the expansion of the Empire.

For centuries it had been assumed that somewhere in the South Seas lay a massive continent, a Terra Australis, which would counter-balance the weight of all the northern continents, preventing the Earth from disintegrating. But where could it be? Had foreign sailors or pirates come upon it in the past, but failed to grasp its full extent? Or did it lie languishing and unexplored, somewhere far from prying Dutch and Portuguese eyes, waiting to be possessed by the manly young officers of the British Navy?

A joint enterprise was agreed on. The Admiralty and the Royal Society would put together an expedition to the South Seas half a world away, to observe the Venus event from Tahiti. This would be such a difficult and dangerous expedition that, in order to pull it off, a robust ship and a captain with first-rate navigational skills were required. But what only the Admiralty knew was that this officer would be given additional top-secret orders that he would be instructed not to open until his scientific mission had been accomplished.

The vessel in which the Admiralty invested was no *QE2*; it was a square stern-backed, single-bottomed tub originally called the *Earl of Pembroke*, but now rechristened HMS *Endeavour*, a name deemed more suitable for its epic mission. It was a mere thirty-two metres long and nine metres broad. For the crew, finding enough space to sleep each night would be a major challenge.

In order to fit out this little collier for her hazardous journey, she was towed to 'Mr Bird's Shipway' and her hull was fitted with thick felt and wooden boards to protect her against the voracious jaws of hungry tropical shipworms. This was a ship designed for hazardous tasks in alien waters, not to flutter the hearts of a nation.

ABOVE LEFT: Notes in Cook's journal recording the transit of Venus, 3rd June 1769
RIGHT: Portrait of Captain James Cook, by William Hodges, c.1775, thought to be a true likeness as it's one of the few painted by someone who knew him well

ABOVE: Fresh off the *Endeavour*, grabbing some much needed scurvy-beating sauerkraut on a hotdog from Sydney's famous Harry's Cafe de Wheels

But if the ship was unglamorous, its captain was even more so. James Cook was the epitome of the dour Yorkshireman. He was born in Middlesbrough, the son of a farm labourer, and at the age of sixteen began work not as a midshipman (as you might have expected of someone destined to become a Royal Navy captain), but as a grocer's boy. He then entered the coal trade, working on board colliers like the *Earl of Pembroke*, which plied their trade between London and Newcastle. But this distinctly unpromising apprenticeship stood him in good stead, because it was at this time that he started studying navigation, a discipline for which he had a rare talent. He was a deeply driven, ambitious young man; indeed, he once said he intended to go not only 'farther than any man has been before me, but as far as I think it is possible for a man to go'.

Soon he was promoted to ship's mate in charge of navigation. Then, just before the Seven Years War broke out between the British and the French, Cook volunteered for the Royal Navy. He saw action in Canada and his navigational skills began to attract the attention of his superiors. He not only surveyed the entrance to the Saint Lawrence River, allowing General Wolfe to make his legendary if slightly sneaky attack on Quebec at the Battle of the Plains of Abraham, but also, over the next five years, often in hideously adverse conditions, produced the first large-scale and accurate maps of the entire jagged coast of Newfoundland.

Given his humble beginnings, Cook didn't have the connections that helped aristocratic young gentlemen gain advancement. Nevertheless, his highly detailed, painstaking and arduous work paid off, and he was offered the post of master of the enterprise. But he was not at this time a captain, even though that's the title with which we so strongly associate him. He wasn't even a first lieutenant, although he was hastily made one in order to lead the expedition.

So what kind of leader would this taciturn, untried Northerner prove to be? He certainly wasn't going to dazzle his subordinates with his charisma. He was thoughtful and serious, and with his towering frame topped by a small head and a big nose, was the embodiment of the quietly confident and rather dull middle-manager. He was seldom fit, suffering from rheumatism, a swelling in his groin and an extremely unpleasant ailment called tenesmus, which made his bowel movements intensely difficult and very painful. This must have been particularly difficult for him on board the *Endeavour*, where it was virtually impossible to find even one moment of solitude. When the ship finally arrived at Botany Bay, the rolling dunes must have offered him intense relief after so many months of close proximity with his fellow officers.

Crammed on board the ship were ninety-four officers, crew, scientists, artists and a one-armed chef, as well as livestock, including a goat that, having already circumnavigated the globe, wasn't designated dish of the day but was treated as an honoured mascot. In fact once back in England the goat became as celebrated as

the returning humans. The British government gave her a pension and she was made a member of the Royal Society – the first animal, indeed the first female, to receive that honour.

This coal boat jam-packed with people and livestock hardly looked like part of an imperial navy that ruled the waves; indeed, when the *Endeavour* arrived at Rio de Janeiro to load more provisions, the crew were banned from landing because the local viceroy thought they must be spies or smugglers. But it was the right ship for the job and, under Cook's efficient and understated leadership, managed to get them to Tahiti seven weeks ahead of schedule. Not only that, but apart from the odd death and one suicide, everyone appears to have remained remarkably fit.

Any sensible sea captain knew that he could sail further and more effectively if his crew were in good

working order, but Cook took the attention to diet and wellbeing to a higher level. Scurvy was a horrible illness whose symptoms included pains in the joints, ulcers, teeth falling out, stinking breath and the failure of various internal organs. Dysentery was an afternoon in the park compared to scurvy. In the late 1700s it would sometimes kill up to a third of a ship's crew on long voyages, but Cook didn't lose a single man to it.

He believed the reason was sauerkraut. He swore by a diet of boiled sour cabbage supplemented by dried-pea soup, and was determined to ensure his men ate it too. His was a tough love; if crew members refused their daily portion he had them flogged. Later, though, these beatings were replaced by a bit of amateur psychology. He'd serve up a plate of the stuff to his officers and petty officers, then invite the lower ranks to take their fill, or miss out altogether. He wrote that the moment his men saw that their superiors put a value on sauerkraut, it became the most delicious dish in the world. I suspect he was a little deluded, though, and that his crew simply thought they'd better shovel the disgusting mess down to make sure he didn't start flogging them again.

The Tattooed Botanist

Although Cook was a big sauerkraut fan, it was another substance that proved far more effective in the fight against scurvy. Joseph Banks, a wealthy young botanist, wrote at the time:

'As I am now on the brink of going ashore after a long passage, thank God, in as good health as man can be, I shall fill a little paper in describing the means which I have taken to prevent the scurvy in particular. The ship was supplied by the Admiralty with sour-crout, of which I eat constantly, till our salted cabbage was opened, which I preferred as a pleasant substitute. Wort [a malt drink] was served out almost constantly, of this I drank a pint or more every evening, but all this did not so entirely check the distemper so as to prevent my feeling some small effect of it. About a fortnight ago my gums swelled, and some small pimples rose in the inside of my mouth which threatened to become ulcers, I then flew to the lemon juice . . . so that I took nearly six

ounces a day of it. The effect of this was surprising, in less than a week my gums became as firm as ever, and at this time I am troubled with nothing but a few pimples on my face, which have not deterred me from leaving off the juice entirely.'

With the benefit of hindsight, it's obvious that there would have been much higher levels of vitamin C, the cure and preventative for scurvy, in lemons than in cabbage, although pickled raw cabbage would still contain a reasonably high amount. How intriguing that in the relatively recent past, a medical cure which we now think of as commonplace should have been trialled, not by doctors in white coats, but by intelligent young laymen.

Once they arrived in Tahiti, the crew, in typical imperial fashion, set about building a fort armed with a four-pound cannon. They then put up a large tent that they used as their

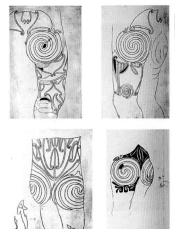

Pl. 8. Black Stains on the Skin called Tattoo

New Zealand

RIGHT: New Zealand Maori tattoos recorded by Joseph Banks, c.1769

Painted by Benjamin West.

Engraved by J R Smith.

M.ʳ BANKS.

Published 15 April 1773, by I. Hooper Nº 25 Ludgate Hill, and J. R. Smith Nº 4 Exeter Court, Exeter Change, Strand.

LEFT: The worldly Joseph Banks, engraved by J R Smith, c.1773, after a painting by Benjamin West

RIGHT: Artist Sydney Parkinson, who died on the *Endeavour*, had been employed to draw specimens by Banks, including this one named after his boss – the Banksia

observatory, with an astronomical clock in it. Facing it was one of the ship's clocks, and a set of reflecting telescopes was set up on a cask full of wet sand.

On the evening of Friday 2nd June everyone was on tenterhooks. They'd sailed halfway round the world to obtain their astronomical readings, but what would the visibility be like the following day? After all this time and effort, would they be forced to point their telescopes at nothing more than ranks of murky clouds? Dawn rose to reveal a blue sky and the scientists got to work.

But not all of those on board were primarily interested in the movements of the planets. Throughout his stay on Tahiti, Joseph Banks concentrated on the flora and fauna. Banks was in many ways the complete opposite of Cook. He had been educated at Harrow, Eton and Oxford, and had an impressive estate at Revesby Abbey

in Lincolnshire. He was a man with all the society connections that Cook lacked (for example, at the tender age of twenty-three he was made a Fellow of the Royal Society). But like Cook, he was an obsessive. From his youth he'd been passionate about all things botanical; when he was a university student he'd even paid out of own pocket for the Cambridge academic Israel Lyons to come to Oxford to give a series of lectures to Banks's fellow students. His subsequent work on an arduous expedition to Newfoundland and Labrador, where he described for the first time its plants and animals, soon qualified him as one of the leading naturalists of his time. This experience as well as his youth, his money and his place in society made him the perfect candidate for the post of chief botanist on the *Endeavour*.

He threw himself into his Tahitian explorations, learned the language and impressed the Tahitians by shooting down three ducks with one shot. He even got himself tattooed. (His excuse for this little piece of self-harm was similar to that of today's adolescents – he wanted to see what it would be like. He discovered it hurt a lot.)

A Major Discovery

Once the astronomical experiment had been completed, Banks and his little coterie of fellow botanists had to set aside their magnifying glasses and paint boxes, because when Cook opened his sealed orders it became clear that there was another long voyage ahead.

He was instructed to steer the *Endeavour* south and west of Tahiti until he found the continent (or land of great extent) thought to exist in southern latitudes. And 'with the consent of the natives, to take possession of convenient situations in the country in the name of the King of Great Britain'. In other words: find the Great Southern Land before the French did and claim it for King George. All this was so secret that upon their return the crew weren't to be allowed to reveal anything about where they had been until they were given permission to do so. In order to ensure that this instruction was obeyed, the journals and logs of all the officers were to be confiscated before they got back to England.

On 9th August they said goodbye to the magical island of Tahiti and their new Tahitian friends, although they found it significantly harder to say goodbye to the 'venereal distemper' (probably gonorrhoea) they'd picked up during their observations of Venus.

The weather alternated between fierce winds, which caused the crew to grumble, and calmer weather, during which Banks circled the ship in a little boat netting jellyfish for dissection and shooting sea birds. At last, though, the boy at the masthead shouted 'Land!', and by doing so earned himself a pint of rum. There ahead was a big land mass complete with snow-topped mountains and dense forest. Could they have found the fabled Southern Continent? Banks certainly thought so.

But whatever excitement coursed through the *Endeavour*, it wasn't shared by the supreme navigator and realist James Cook, who swiftly worked out that they'd hit upon a place the Dutch had discovered previously and which they'd called New Zealand. It certainly wasn't Terra Australis, but it was a very significant find, one which both the Navy and the Royal Society would be keen to know more about. New Zealand was almost completely uncharted, and its unique wildlife and plants seemed tailor-made to be stuffed and pressed for the perusal of the earnest academics back in London.

Cook was confident he could explore the place with alacrity, but he hadn't taken the Maori into account. Unlike Dampier's Aboriginals, these were a warrior people who responded to any perceived slight with outrage and a blow on the head with a club. The *Endeavour*'s officers were not trained in the art of diplomacy. Guns were fired and spears thrown, and although Cook was clearly uneasy about his own contribution

to the violence – 'I am aware that most humane men who have not experienced things of this nature will censure my conduct' – nevertheless he was constrained by his sense of responsibility towards the honour and dignity of his little coal-tub, which in his eyes represented not only the person of the British monarch but European civilisation itself. Consequently, no one was going to be allowed to mess with him and his boat, an attitude that in later years would have fatal consequences for him.

During the last month of 1769, Cook mapped as much of New Zealand as he possibly could, sailed between North Island and South Island in order to establish that they were separate bodies of land, and planted Union Jacks on them so that from now on everyone would know they were British possessions. Then, when his job there was done, it was time for a major decision to be made. He called his officers into his cabin for a conference. They had been away for a year and

a half in what was now a leaky ship. Should they continue battling their way west through the bleak southerly ocean in order to have another stab at finding the Southern Continent, or should they turn north and return to England?

They'd already taken part in a successful international scientific experiment, and they'd mapped a colossal pair of islands which would undoubtedly have strategic importance over the next few decades, and yet on 31st March 1770 they headed west.

Why did they make such a life-threatening decision? Why didn't they just go home? The answer is epitomised by the character of Joseph Banks. Here was a man of insatiable curiosity who found himself surrounded by natural wonders few Europeans had ever seen before. He had a passionate desire to map them, weigh them, draw them and paint them. He and his team were imbued with the philosophy of the Enlightenment. If they had a god it was science; they believed they had a moral duty to seek out scientific truth regardless of the cost. Consequently, they were prepared to forego their luxurious London life in exchange for a ridiculously small sleeping space and the chance to see all that the natural world had to offer.

Botany Bay

On the evening of 18th April 1770, in the middle of the open ocean, Cook ordered the 'close reef-top sails to be set' and the *Endeavour* slowed down. He clearly knew, or at least suspected, that there was land ahead. At 6 a.m. the following morning, Lieutenant Zachary Hicks confirmed Cook's hunch – there was definitely land ahead, and it looked very substantial. Whatever it was, and it was certainly virgin territory. The Dutch hadn't been here, nor the Chinese or the Portuguese – probably not even the Egyptians! This was something even the phlegmatic James Cook could get a little excited about.

He edged his ship along the coast, looking for a safe place to disembark, but the surf was so violent that landing proved a major problem. Banks and a few of his comrades attempted it in a little boat, but to no avail. Finally, on 28th August a party led by Cook found a small bay that appeared much more promising. He anchored off the south shore and a boat full of 'natives' painted with white stripes rowed towards them in a canoe. Cook ordered small presents to be thrown at them, but this was not an auspicious start. The locals seemed offended by the gifts. 'All they seemed to want from us was to be gone,' he later reported.

BELOW: *Captain Cook taking possession of the Australian continent on behalf of the British crown, AD 1770, under the name of New South Wales,* by Samuel Calvert, 1865

London. Published by Alex.r Hogg at the Kings Arms, N.o 16 Paternoster Row.

View of ENDEAVOUR RIVER, on the Coast of New Holland, where Captain Cook had the Ship laid on Shore, in order to repair the Damage which she received on the Rock.

ABOVE: The stricken *Endeavour* on the shore of its now eponymous river, near Cooktown, Queensland, after striking the Great Barrier Reef in 1770

Nevertheless, he ordered his boat to land and, in a rare display of nepotism, gave Isaac Smith, his wife's seventeen-year-old cousin, the honour of being the first person to step ashore onto this new territory. He and Smith spent the rest of the afternoon exploring the bark huts they came across on the beach, where they found some small children hiding behind a bark shield and gave them a few beads.

Cook was pleased with his bay. The soil was sandy, there were plenty of trees and shrubs, and pelicans, parrots and cockatoos abounded. Initially he named it Stingray Harbour, because of the numerous scary-looking but harmless rays sheltering in its shallows. But later he decided he wanted to call it something that reflected the abundance of trees, shrubs and wildlife there, and renamed it Botany Bay.

How refreshing that he wasn't tempted to do what so many later explorers did, by naming his discovery after some bureaucratic nonentity in Whitehall.

When the Sailors Stopped Swearing

The expedition remained based in the bay for two weeks, but when the wind changed, Cook sailed northwards. As each day passed, more Australian territory was revealed. This might not be a continent the size of Asia or Africa, but it was still vast. But then disaster struck. On 12th June they were off what we now know as northern Queensland, when there was a grinding sound that was the dread of every sailor in a wooden ship. They had hit a reef.

To prevent the *Endeavour* sinking,

27

It wasn't only Banks who had a hard time explaining what these outlandish creatures looked like. Most early visitors, however erudite, struggled to describe them accurately, and had an even harder time drawing them.

1. 'I saw myself one of the animals . . . the full size of a greyhound . . . with a long tail which it carried like a greyhound. In short, I should have taken it for a wild dog but for its walking or running, in which it jump'd like a hare or deer.' – James Cook, 1770

2. 'The Wombat is about the size of a turnspit dog; it is a squat, thick, short-legged and rather inactive quadruped with an appearance of a great, stumpy strength. Its figure and movements, if they do not exactly resemble those a bear, at least remind one of that animal . . . The hair on the face lies in regular order, as if combed.' – George Bass or John Hunter to Joseph Banks, 1802

NOUVELLE-HOLLANDE : le King.

LE WOMBAT. *(Dasuus Ursai ?)*

3. 'Of this extraordinary genus . . . it was impossible not to entertain some distant doubts as to the genuine nature of the animal, and to surmise, that, though in appearance perfectly natural, there might still have been practised some arts of deception in its structure.' – George Shaw, 1800

4. 'As may be imagined, from the very expressive name which has been appropriated to the animal . . . Native Devil . . . its character is not of the most amiable, nor its appearance the most inviting. Few animals have deserved their popular titles better . . . The innate and apparently ineradicable ferocity of the creature can hardly be conceived . . . Even in captivity its sullen and purposeless anger is continually excited, and the animal appears to be more obtuse to kindness than any other creature of whom we have practical knowledge.' – John George Wood, 1861

5. 'Wholly without a tail, and indeed the possession of such appendage . . . would be of little use, but rather as annoyance, as it is sufficiently defended from the flies by the length and thickness of its furry skin.' – George Perry, 1811

they threw everything they could overboard, including stores and casks, the guns and their carriages, and the iron and stone ballast. But they were completely stuck. Then the ship heeled starboard and began to take on water. Even the young scientific gentlemen, aware of the extreme danger they were in, took their turn manning the pumps, and Banks noticed that the sailors stopped swearing – presumably because if they were about to meet their maker, they wanted their souls to be untainted by bad language.

Their only chance was that the next tide would be high enough to lift them off the coral, but that would bring its own dangers, because if a large hole was revealed then the ship would sink and leave them stranded among 'the most uncivilised savages in the world'.

Fortune was on their side, though. The ship came away from the reef and took with it a large lump of coral that plugged the hole and bought them some time.

As the *Endeavour* edged towards the shore, the crew 'fothered' her, passing a sailcloth under her keel and back up the other side, and fixing it fast until she was as tightly bandaged as a footballer's knee. Finally, the battered ship made land and the carpenters could get to work mending her hull. Throughout this crisis the crew behaved well and didn't panic, something Cook remained proud of for the rest of his life.

Exotic Species

While the ship was being repaired, Banks and his fellow scientists were

free, like Dampier, to enter into a full-scale investigation of the surrounding jungle and mangrove swamp. Previous explorers had been extremely sniffy about Terra Australis, but all that was about to change. Banks fell in love with it. He identified and named more than 1400 species of trees and plants previously unknown to Western science, including no less than a hundred different types of gum tree.

And as for the animals, the excitement he felt when confronted by evidence of all those exotic species is

Cook's Death

After the discovery of Australia, Cook becomes famous (although not as famous as Banks).

In 1772–5 he makes a second voyage to the Southern Ocean.

Eventually promoted to captain and given a pension.

Following a brief and reluctant retirement, makes a third voyage 'to discover the North West Passage' from the west to east coast of America . . . Can't find it because there isn't one!

Charts majority of north-west American coastline for first time. Determines extent of Alaska. Grows irritable and a bit irrational; bad stomach. Forces crew to eat walrus meat, which they find disgusting.

Sails to Hawaii. Locals treat him as incarnation of the god Lono. Leaves, but mast breaks and he returns to Hawaii. Tensions rise. Quarrels break out. Locals steal one of his rowing boats. He attempts to take hostages until his boat is returned. But is struck on head by a villager, 'falls on his face in the surf' and dies.

Why did Hawaiians change their attitude towards him? No one knows. Perhaps because he returned to Hawaii outside the season of the worship of Lono (synonymous with peace) and they were now in the season of Ku, the God of War?

In a demonstration of the regard the Hawaiians had for him, his body is disembowelled and the flesh removed after being baked. His remains were passed around the island chiefs (and eaten, by some accounts) and the bones cleaned (like a medieval saint). Some bones and two parcels of flesh eventually returned to England were buried at sea.

RIGHT: A statue of the captain forever on the lookout in Cooktown, Queensland

vividly expressed in the words of
his journal:

'We saw one quadruped about the
size of a rabbit. My greyhound
just got sight of him and instantly
lamed himself against a stump
which lay concealed in the long
grass. We saw also the dung of
a large animal that had fed on
grass which much resembled that
of a stag; also the footsteps of an
animal clawed like a dog or wolf,
and as large as the latter; and of a
small animal whose feet were like
those of a polecat or weasel.'

Possession Island

Eventually, the *Endeavour*'s crew were
able to tow the repaired hulk off the
beach, rig the sails and set off north
again, but they were now travelling
painfully slowly. The Great Barrier Reef
was an uncharted maze of knife-edged
coral, cul-de-sacs and other hidden and
not so hidden dangers. Cook wrote: 'A
reef such as one speaks of here is scarcely
known in Europe. It is a wall of coral
rock rising almost perpendicular out of
the unfathomable ocean . . . The large
waves of the vast ocean meeting with
so sudden a resistance makes a most
terrible surf, breaking mountains high.'

Finally, as the *Endeavour* reached
the northernmost extremity of
Australia around Cape York, their

passage began to broaden out. But
this time Cook didn't turn west and
continue exploring along the north
coast; the whole of that seaboard had
already been claimed by Holland. He
was fairly confident he would now be
able to find a route north to the Indies
and then on to England, and that was
the direction in which he ordered the
ship to head. It was time to go home.

To seal the deal for Britain, Cook
landed on what became known as
Possession Island, and fired three
volleys of small arms from the beach.
His crew fired three more shots from
the ship, and that was that. The crown
was suddenly in possession of a north
to south slice of land thirty times the
size of England, Scotland, Ireland and
Wales put together.

Whatever would King George do
with all that space?

1770–1788

The Finest Harbour
in the World

It was eighteen years before the sails of any more British ships were to be seen fluttering in the harbour of Botany Bay, and once again their arrival was motivated by a grand experiment. This time the scientists weren't young gentlemen clutching telescopes and sketch pads, but gnarled prison warders dragooning their battered and disorientated charges.

In the 1770s Britain's penal policy was in crisis. Thousands of labourers had been made homeless as the land-owning elites fenced in their great farming estates and repopulated them with sheep. The redundant farm workers attempted to find jobs in the overcrowded cities, and in order to survive many resorted to petty crime.

BELOW: The annual Tall Ships Parade to celebrate Australia Day, on Sydney's famous harbour

LEFT: HMS *Discovery* at Deptford, in use as a convict hulk 1818–34

But in those days there was no such thing as probation. Felonies like stealing a fancy handkerchief or treating your employer with disrespect got you thrown into gaol. But imprisonment was only possible if there were prisons available in which to lock people up, and most gaols were overcrowded and burdened by debtors waiting to pay off their debts. Thousands were incarcerated in prison ships around the Thames Estuary, but these were rotting hulks, well past their sell-by date, and there was a limit to the number of felons you could put in them. And anyway, the inhabitants of Kent and Essex weren't that keen on having so many ne'er-do-wells within swimming distance. The hulks were seen as, at best, a temporary expedient.

A Fashionable Solution

Nowadays we tend to look back on penal transportation with horror and disdain, but in the late 1700s it was like community sentencing – liberal people's fashionable solution to the mushrooming law-and-order problem. Enforced exile as an alternative to execution had been popularised a hundred years previously, under Oliver Cromwell, with criminals being sent to the American colonies to work as indentured servants. This had been relatively successful, albeit on a small scale. But when America declared her independence and would no longer accept Britain's social and political misfits, a new and more effective solution was required.

Alternative transportation sites were looked at. Two hundred prisoners were sent to the Gambia in West Africa, but a year later only thirty were left alive, which many people of a reforming bent found a considerable embarrassment.

But another, far more practical location was on offer: Botany Bay. And who argued most forcefully for it to become the new haven for Britain's convicted classes? None other than Joseph Banks. Australia was not only very big, he argued, thus offering thousands of square miles of virgin territory in which penitents could start a new life, but it had a climate similar to Toulouse and was so far from any part of the globe occupied by Europeans as to make escape virtually impossible.

Dodgy Banks

(This episode is taken from *Coleridge*, a biography by Richard Holmes)

The poet, essayist and habitual drug-user Samuel Taylor Coleridge wanted to go on a drug-fuelled weekend with his rich young sponsor, the porcelain heir Tom Wedgewood. Their usual drug of choice was opium but they wanted to experiment with bhang (hashish) and wrote to a few well-travelled acquaintances to try and obtain some.

Who came up trumps? Joseph Banks, the world-famous botanist, prison-reformer and tattooed dope dealer!

Inspiration or Desperation?

The previous transportations to America had established colonies in relatively accessible locations, where prisoners could be easily controlled and absorbed into the community. This proposal was entirely different. No European had ventured further than about a mile inland of Botany Bay – who knew what problems might lie there?

The Cabinet certainly wasn't convinced; not because of the cruelty involved in abandoning so many of the nation's citizens to an uncertain fate, but because they thought it would involve considerable expense (and in this they were absolutely right). But the public liked the idea. Indeed, a new opera had opened at the Royal Circus theatre in London entitled 'Botany Bay'. And a new force had entered into politics in the person of the boy wonder, William Pitt, Prime Minister at the ridiculously young age of twenty-four years, a time of life when young men should be out on the lash, or round their mum's getting their washing done. Pitt was confronted by a host of political problems, and wanted the issue of the overcrowded prisons sorted out – and sorted out quickly.

Transportation was the responsibility of the Home Secretary, Lord Sydney. To send hundreds of prisoners to Botany Bay was either an intelligent and audacious move on his part (although neither of these qualities was considered his strong suit), or an act of desperation (and certainly the intractable crime wave of prisoners was a challenge of gargantuan proportions).

Whether driven by inspiration or desperation, Sydney eventually pressured the Treasury, and screwed enough money out of them to realise the project. 'I am commanded', he wrote, 'to signify to your Lordships His Majesty's pleasure that you do forthwith take such measures as may be necessary for providing a proper number of vessels for the conveyance of 750 convicts to Botany Bay, together with such provisions, necessaries and implements for agriculture as may be necessary for their use after their arrival.'

This historic decision not only removed a thorny political problem from Sydney's backside, but eventually immortalised him in the name of one of the world's most beautiful and successful cities.

The First Fleet

The First Fleet of eleven small ships left Portsmouth at 6 a.m. on 13th May 1787 under the command of Captain Arthur Phillip. There were 775 convicts, 247 marines, 323 crew members, and some wives and children, all sharing the cramped confines of the ships with horses, dogs, cats, cattle, sheep, pigs,

goats, turkeys, geese, ducks, chickens, rabbits and pigeons.

It was no luxury cruise. The ships were riddled with rats, lice, fleas and cockroaches. Below decks it was so low that only a child could stand upright, and the place was swimming with bilge water full of human and animal sewage.

In such conditions it was difficult for Captain Phillip to preserve the physical and moral health of his human cargo. Two weeks out from England, he insisted the convicts be unshackled and be given time in the open air. But his liberal sensibilities had their limits. He separated male and female convicts into different ships, nailed down the hatches and erected pronged barriers to prevent the sailors and prisoners from interacting.

But interact they did, and quite openly. One of the ships, the *Lady*

Penrhyn, contained 109 female convicts. The only men on board were crew and marines. With up to 210 people packed into one 'pygmy-sized' sailing ship, sexual tension was inevitable. Punishment was no deterrent to desire. Alliances between the female convicts and the marines and sailors were quickly forged. Some women offered sexual favours in exchange for extra rations. Officers acquired 'housekeeper lovers' or 'sea wives' to keep their bunks warm.

This litany of misery, disease and sexual desperation may seem somewhat remote from life in Australia today, with its bustling markets, its optimism and its cheery safe-sex posters. But the reality is that thousands of those shopping in Myer or basking on the beaches at Bondi and Manly today are the direct descendants of the convicts who became the first white Australians.

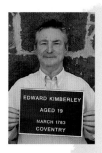

1. **Phillip Lock** worked for Goodyear for many years as a component die designer in their tyre plants. He has now retired, and enjoys welding, plastering and repairing old jewellery and clocks. He has five grandchildren — Max, Kimberley, Courtney, Byron and Charlize.

   Phillip is descended from Edward Kimberly. Edward was aged nineteen when he was sentenced to seven years' transportation for stealing muslin from a milliner's shop in Coventry. He had the advantage of being able to read and write, which eventually propelled him to the position of chief constable on Norfolk Island.

2. **Cheryl Timbury** spent three years in Papua New Guinea, and ten years working at the Geelong Heritage Centre. She enjoys caravanning, particularly to Queensland, and is involved with the Lions Club and her local church.

   Cheryl's great-great-great-grandparents were Lydia Munro, off the *Prince of Wales*, and Andrew Goodwin, off the *Scarborough*. Lydia was born in 1767 and was convicted of stealing ten yards of printed cotton valued at twenty shillings in October 1786. She was sentenced to be hanged, but was reprieved and the sentence was commuted to fourteen years' transportation.

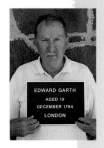

3. **Wayne Hughes** was born in Hobart and was raised on a berry farm. He spent seven and a half years in the RAAF, and in 1965 began a lengthy career with a greeting card and gift-wrapping firm. There are nineteen different convicts in his family tree.

   He is descended from Edward Garth, who was born in 1763 and sentenced to death by hanging — at the Old Bailey on 8th December 1784 for the theft of two cows. His sentence was commuted to transportation for seven years and he was sent out on the *Scarborough*. (On 6th July 1789 he was ordered to receive one hundred lashes for the theft of three quarts of wheat.)

4. **Helen Lucas** has worked as a sales assistant, dressmaker, mothercraft nurse, primary-school teacher and embroiderer. She has now returned to live in her birthplace, Camperdown in Western Australia, where she has opened a community craft shop.

OLIVIA GASCOIGNE
AGED 25
MARCH 1785
WORCESTER

She is descended from Olivia Gascoigne, who went before the Worcester Court on 5th March 1785 charged with robbery of coins with a total value of 277 shillings. She gained a royal prerogative of mercy from the King and, instead of death, the sentence was commuted to transportation for seven years. *'His Majesty hath been graciously pleased to extend Royal mercy to her on the condition of her being severally transported beyond the seas for and during the term of 7 years.'*

The Birth of Sydney

Governor Phillip had a big problem with Botany Bay. Cook may have sung its praises, and Joseph Banks may have lauded it to the skies as the perfect spot for the new colony, but Phillip wasn't impressed. The bay is wide, featureless and vulnerable to the fierce waves that so often gather on that coast. They may be a surfer's dream today, but two hundred years ago they were a serious marine hazard.

In many ways, Botany Bay now offers an even less promising vista than the one on which Phillip cast his eye. Close to shore it's too shallow for ships to berth (a point Banks appeared to have forgotten to mention when lobbying the great and the good), but at its mouth it's very deep – big enough for tankers and container vessels. Consequently, the coastline is now dominated by the shiny domes of a big oil-storage depot, and murky grey jetties and groynes. Where Banks once watched awestruck as marsupials hopped and gambolled, now enormous carriers offload imported Japanese cars.

Shortly after the First Fleet convened there, Phillip took three open boats and sailed further north in search of something better, and fortunately he didn't have to go far. Cook had spotted a harbour just up from Botany Bay, which he named Port Jackson but didn't explore. But Phillip took a look, and when he did he became very excited about its suitability. He said it was 'the finest harbour in the world, in which a thousand sail of the line may ride in perfect security', and tucked away deep inside this elaborate harbour was a cove of which he became particularly fond. This, he decided, was where the First Colony should situate itself. He called it Sydney Cove, eschewing Cook's example and, with typical explorer's obsequiousness, naming it after the fleet's sponsor. The new colonists had found their home.

The Tank Stream

The swarming crowds of tourists who shuffle through the automatic ticket barriers at Sydney's ferry terminal today are blithely unaware that deep below it lie the sandstone rocks on which Captain Phillip trod.

He liked the protection the cove gave him, there was good anchorage close to shore, the ground was level and looked suited for cultivation, and it was altogether less swampy than Botany Bay. But there was another reason Sydney grew up there rather than adjacent to any of the other little inlets around the vast harbour of Port Jackson.

The most important factor to consider when you're setting up a new colony is whether you've got sufficient access to a reliable fresh water supply. Paris boasts the River Seine, London's got Old Father Thames, but Sydney's foundation waterway is a little less spectacular.

On landing at Sydney Cove, Phillip noticed a profusion of wildlife gathered around a freshwater creeklet flowing out of the swampland. He immediately declared a 'green belt' fifteen metres wide on either side of it. Polluting activities like cutting trees and grazing stock would from now on be banned there.

But what had seemed like a secure water source started drying up within a year. So, to preserve the supply, Phillip ordered three huge water-storage holes, or 'tanks', to be excavated in the sandstone rock adjoining the stream; hence the little river's subsequent name, 'The Tank Stream'.

It soon became an unofficial social divide bisecting the settlement. Officers and governors lived to the east of it because the sea breezes made the place less pungent, and to the west where it was often much smellier, lived the soldiers and convicts. (Incidentally,

BELOW: *Old Tank Stream, Sydney*, by John Black Henderson, c.1852

RIGHT: Sydney Cove's once life-giving Tank Stream is now a trickling underground drain

that social divide is still perpetuated today. The eastern suburbs are predominantly the wealthy areas; the west is the preserve of the working classes.)

Phillip worked hard to keep the Tank Stream in good condition, but subsequent governors weren't so environmentally minded. The green belt was soon breached by the military, who were given permission to build houses and pigsties adjoining it. By the 1820s it was so polluted that even the least discerning convict would have spat out its water and declared it foul. Other water sources were found and the Tank Stream became an open sewer. But of course that made it stink even more, and as the city grew and town planners began to take ideas about sanitation and water-borne diseases more seriously, it was covered with a series of stone archways and culverts. It was effectively buried and the city swiftly developed on top of it.

Nowadays, it's a stormwater drain, but it's also become part of Sydney's tourist industry. Today's visitors not only want to wallow in the sense of the heritage offered by the Harbour Bridge and the Botanical Gardens, they also like to bask in the history of Sydney's effluent. For the two days a year on which it's opened to the public, tours of the Tank Stream are so over-subscribed that a ballot has to be conducted to allocate tickets.

The French Are Coming!

Phillip was so enthusiastic about Sydney Cove's prospects as a potential new base that he returned to Botany Bay and ordered his fleet to move there, but as they prepared to set off, one of his sailors shouted something entirely unexpected: 'Another sail!' On the horizon was a most extraordinary and improbable vision. Imagine if Neil Armstrong, when he landed on the

moon, had stuck his head out of his Apollo spacecraft, walked round the nearest crater and bumped into a party of Russian astronauts. This was just such a moment. Two French ships were approaching, thousands of miles from where they should have been.

Before the First Fleet departed Portsmouth, rumours had been flying around that France might have an interest in the Southern Continent. The Duke of Dorset informed the government of a journey to the Pacific by a French nobleman, Jean-François de Galaup, the Comte de La Pérouse. He was supposed to be mapping the coast of North America, or possibly exploring the East China Sea. Yet here were two French vessels, in broad daylight, loitering with intent.

Their presence was baffling. Were they spy ships? Were the French intending to set up a rival colony? Had Britain and France gone to war? Was there the possibility of a military engagement right here in Botany Bay? La Pérouse had form – he had previously engaged the British off the French coast and around Canada. The ships may have looked battered and dishevelled, but they were certainly capable of putting up a fight.

In fact, La Pérouse's intentions were far more benign. Under the patronage of the King of France, he had planned a great scientific voyage, not unlike Cook's (only without the Machiavellian secret instructions). The French-speaking scientific world had been given instructions to draw together research programmes in geography, physics, astronomy, botany and zoology, and had responded with gusto.

La Pérouse was deeply influenced by Cook. Following the Englishman's example, he had selected solid, heavy vessels and had sent a spy to London to purchase scientific instruments and books on scurvy prevention. His enterprise was intended to be one of the major scientific undertakings of the Age of Enlightenment, the quality of scientists he took with him was first-rate, and hopes were high. But by the time he arrived in Botany Bay, two and a half years later, his expedition was in a very sorry state.

'Whatever professional advantages this expedition may have brought me, you can be certain that few would want them at such cost, and the fatigues of such a voyage cannot be put in to words. When I return you will take me for a centenarian. I have no teeth and no hair left and I think it will not be long before I become senile . . . farewell until June 1789. Tell your wife she will mistake me for my own grandfather.'
— LA PÉROUSE 1788

The most severe blow to the expedition had fallen some six weeks previously when it had pulled in to Tutuila, part of the chain of Samoan islands. La Pérouse had been suspicious of the intentions of the islanders, but trading proceeded without too many problems, and some of his senior officers, in a fit of Rousseau-esque romanticism, became convinced that these were noble savages untainted by the ferocity and aggression of European life, and would do their

visitors no harm. La Pérouse noticed that the bodies of these men appeared to be covered in battle scars, which he thought rather undermined this charming thesis. Nevertheless, he allowed his friend Paul-Antoine Fleuriot de Langle to lead a party of men to a nearby village to take on casks of fresh water. De Langle argued that the islanders wouldn't object – his sailors would merely be collecting a resource that flowed abundantly. La Pérouse concurred. 'Monsier de Langle is a man of such excellent judgement and ability,' he wrote, 'that these considerations more than anything else finally caused my own will to bow to his.'

Once de Langle's men were out of sight of the two frigates, the villagers gave a ferocious roar and attacked them. By the time the survivors had made it back to the ships, twelve

men – including de Langle – were dead, many others were wounded and the padre Father Receveur had lost an eye. Boat-loads of Samoan traders were still doing business with the traders in the frigates, so it would have been easy to administer some kind of rough justice. But La Pérouse made the kind of noble decision that wasn't uncommon among the more enlightened colonial adventurers (indeed, Phillip himself would make similar decisions in the weeks and months to come). Though both he and his crew were profoundly angry about what had happened, he didn't fire one bullet in revenge, merely a single blank shot to warn the Samoans to retreat.

'I could have destroyed or sunk a hundred canoes, with more than five hundred people in them,' he wrote, 'but I was afraid of striking the wrong victims; the call of my conscience saved their lives.'

La Pérouse sailed on southwards, and now two dispirited little fleets, one English the other French, confronted each other on that bizarre morning in January 1788, their sails torn and grimy, their paintwork bleached and peeling. Philip soon realised that La Pérouse had no hostile intentions. Granted, the Frenchman wanted to report the progress of the British colony to his king; indeed, he was surprised it was in such a rudimentary state of development. But equally importantly, he needed to rest his crew, carry out repairs and take on food and water.

There was little the First Fleet could do to help him; the straits they were in were similarly dire. Not that Phillip wanted to give La Pérouse, an old adversary from his spying days, too

much assistance. The British captain needed to make sure he had properly claimed his wonderful new harbour before the Frenchman did. But his men agreed to take La Pérouse's letters and reports back to Europe, and had they not done so, the story of much of his tragic voyage would have been lost.

The behaviour of some of the newly arrived convicts was a source of irritation to both captains. The idea of stowing away on a French ship and returning to Europe was overwhelmingly attractive to them. But the punctilious La Pérouse returned those he found smuggled away on his ship to Phillip, who had them flogged.

Eventually, on 10th March 1788, La Pérouse's ships, the *Boussole* and the *Astrolabe*, weighed anchor and set off again for the open sea. The First

BELOW: A typical Aussie spread, if the French had landed in Botany Bay first

Fleeters were the last white people ever to see them. La Pérouse, his ships and their crew all vanished somewhere in the Pacific. Searches for them were to no avail, and their disappearance became one of the great mysteries of the sea. It wasn't until forty years later that remains of the two ships were found off the coral atoll of Vanikoro in the Solomon Islands, and not until 2005 that the underwater wreck of the *Boussole* was confirmed.

But who knows? If the winds had been kinder, La Pérouse might have arrived in Australia before the First Fleet, and planted the Tricolore on the sands of Botany Bay instead of the Union Flag. Had he done so, the course of history might well have been changed, and Australians today would *parles français* and eat coq au vin, rather than speak English and wolf down pie and sauce.

The Founding Orgy

The raggle-taggle army of First Fleet miscreants was never meant to be the start of a nation. When the ships had pulled into Sydney Cove, their task had been simply to set up a penal colony. But things don't always go to plan. Right from the start, human nature began exerting itself in unpredictable and ungovernable ways.

On arrival, the male convicts were expected to obey orders just as they had on board. But having spent almost nine deranged months at sea segregated from the female convicts, they were now possessed by a powerful force that meant that once they'd landed, their obedience could

no longer be relied upon. And that mighty force was, of course, sexual frustration.

The men were disembarked first. They were to be the advance party sent ashore to erect storehouses and tents, the first tentative step in creating the infrastructure of the new colonial open prison.

The women were kept on board for eleven more days. When they came ashore they had changed out of their prison rags into their best clothes and were carrying hat boxes. It was said that 'a few amongst them were surprisingly well dressed'.

Their good mood had doubtless been enhanced by the generosity of the sailors of the *Lady Penrhyn*, who had been rewarded with a double ration of rum to celebrate the offloading of the female convicts and had shared it with them. It was the makings of an all-night party that became known as the Founding Orgy.

But these cavortings didn't take place unobserved. Imagine Manhattan's Central Park carefully manicured, jacked up twenty degrees along its west side, with Fifth Avenue demolished and replaced by an undulating sea wall – that's Sydney's Royal Botanic Gardens, one of the most beautiful city parks in the world, with its sloping lawns running down to Sydney Harbour. Its most stunning natural features are the clumps of sandstone rocks running parallel to the water, eroded by stormwater and prehistoric floods so that they form recesses and caves, the roofs of which are stained black with smoke from centuries of campfires.

Aboriginal clans had lived there for at least ten thousand years. They called themselves the Eora, which means 'of this place'. They were in a perfect position to observe the fleet of sailing boats, graced by what appeared to be hordes of monkeys or possums swinging through the rigging wearing peculiar hats – and they had a ringside view of the Founding Orgy.

The day had been sunny when the convicts first landed, but there were storms on the horizon and by evening all hell had broken loose. A Sydney thunderstorm can feel like the end of the world. Lightening, thunder and rain that you can hardly see through. A giant bolt of lightening struck, hitting a sentry on duty, blinding him and killing six of the colony's sheep, two lambs and a pig. The officers weren't going to come ashore in

that kind of weather, and remained cowering from the storm in their ships, while the sailors stayed on land with lots of rum and a ship-load of recently liberated women. Up until a few days previously, the little settlement had been a scrubby forest. But the convicts had cleared the undergrowth, and once the rain began to tip down and people started churning up the earth, it rapidly turned into a sticky soup. So not only did a wild party break out, but it took place in a sea of mud.

The next morning, Captain Phillip, in a desperate bid to reassert his authority, sent his marines ashore to put a stop to the philanderings. They marched around the little clearing, prising various couples apart, opening the flaps of tents and peering inside, and finally they came to one where they discovered the senior carpenter

THE FINEST HARBOUR IN THE WORLD: 1770–1788

of the *Prince of Wales*. This must have come as something of a shock because he was of officer rank, the kind of person who was supposed to be keeping order in the middle of this mayhem. Then they realised that someone else was lurking in the tent, and that someone came as an even bigger surprise – it was a cabin boy dressed in a woman's petticoat. Finally, to cap it all, out staggered a woman convict, uttering oaths and other profanities.

Phillip hated sodomy. He'd previously served with the Portuguese navy, where the punishment for bloke-on-bloke hanky-panky had been for the two men involved to be tied together back-to-back and thrown overboard. Indeed, in one of his less liberal moments he threatened to ship anyone found guilty of homosexual activity to New Zealand, where they'd be fed to the supposedly cannibalistic Maori.

But he didn't carry out this threat. Indeed it was difficult for him to know what punishment was appropriate, and who should receive it, because he couldn't prove who'd had sex with whom. Eventually, perhaps in an unconscious parody of the Portuguese system, he instructed the hands of the three gang-bangers to be bound and, accompanied by the ship's band playing 'The Rogues March', they were paraded through the colony watched by the assembled convicts; the solemnity of this event being only slightly marred by the fact that the cabin boy was still wearing his petticoat. Then, when they reached the trees at the furthest edge of the

tiny colony, the sorry trio were turned round and marched back again.

Farce on the Beach

The orgy and its consequences must have seemed slightly ridiculous to the observing Aboriginals, but the events of the following day were pure farce. Before the First Fleet set sail, the colonial authorities had decided that once disembarkation had taken place, Captain Phillip should be appointed the colony's leader. But this being an edict of Her Britannic Majesty, everything needed to be done by the book. So on the morning of 9th February, a very serious but very absurd ritual took place.

A folding table was set up on the beach, along with a couple of suitcases and some chairs. All the convicts were gathered in a big huddle surrounded by the ship's company of soldiers, and Captain Phillip and his senior officers stood to attention next to the table.

Surrounded by eucalypts and cabbage trees, and with steam rising from the humid ground, Captain Collins read 'The Commission', a set of instructions from the Crown that were to be the rules of the new penal colony. They were very long and written in imperial jargon.

'With these Our Instructions you will receive Our Commission under Our Great seal constituting and appointing you to be Our Captain General and Governor in Chief of Our Territory called New South Wales, Extending from the Northern Cape or

Extremity of the Coast called Cape York in the Latitude of Ten Degrees thirty-seven Minutes south, to the Southern Extremity of the said Territory of New South Wales, or South Cape, in the Latitude of Forty-three Degrees Thirty-nine Minutes south, and of all the Country Inland to the Westward as far as the One hundred and Thirty-fifth Degree of East Longitude . . .'

It would have taken Collins over an hour to read it all, and must have been particularly irksome for those still nursing hangovers. But once he'd finished, one of the biggest land grabs in the history of the British Empire could begin, although at that moment the locals who had lived in this land for the previous fifty millennia were blithely unaware of its significance.

1788–1790

Soak the Pork Overnight to Reduce Excess Saltiness

The First Few Days

From the moment the First Fleet anchored, Captain Phillip was eager to cultivate good relations with the Eora. He went ashore to try to woo them, along with Lieutenant Philip Gidley King and a party of seamen, and instead of letting fly with shot, as Cook had done, they laid down their weapons and approached the Aboriginals who had gathered on the beach with their arms outstretched like cowboys attempting to negotiate a parley with a party of Indian warriors. Not that this was entirely Phillip's own idea – he had been explicitly instructed by the Crown to act in a friendly manner.

BELOW: *First interview with the Native Women at Port Jackson New South Wales,* by William Bradley, c. 1802

'You are to endeavour by every means to open an intercourse with the natives, and to conciliate their affections, in enjoining all our subjects to live in amity and kindness with them.'

They gave the Aboriginals the usual colonial car-boot-sale offerings of beads, looking glasses and assorted trinkets, as well as a number of hats they apparently took quite a shine to, at least according to Lieutenant King, who later described the incident in his journal.

But then the be-hatted natives began pointing at the trousers of the two naval officers, particularly at their crotch area. Eventually it dawned on Lieutenant King that they were enquiring about the officers' gender, their confusion stemming from the fact that none of the English party wore beards. In true officer fashion, King delegated the responsibility of demonstrating their sex to one of his men. When this plucky tar dropped his trousers there was, according to King, a shout of admiration, although I suspect this little detail might have been a piece of imperial spin to reassure his readers that the British were not only more civilised and capable than the natives, but also had bigger willies.

Whether the Aboriginals were impressed by the sailor's girth or not, the little demonstration had an instant effect. They pointed to the shoreline from where a group of Aboriginal women were approaching 'in puris naturalibus – pas même la feuille de figuer', a coy piece of phraseology in which King deployed both Latin and French to explain that the women were stark-naked – without even a fig leaf! The Aboriginal men then engaged in a series of graphic mimes to explain to the sailors that the women were at their service, but King declined on behalf

of the party and instead produced a handkerchief, which he offered to one of the young women who 'suffered me to apply the handkerchief where Eve did ye fig leaf'.

Apart from the stiff-upper-lip absurdity of this story, it's rather curious. Why were the women offered for sex? Was it a misunderstanding? Was it part of a traditional exchange of gifts, or was there more to it than that? Maybe the Aboriginals thought that if the Europeans' lust was satisfied, they might go back where they came from. It's believed they offered the convoy fresh water with that hope, so perhaps they were prepared to offer a few personal services too.

Phillip was genuinely impressed by the confidence and bearing of many of the Aboriginals. He didn't believe they were the 'cowards' Cook and Banks had concluded they were. He thought they displayed the kind of qualities he most admired in an English gentleman. He even named a cove in which he had seen them after the attribute that he felt they most epitomised. Thus the suburb of Manly was born.

An enthusiastic young lieutenant, William Bradley, recorded these first encounters.

'We saw several of the Natives on the upper part of the rocks who made a great noise & waved to us to come on shore . . . The Natives were all much disposed to good humour & pleased with us.'

There was even a touching and innocent moment when the Aboriginals and the settlers danced together.

LEFT: *A Family of New South Wales*, engraved by William Blake after a painting by Philip Gidley King, 1793

'In the course of the forenoon we went to a Cove . . . where we were cordially received by 3 Men, who left their women sitting in a Canoe at the other end of the beach. We made a fire on shore & dined in the Boats. While our people were cooking the dinner, the natives were amongst them playing, looking at the Boat, manner of Cooking &c. & were without any weapons the whole time, they laid their Spears down on the sand between the women & the place they met us at . . .'

But Phillip's attempts at engaging with these enigmatic people began to prove futile. Two clans of Eora, the Gweagal and the Bidjigal, lived on the shores of Botany Bay, and they swiftly became uneasy about the presence of the red-coated 'People of the Clouds' who had arrived uninvited in the midst. 'Get out! Be gone! Clear away!' they yelled at their ghostly-looking visitors.

Relations soon began to deteriorate. One day Phillip's men had been fishing in the bay and dragged their net full of fish up the beach. When they saw the quantity the sailors had caught, the Aboriginals 'were much astonished, which they expressed with a loud and long shout'. They took some for themselves. A few days later, a lieutenant fired a musket in their direction, and the Aboriginals hit the Fleet's fishermen with spear shafts and ran off with more fish.

The presence of the white-faced strangers raised a number of difficult questions for the Eora. Who were they? Were they spirits? Were they just passing through or were they planning to stay? Why did they feel they could plunder the waters with such impunity when the fish clearly belonged to the Eora?

Then there was the puzzling question of the white men's leader. Aboriginal men of the Sydney region had their front tooth knocked out to mark their coming of age. Arthur Phillip was missing the same front tooth. So what did this make him? Was he some ghostly ancestor of theirs? If so, why had he returned?

A kind of stand-off developed, with the two sides equally fascinated by each other, but with totally different agendas.

William Bradley

The various descriptions of these first few weeks, eventually published on the officers' return to England, may be remarkably vivid, but we are fortunate to have more. Lieutenant William Bradley was not only a diarist, he was also a watercolourist; indeed, it could be said that he was Australia's first photo-journalist.

To me, his paintings seem a little gloomy and desolate, which is understandable given that he was a young man far from home in an alien environment. But maybe there's more to it than that. Perhaps they prefigure the man he eventually became – because Bradley's was not a happy life.

In 1790 Phillip despatched him to Norfolk Island, a remote Pacific island far to the west, in a bid to find better food supplies, but his ship was caught in a storm and wrecked. He

Sydney Cove, Port Jackson. 1788 — W. Bradley

RIGHT: *Sydney Cove, Port Jackson. 1788, by William Bradley, c 1802*

and his crew spent eleven months marooned on the island, and when they were finally rescued and returned to Britain they were court-martialled for the loss of the ship. Eventually, they were all 'honourably acquitted' and Bradley was promoted to master and commander, in which capacity he remained for many years, although his fellow officers often found him disagreeable and standoffish.

But in 1809 he suffered the first of many mental disturbances, which continued until 1812 when he was retired with the rank of rear admiral. Two years later, in an act which appears completely out of character, he was caught trying to defraud the postal authorities. He had forged a receipt in order to collect 411 ships' letters from the postmaster at Gosport, and even though this was a relatively

minor offence, he was stripped of his rank and pension, and sentenced to death. His family appealed, pleading that he had served the navy for forty-two years, was the great-nephew of the Astronomer Royal, and anyway, 'the letters cost the prisoner more to fabricate than he received for them'. The judge must have been moved by at least one of these pieces of mitigating evidence, because he reduced the sentence to exile.

Bradley retired to Le Havre in France and spent his sane hours trying to find a way to make it easier for sailors to calculate longitude by using an hourglass. He thought if he was successful, he'd be forgiven and would be able to return home. But his attempts were fruitless and he eventually gave up. He died a recluse, in France, in March 1833.

But his legacy is his journal, with twenty-nine of his watercolours inserted between the pages. It was unknown to the general public until the early twentieth century, but a bookseller eventually realised its significance and it now rests in Sydney's Mitchell Library.

Food

In those first few months, Phillip's most pressing concern was not his relations with the local population. He needed to ensure there was enough food available for his little colony. He'd certainly packed a colossal amount of basic foodstuffs before he left. In today's terms, the beef alone would have required five twenty-foot dockyard containers, six for the pork and fourteen for the flour.

A huge amount of organisation and time had been put in ensuring everything was properly organised. Phillip continually delayed starting the voyage in order to ensure everything had been made ready. Even so, the lime for the mortar was left behind, as well as wood for the carpenters and even balls for the muskets (an omission Phillip kept to himself throughout the journey for fear of mutiny if the convicts discovered the marines weren't properly armed). In addition, the convoy stopped off at Rio de Janeiro and bought plants and seeds for cultivation, including coffee, cocoa, cotton, banana, orange, lemon, guava, tamarind and prickly pear, not forgetting a hefty investment in 65 000 litres of rum – all this for the

BELOW: My colonial gastronomic guide, Jacqui Newling, from the Historic Houses Trust

RIGHT: An appetising spread! The colonists' original weekly rations: flour, rice, dried pork, butter and dried peas

remainder of the voyage and for the first few years of the new settlement.

On their arrival, Phillip had to organise the division of the food. He relied on the ancient naval tradition of rationing. Each man was given a weekly ration of four pounds of dried pork, three pints of dried peas, seven pounds of flour, six ounces of butter and half a pound of rice. This applied to both convicts and officers, an extraordinary piece of egalitarianism on Phillip's part, but it was also highly practical. He was well aware that the convicts were about to embark on a life of hard, physical activity in a difficult climate. If the colony was going to be built swiftly and to a high standard, it would require men and women (wives and 'fallen women' received seventy-five per cent of the men's rations) who were fit and well fed. Indeed, although we tend to think of nineteenth century convicts as underfed, the food they ate here was much higher in calorific value

than that which most of them had been used to back in England.

But rationing was also a shrewd exercise in social control. The area around Sydney Cove was essentially a prison without bars, and the convicts were unlikely to wander off too far if they had to soon return to base for their ration.

To us, a combined diet of dried peas and year-old dried pork may seem pretty oppressive, but despite the rudimentary nature of the ingredients, it was possible to cook some relatively appetising dishes, including a very tasty pea and ham soup, washed down with tea from the leaves of the local sarsaparilla vine. In fact, being British, the colonists drank so much of the stuff that sarsaparilla remains almost extinct in the area around Sydney.

The original plan wasn't for the colony to rely solely on the provisions they'd brought with them. Food restrictions were to be gradually eased

Convicts' Pease Soup

In separate containers, soak the peas and pork in a generous amount of fresh water overnight.

Drain the peas and place in large pot with 4 cups of fresh water. Rinse the pork bones and add to the peas. Bring to the boil, reduce heat and skim if necessary. Simmer for 2 hours on a low heat with the lid on, stirring occasionally to prevent catching on the bottom of the saucepan, and add water as needed to prevent the soup becoming too thick, until the peas have broken down and become soft.

Remove any meat from the bones, discard bones and shred the meat through the soup.

Note: Bones from a hand of pickled pork may be substituted for salt-pork bones, or use bacon bones, which will give a more smoky flavour. Overnight soaking should not be necessary with modern substitutes, but add salt to taste once the soup is cooked. Salt was the only flavouring available to First Fleet convicts, but a clove, 2 bay leaves and some freshly ground pepper will improve the flavour.

200g (7oz) dried split peas
55g (2oz) salt-pork or meaty salt-pork bones

A Convict's 'Mess'

Soak the salted pork overnight in fresh water to reduce intense saltiness. Drain and transfer to a pot with 2 litres (8 cups) of fresh water. Add whatever vegetables are at hand – onions, turnips, potatoes, carrots, celery, cabbage – and bring to the boil. Add rice, reduce heat and simmer until meat, rice and vegetables are soft. Leafy greens may also be added once hardier vegetable are cooked, simmer for a further 5–10 minutes. Dumplings made with flour and water may also be added – simmer in the broth until they float to the top.

200g (7oz) of salt-pork (or substitute – pancetta or kassler / uncut bacon)
1 cup of roughly chopped vegetables – onions, turnips, carrots, potatoes, cabbage, celery.
2 tablespoons (1oz) of rice
Dumplings (optional – see method below)

Hard Dumplings

Place flour and salt in a bowl. Add a splash of water and mix into the flour, adding extra water in small amounts, as needed, to make a soft dough. Form into walnut-sized balls and add to the simmering broth. They are cooked when they float to the top.

½ cup of flour
A pinch of salt
Water

Damper

Place the flour in a deep bowl. Add enough water to make soft dough. Knead until smooth and form into a round ball about 3cm high. Bake in a very hot oven, or place on a shovel laid over hot embers, turning frequently. Damper is cooked when it sounds hollow when tapped.

2½ cups of flour
1 teaspoon of salt
water (50–60ml / 2oz – the quantity will vary with the flour used)

Note: First Fleet convicts had no baking powder or yeast to help their damper rise, so it tended to be very dense. Add 2 teaspoons of baking powder per cup of flour or use selfraising flour for a lighter version.

Recipes courtesy Jacqui Newling, Colonial Gastronomist, Historic Houses Trust

TOP: Jacqui demonstrating some surprisingly tasty recipes using only first colonists' rations

as the colonists developed their own food supply. And this didn't just mean sowing wheat and growing bananas. The ships of the Fleet were together a Noah's Ark of animals that it was hoped would thrive and multiply once the convicts reached their new home. But there was only a limited amount of space on board for the animal feed, and it ran out before the ships reached Botany Bay. Soon there was nothing for them to eat but handfuls of stale bread, and many died or became very emaciated.

When the ships pulled into the bay, a desperate attempt was made to get the rest of the livestock onto the beach. They were lowered into boats, albeit in a clumsy fashion, and those that survived were rowed ashore and left to graze on the first fresh grass they'd tasted for months. But looking after them was a struggle, particularly as most of the settlers were from the big industrial cities and hardly knew one end of a horse from the other. Indeed, there were only two farmers among the entire group of colonists, so not only were the animals poorly maintained, but most of the plants and seeds went to waste too.

Bread, in particular, was a big problem. They'd brought seed corn with them, but some had rotted or been eaten by animals and, because of the sandy soil, the rest didn't take. Instead, they had to rely for their flour on maize that they'd picked up in Rio de Janeiro. A problem arose when the settlers were affronted by the cornbread. They may have been convicts, but they were English and were outraged that they weren't being offered the eighteenth century equivalent of Tip Top.

LEFT: *Governor's House at Sydney, Port Jackson. 1791*, by William Bradley, c.1802

Governor's House at Sydney, Port Jackson. 1791. W.B.

SOAK THE PORT OVERNIGHT: 1788–1790

Then they were hit by drought, not once but twice, and their first two crops withered on the stalk. Soon the food started to run out and they had no idea when the next supply ship would arrive. So Phillip had to start cutting the rations.

1789 came and went, and still no ship. By 1790 the whole colony had sunk into a deep depression as the realisation grew that they might well starve to death. If there was a clap of thunder or someone fired a weapon, the shout would go up – 'A gun from a ship! A gun from a ship!' – and the settlers would stare at the horizon. But of course, no ship came.

Finally, on 1st April 1790, Phillip had to cut rations even more dramatically. The good news was that you were now given more rice, but there would be no more dried peas, no butter, only a third of the flour and a drastic cut in the amount of meat. Life had been difficult; now it became desperate. Every grain of rice was a moving body due to its living inhabitants. But then, on 3rd June of that year, another cry echoed through the little settlement: 'The flag's up!' It was a signal from the harbour look-out that, at long last, a ship was coming in.

There was an immediate outpouring of emotion unlike anything that had previously occurred. On the little streets of Sydney there was kissing and crying, and even Phillip's public-school-educated officers 'wrung each other by the hand, with eyes and hearts overflowing'. And when the word 'London' was finally made out on the ship's stern, the population was completely overwhelmed. It was

the *Juliana*, the first of five ships that would arrive over the next few weeks, bringing with them their long-awaited famine relief, enough people to quadruple the size of the population, and more degradation and misery than anyone could possibly have imagined.

The First Hanging

In the first few months of the settlement, crime was remarkably low, with one exception – the theft of food. Whereas in other circumstances this might have been seen as a trivial offence, here it was treated with deadly seriousness. Putative colonies elsewhere in the Empire had been wiped out by the kind of food shortages the new colony experienced, and Phillip wasn't prepared to take any chances. He was in many ways a liberal man and certainly didn't want to impose heavy-handed edicts on his charges, but when it came to those stealing food, he felt obliged to be firm – although clearly with a heavy heart.

He assembled all the convicts and, adopting a tone reminiscent of a public-school headmaster, made a statement on the subject of food theft. Many of those in front of him, he said, were incorrigible, and he was convinced nothing but absolute intolerance would make them behave properly. Food was of the utmost consequence to them all, so stealing even the most trifling amount would be punished with death, 'however much this severity might militate against my own humanity and feelings'.

It wasn't long before his humanity and feelings were put to the test in

LEFT: An early photograph of the corner of Harrington and Essex Streets, in Sydney's The Rocks, where Thomas Barrett became the first man to be hanged in Australia

the person of Thomas Barrett. In 1782, at the age of twelve Thomas had been condemned to death for stealing a watch, a hook, two shirts and a nightdress, a sentence that was commuted to transportation to the American colonies. But he became involved in a mutiny on board the transport ship *Mercury*, when the mutineers forced the ship to put in to Torbay shortly after it left for North America. Barrett escaped, was captured and was once more sentenced to death, this time for 'being criminally at large in England'. Again his sentence was commuted to transportation, apparently because the court recognised that he had intervened when a fellow mutineer was intent on souveniring the captain's ear, using a pair of scissors.

While on board the prison hulk *Dunkirk* waiting to be transported (this time to Australia), Barrett began to learn how to work metal. Prisoners made little discs out of salvaged copper alloy or low-denomination coins, which were polished and inscribed with poems or affectionate phrases. These 'love tokens' were then sold to other convicts who gave them to their sweethearts as mementos of the fact that they were about to be sent away, maybe forever. Barrett had never been trained in this kind of craft, but he not only picked it up very quickly, he rapidly became a talented forger.

In March 1787, he boarded the *Charlotte* bound for Botany Bay, and by the time it got to Rio de Janeiro, he'd been caught making counterfeit coins, which he'd managed to manufacture out of pewter spoons and old buttons.

He seems to have found it utterly impossible to stop this life of crime, because shortly after he arrived in the new colony he was in trouble once more, this time for stealing peas, butter and pork from one of the public stores. Yet again he was found guilty, and even though he was one of very few craftsmen in the colony and was consequently highly valued, Phillip felt obliged to sentence him to death.

On a late February day at six in the evening in the year 1788, Barrett was marched by the marine garrison to the junction of Essex Street and Harrington Street. The entire convict population had been ordered to gather there, so they could witness the ultimate punishment for the theft of food.

A young convict called James Freeman was the hangman. Like Barrett, he'd previously been sentenced to death for stealing food from another convict. But Phillip had pardoned him on condition he become the colony's public executioner. This might appear to have been a pretty good trade-off, but Freeman didn't want to be a hangman – he thought it would make the other convicts hate him, an apprehension with which one can sympathise.

You can imagine Freeman's dilemma. He was standing in front of the man who'd pardoned him, and who could rescind the pardon if he didn't do his job properly. On the other hand, he probably believed that if he killed Barrett he'd end up lying in the bush somewhere with a knife through his shoulder blades. So, rather pathetically (if understandably), he tried to stall. He procrastinated, fiddled about and

generally took so long to get Barrett, the gibbet and the rope sorted out, that eventually Major Ross, the head of the marines, threatened to shoot him if he didn't get on with it.

Up to this point Barrett had been noticeably relaxed – presumably he thought he'd get a last-minute reprieve, as had happened to him twice before. But Freeman now speeded up, at which point Barrett realised it was third time unlucky, and suddenly he became terrified. Freeman yanked on the rope, Barrett was asphyxiated and lost control of his bowels, and the entire captive audience, including the First Fleet children, were treated to a vivid example of Phillip's justice.

Some time before he had arrived in Australia, and with the active encouragement of one of the Fleet's officers, Barrett had etched the magnificent Charlotte Medal. It's an elaborate and extended version of a convict love token made out of a flattened medical kidney dish, and shows a fully-rigged ship of the First Fleet in exquisite detail. It's widely regarded as the first work of art to be created by a colonist, and the Sydney National Maritime Museum recently bought it at auction for three quarters of a million dollars.

So Barrett has two claims to fame. His Charlotte Medal is the most valuable object in the National Maritime Museum's collection, and he was the first European to be executed in Australia – a celebrity indeed!

1789–1802

A Bold Intrepid Countenance Which Bespoke Defiance and Revenge

Arabanoo

There was a serious disagreement among the First Fleeters, one that even today continues to rumble on around Australia, generating long embarrassed silences whenever the subject is mentioned. Some of the early white settlers held the Aboriginals in absolute contempt. They said 'the natives' were feckless, lazy and stupid. Others, including Governor Phillip, thought this kind of talk was ignorant nonsense. He wanted to learn their language, discover what they ate, understand

BELOW: A painting of unknown provenance of one of the Aboriginals befriended by Governor Macquarie, c.1810–21

their mysterious rituals, even make friends with them. This wasn't just out of idle curiosity. The colonists were perched precariously on the edge of a vast unknown continent; Phillip calculated that it would be much safer for them, if they could convince the locals that they were friends, rather than enemies who deserved to be run through with a spear.

Unfortunately, winning the Aboriginals over didn't prove easy. A year after the Fleet had landed, they still showed no inclination whatsoever to engage with the Europeans and their little colony. So Phillip devised a hands-on adult-education scheme – he identified a likely-looking Aboriginal and kidnapped him. The victim's name was Arabanoo, and on New Year's Eve 1788 he was snatched from his people's territory in Manly and brought to the settlement in chains.

His arrival caused a sensation; women, children and soldiers mobbed him. Not surprisingly, he was deeply distressed, but he was a resilient man and the following day gave a superb performance at the formal New Year's Day lunch held at the governor's home. Everything in the room was alien to him, including the knife, fork, plates and napkins. But he was treated as an honoured guest who would immediately appreciate the etiquette of European table manners, and was even offered a glass of liquor, which he smelled, found repulsive and declined.

Aboriginals commonly interact with others from different kinship areas, and tend to be far more adept than Westerners at picking up new customs. Arabanoo was particularly quick on the uptake, and managed to get through the entire meal without mishap, including the toast to the King, which he performed with his glass of water. But when he'd finished eating, he picked up his plate and made to throw it out of the window, an appropriate thing to do if your usual tableware is a large leaf or a piece of bark. However, the diners were eating off the only china service in the colony, so those nearby swiftly grabbed his arm and saved the valuable plate – a

BELOW: Australian Aboriginals, attributed to George Charles Jenner and William Waterhouse, pre-1806

story that must have grown even more hilarious with each telling.

Naval Officer Watkin Tench, who wrote some of the shrewdest reports about the early months of the colony, gave a well-observed account of Arabanoo's behavior as the governor's house guest:

'Our dogs and cats had ceased to be objects of fear, and were to become his greatest pets, and constant companions at table . . . Much information relating to the customs and manners of his country was also gained from him . . . He knew that he was in our power; but the independence of his mind never forsook him. If the slightest insult were offered to him, he would return it with interest.'

He was an odd kind of guest; one who was kept in handcuffs, with a convict specially assigned to make sure he didn't escape. Yet despite his fetters, his gaolers were absolutely convinced he was happy. He had his own quarters in Government House, enjoyed playing with the domestic animals, and gave little treats from his plate to the small children. He even began to adopt European fashions – his beard was shaved and his hair was cut short – although he had to be prevented from picking up his shorn locks and eating the lice.

Unfortunately, he never became the Aboriginal diplomat Phillip had hoped for. He struggled to learn English, and so couldn't understand what the colonists wanted him to communicate to his fellow Aboriginals, and when he returned to his home, his visits were a failure. Phillip had taken him back to Manly to show his clan that he'd been treated well, but Arabanoo's clan wouldn't even come out to say hello to him, even though he'd left them a present of three birds in a basket. Perhaps they felt he'd sold out. His

capture had trapped him between two cultures – his old one disowned him, and as for his new one, he soon discovered that European life wasn't all about stroking puppies and playing with babies.

Some convicts were convicted of plotting to assault a party of Aboriginals and steal fishing tackle and spears from the Aboriginals and were sentenced to a hundred and fifty lashes. Arabanoo was invited to watch the punishment being administered, so that he could see that white people's justice applied not only to those who mistreated other whites, but also to those who did Aboriginals

BELOW: *Taking of Colbee & Benalon. 25 Novr 1789*, by William Bradley, c.1802

Were the Aboriginals Right?

What caused the smallpox epidemic?

1. *It could have been spread from a smallpox scab carried in a sealed bottle for immunisation purposes. Aboriginals at the time (and some today) say it was deliberately spread by the British, but Phillip's doctor insisted that the flask was unbroken and secure on a shelf.*

2. *Did convicts or crew accidentally pass it on? Smallpox wasn't ever recorded among them, and the outbreak was over a year after the First Fleet arrived – too long a gap for the FF to have been the source?*

3. *The French? There's the same big gap between La Pérouse and the outbreak. N.B. Respected scientist Tim Flannery believes it's possible the disease spread slowly from Botany Bay to Sydney because of the Aboriginals' strict quarantine rules. If so, the long gap isn't so relevant.*

4. *The Macassans (Indonesian visitors)? They traded with Aboriginals along the Australian north coast. But could the infection have come from the north? Unlikely – it seems to have started in Sydney.*

5. *Accidentally spread by the British? Perhaps the virus lay dormant in clothing and bedding given by them to the Aboriginals.*

Whatever the cause, it's estimated two thousand Aboriginals perished.

harm. But unfortunately this little demonstration didn't go well. Far from being comforted by its firmness and fairness, he was appalled by its barbarity and made his disgust plain.

Phillip was certainly insensitive in his dealings with Arabanoo, but at least he was trying in his ham-fisted way to bridge the cultural abyss that existed between the Aboriginals and the Europeans. Sadly, though, his attempt came to nothing. Arabanoo's time with his captors ended a few months later when the local Aboriginal population was almost wiped out by smallpox.

Many colonists had the pitted faces of smallpox survivors, but by and large they were relatively immune to its worst effects. Not so the Eora people, who had no protection from it. Dead Aboriginal bodies, particularly those of women, children and the old, piled up around the shores of Sydney Harbour.

The question on everyone's lips was where had it come from? Watkin Tench wrote: 'An extraordinary calamity was now observed among the natives . . .

ABOVE: Painting of Bennelong, by
William Waterhouse, c. 1793

Pustules similar to those occasioned by the smallpox were thickly spread on the bodies; but how a disease, to which our former observations had led us to suppose them strangers, could at once have introduced itself, and have spread so widely, seemed inexplicable.'

Whatever its cause, its effect was devastating. Death was so widespread there weren't enough people available to bury the bodies, many of which were left lying where they fell, which was completely at odds with the usual quarantine practices among the Aboriginals. Others fled the region, leaving their dying family members with nothing but a small fire to warm them and a container of water to drink. And of course, those who left spread the disease further afield.

Arabanoo was taken back to Manly for one final visit, ostensibly to try to find his family and friends, although Phillip wanted him to assure the Aboriginals that it wasn't the British who had started the epidemic. But there was no one left to tell. Arabanoo found his home deserted. When he looked around, all he saw were dead bodies. 'He lifted up his hands and eyes in silent agony for some time; at last he exclaimed, "All dead, all dead!" then hung his head in mournful silence.'

A number of sick Aboriginals were being treated close to the settlement and Arabanoo spent the few remaining weeks of his life attending to them. Then he became ill. At first his new friends believed he was suffering from a minor ailment, but it soon became clear that he too had fallen victim to the disease. He died on 18th May 1789. Governor Phillip arranged for him 'to be buried in his own garden, and attended the funeral in person'.

Bennelong

After Arabanoo's death, Phillip was once again left without a line of communication to the Aboriginals. He was still determined to set some of them up in Sydney with all the comforts of Western society, as an example of how good such a life could be. But since none could be persuaded to move there, Phillip, undeterred by the failure of his first kidnapping experiment, sent another snatch squad out to Manly Cove. They tempted two local men with gifts of fish, grabbed them and rowed away again, hotly pursued by the captives' spear-throwing kinsmen.

Phillip himself, of course, took no part in the mugging and hijacking, but his men had to face the brutal reality his orders entailed. The artist and diarist William Bradley led the party of sailors, and wrote: 'The noise of the men, crying and screaming, of the women and children, together with the situation of the two miserable wretches in our possession, was really a most distressing scene . . . by far the most unpleasant service I was ever ordered to execute.'

The two captured men were called Colebee and Bennelong, and they were both survivors of the smallpox. Colebee's face in particular was heavily marked by it. Bennelong was about twenty-six years old, 'with a bold intrepid countenance, which

ABOVE & OPPOSITE:
Eminent author
and historian Thomas
Keneally gamely stands
in for Cook to help
explain the Captain's
spearing in Manly

bespoke defiance and revenge'. He was a funny and charismatic character, and was well-liked among the different clans around the harbour, even though he had a reputation as a serial womaniser.

On their arrival in the settlement, both men were chained up, but seventeen days later Colebee managed to escape (the convict looking after him received a hundred lashes for 'excessive carelessness'). Bennelong stayed put. Unlike Arabanoo, he picked up English very quickly, interacted with everyone, told them about his life and enthusiastically mimicked the British lifestyle, dressing up in trousers and a jacket for regular dinners at the governor's table, at which, unlike Arabanoo, he toasted the King with a glass of wine.

At last the governor had found an Aboriginal who seemed to want to engage in his cross-cultural experiment. Indeed, a strong bond seems to have developed between the two men; Bennelong called Phillip *Beanna* (father), and Phillip called Bennelong *Dooroow* (son).

By April 1790, Bennelong was considered loyal enough to be released from his chains, although he was still closely guarded. A month later, he completely nonplussed Phillip by feigning illness, requesting permission to go outside to the toilet, climbing over a fence, taking off his clothes and leaving the settlement to rejoin his own people. Clearly the experiment had failed. Bennelong had been showered with the comforts of European life and, even though 'a whole world was opened up to him', he had obviously not given up his 'savage' ways. Had Phillip failed to see the reality behind this relationship – that beneath Bennelong's conviviality was a desire to learn what the British wanted, look for a way to appease them and maybe even find out how to make them leave?

Search parties were sent out around the harbour to look for him. But all they heard in reply when they called out to him, were the high, teasing voices of the fisherwomen in the harbour mimicking their clumsy attempts to pronounce his name. Bennelong had disappeared.

A couple of months later a tragedy occurred in the harbour. Four of Phillip's men were rowing in a small boat, when a whale that had eluded harpooning only days earlier, loomed out of the water close by them. They tried to avoid it by tacking this way and that, but the next time it surfaced, it was so close that the wash poured into their boat and they could only prevent themselves from sinking by furiously bailing out. The whale then disappeared and they gradually became convinced it had swum off. But like the scary climax of a horror-at-sea movie, it suddenly rose out of the water for a third time, only this time it did so directly under their boat, which was lifted high in to the air, until it slid off the creature's back, dropped like a stone into the water, and immediately sank. Two of the men were sucked into the vortex and never reappeared. The other two swam for the shore, but only one reached it alive.

Eventually, the whale washed up on Manly beach, where it was killed by local Aboriginals, who, over the ensuing weeks, hacked it to pieces for a feast. Bennelong was seen among them, and on 7th September, he sent Governor Phillip a large piece of its stinking blubber.

Who knows whether Bennelong's present was a token of affection or a ploy to lure Phillip to Manly? Certainly Phillip seems to have been relaxed about the situation. Although he had some musketeers with him when he set out to see Bennelong the same day, he left them in the boat while he and two fellow officers went ashore. Bennelong approached Phillip, who didn't recognise him at first because the Aboriginal's beard had re-grown and he no longer had respectably coiffured European hair.

They began a good-natured conversation about Bennelong's Sydney days, but then the mood changed. There were other Aboriginals on the beach who had been engrossed in butchering the whale. Now they

began to encircle Phillip and the officers he had brought with him. On the ground in front of Bennelong was a barbed spear of 'uncommon size'. Phillip asked if he could have it, but Bennelong picked it up and placed it down in front of an older, rather corpulent man who appeared tense and agitated.

Phillip tried to calm him down by dropping his sword and approaching him with arms open, whereupon the man, who was named Willemerring, picked up the spear, stepped back onto his right leg and hurled the weapon at Phillip with such force that it went through his shoulder just above the collarbone and downwards through his body, with half of it protruding from his back. Willemerring stared at his victim for long enough to ensure he'd done his job properly, then hared off into the bushes.

Phillip tried to retreat to his boat, but the spear was so long (almost four metres), that he couldn't move without it scraping on the ground. He begged Lieutenant Waterhouse, 'For God's sake, haul out the spear.' The young man attempted to do so, but by now they were under fire from other Aboriginal spears.

Waterhouse described that moment with military precision:

'I then determined on breaking it off and bent it down for that purpose, but owing to its length could not effect it. I then bent it upwards but could not break it owing to the toughness of the wood. Just at this instant another spear came and just grazed the skin off between the thumb and forefinger of my right hand. I must own it frightened me a good

BELOW: Aboriginals cooking and eating beached whales in Newcastle, by Joseph Lycett, c.1817

deal and I believe added to my exertions, for the next sudden jerk I gave it, it broke short off.'

Once back in the boat, the crew rowed as fast as they could back to Sydney. Waterhouse supported the governor in his arms the whole way. Phillip was completely lucid, but both he and his men were aware that the spear could have caused serious internal damage, and that attempting to remove it might kill him.

As soon as he arrived back in Sydney, and still believing his life was about to end, the governor ordered that no native should be attacked in retaliation for the wounding. Had he wanted an excuse to launch a punitive strike, now was the moment he could justifiably do so, but he chose not to, even though some of his officers saw the spearing as a terrible act of betrayal.

The weapon was finally removed, and when the spear point was examined, it was discovered that it didn't have the jagged stones of an Aboriginal death spear. It seemed that Willemerring's thrust was specifically designed not to kill.

The Aboriginals' behaviour after the attack baffled the British. They didn't run away, they didn't attack anyone else, but they all carried on with their ordinary lives, including Willemerring, the perpetrator. Phillip's initial thought was that Willemerring had thrown the spear out of panic, fearing that he too might be kidnapped, but the governor soon came to the opinion that he had been on the receiving end of a piece of 'payback', a ritual punishment for a perceived wrong inflicted without malice. Phillip concluded that such assaults weren't attempted murder, but that the Aboriginals were guilty merely of 'occasionally taking a life in their quarrels', like the poor in England did when they stripped to the waist to give each other a good hiding. If this was the case, then Willemerring was probably a 'wise man', brought in from another clan to inflict retribution on the British leader for the crimes of his people – camping on land without permission, the stealing of fish and game, random shootings and the curse of smallpox and other diseases.

If this is so, it seems to have worked in the way Bennelong and Willemerring intended, because the result of this violent and potentially explosive event was an increase in harmony and interaction between the two races, at least for the next few months.

'This accident gave cause to the opening of a communication between the natives of this country and the settlement, which, although attended with such an unpromising beginning, it was hoped would be followed with good consequences.'
– CAPTAIN COLLINS

Once Phillip had fully recovered, he sent his men to give Bennelong an invitation to visit his home, to show him there were no hard feelings. But Bennelong insisted that Phillip come to him. Eventually, a compromise was reached and the two men met out in the harbour, Phillip in his boat and Bennelong in his canoe. Their friendship swiftly resumed.

The governor even ordered a brick house to be built for his friend, which was erected on one of the most iconic spots on the harbour, where the Opera House now stands. 'He has lately become a man of so much dignity and consequence,' one of Phillip's lieutenants wrote rather peevishly, 'that it was not always possible to obtain his company.'

Bennelong remained close to Phillip for as long as he was governor, and was an influential figure in the colony. His opinion was sought by the British and he became a major player among his own people (although his manipulative and sometimes brutal treatment of native women was a constant problem).

When the governor finally returned to England, Bennelong went with him. He lived in London, and went on trips to the Houses of Parliament and to the home of the prime minister. Back in Sydney, he described one episode, a visit he made to the house of 'a very respectable gentleman', where he was surrounded by a crowd of curious guests, eager to observe this exotic trophy. But one old man, unmoved by all the fuss, ignored him, and instead helped himself to large quantities of snuff, while requesting the other guests to pour him another drink. If that was the one incident that stuck in Bennelong's memory, it sounds as though his stay was a pretty appalling one.

Back home, Bennelong was a changed man. He now affected the style and manners of an English gentleman, and was seriously put out by 'some little indelicacies of his sister Carrangarang', who visited him to say hello, having 'left her habiliments behind her'.

Sydney had changed too. A new class of settlers and officers had arrived, for whom the acquisition of land was an absolute priority, regardless of who might have been living on it for the previous few thousand years. The door to good relations between the Aboriginals and the British had been kicked firmly and catastrophically shut.

Bennelong took up residence in Government House again, but now he had become an irrelevance, and the prestige that went with his former role had drained away. He took this hard, stalking the streets naked, clutching his spear and threatening to kill the new governor.

Eventually, he turned his back on Government House, discarded his European clothes for good and went to live back with his own people. Many Europeans accused him of descending into a liquor-driven decline and said he had lost his influence over his fellow Aboriginals. On his death, the *Sydney Gazette* even wrote: 'Of this veteran champion of the native tribe little favourable can be said. His voyage and benevolent treatment in Britain produced no change whatever in his manners and inclinations, which were naturally barbarous and ferocious.' But this doesn't seem to be borne out by the evidence. On his death bed Bennelong was surrounded by at least a hundred of his kinsmen – hardly the response of an alienated family.

ABOVE: Pemulwuy, by
S J Neele, 1804

Pemulwuy

Early in his career with the British, Bennelong had developed a profound dislike for a fellow Aboriginal called Pemulwuy. It's not difficult to see why the two men developed a mutual antipathy. Bennelong was by nature a conciliator who wanted to try and understand the colonists and negotiate with them. Pemulwuy was a radical, hell-bent on driving them out of his country.

But what the two men had in common was a loathing for Governor Phillip's gamekeeper, John McEntire. There was a long list of offences of which he stood guilty in Aboriginal eyes. He slaughtered animals they considered for their use alone. He killed dingoes, which only male initiates were allowed to do. Worst of all, he had raped Aboriginal women and killed Aboriginal men. In the eyes of the Eora, he deserved to die. But he was popular among the colonial officers, not least because he shot birds and animals that the more scientifically minded among them could study, and the rest could pluck and eat.

Pemulwuy was a *carradhy*, a special person chosen by the clan in childhood to be trained in sacred rites and the interpretation of dreams. His strangeness was accentuated by a deformed foot and a flawed eye. He was charismatic and believed himself invincible. It's hardly surprising that it was Pemulwuy who led the punishment attack on the gamekeeper.

A sergeant had taken a number of convict hunters including McEntire to shoot game. They had built a hide out of branches, and, as hunters often do, they fell asleep in it. They were eventually woken by the approach of five Aboriginals. McEntire wasn't panicked by this – he was already familiar with Pemulwuy and didn't regard him as dangerous. But his complacency proved misplaced when Pemulwuy ran him through with a spear. 'I am a dead man,' McEntire is reported to have groaned.

Unlike on previous occasions, Phillip was furious about this attack. Indeed, he was so angry that it was almost as though he had suddenly been transformed into a cartoon dictator. He immediately jettisoned his policy of fostering good relations with the Aboriginals and instead ordered bloody revenge attacks. Punishment expeditions were sent out into the

bush complete with hatchets and bags, in order that the pursuers could bring back the severed heads of Pemulwuy and his cohorts. But these expeditions soon degenerated into pantomime. The soldiers were carrying sixty-pound packs and had to wade through rivers and mosquito-ridden swamps, where they got stuck waist-deep in the mud, while Pemulwuy's men easily eluded them.

Unlike the weapon thrown at Phillip, McEntire had been on the receiving end of a death spear with stone flakes embedded in it which disperse like shrapnel on impact. It took McEntire a long time to die, during which time he made a deathbed confession of his crimes. Watkin Tench wrote: 'The poor wretch now began . . . to accuse himself of the commission of crimes of the deepest dye, accompanied with such expressions of his despair of God's mercy as are too terrible to repeat.'

Why Phillip chose to go down the path of savage reprisals isn't clear. At the time, he justified his actions to the appalled Watkin Tench by explaining: 'I am fully persuaded that they [McEntire's attackers] were unprovoked, and the barbarity of their conduct admits of no extenuation.' But this doesn't explain his desire for mass decapitation. Perhaps his response was that of a man distressed by the death of someone he cared for. We know he was often a poor judge of character and could be remarkably loyal and affectionate to people who hardly deserved it (like the

nondescript alcoholic Henry Brewer, who he appointed provost marshal of the colony even though he had no qualifications for the job). Perhaps he held McEntire in similar esteem.

Whatever the reason, the outcome was disastrous, because there now followed a twelve-year war between the British soldiers and Pemulwuy. His resistance army grew, swelled not only by warriors from other clans, but also by escaped and disaffected Irish convicts. They ambushed colonists, burned down maize fields, and at one time came so close to the Sydney settlement that they were able to attack a man near a brickfield on the perimeter of the little town.

Then, in 1797, Pemulwuy led one hundred fighters in a pitched battle against the British on open ground near the Parramatta River. He was shot seven times in 'the Battle of Parramatta' and presumed dead. But in a remarkable display of admiration, the soldiers took him to the nearby hospital, where he healed against all expectations and, although in chains, managed to escape. According to his clan, the Bidjigal people, he achieved this apparently impossible escape by turning into a crow.

His ability to recover from his wounds gave him a superhero reputation. The Aboriginals believed that bullets couldn't harm him, nor could chains hold him. Even the colonists started believing the myths. John Washington Price, a surgeon on the transport ship *Minerva*, wrote, 'He has now lodged in him, in shot, sluggs and bullets, about eight or ten ounces of lead.'

But Pemulwuy was eventually proved human. His resistance came to an end in 1802, when he was killed by Henry Hacking, a seaman, bounty hunter and drunk. He was decapitated, and his head was put in a jar and sent to Joseph Banks in London.

It is remarkable that, although the Aboriginals conducted organised resistance against the British colonists for twelve years, this war is just a footnote in most histories of Australia. And few people are aware that the rebel leader's head was severed from its body, pickled, sent to England and kept in the British Museum until it was lost.

But there's an interesting twist to this story. Recently, the grandson of the present Queen of England – Prince William – has been enlisted to try to find Pemulwuy's head and return it to Australia. I hope he's successful.

A Man of Honour

Governor Phillip

There now follows a chapter in praise of Arthur Phillip. This may come as a surprise to my more attentive readers, given his puzzlingly barbaric response to the killing of John McEntire. Indeed, his entire relationship with the Eora people is hard to fathom – sometimes he was austere, at other times open-hearted, sometimes forgiving, at others vengeful. I suspect the Eora were as confused by him as he was by them.

And yet, for all his inconsistencies, under his influence relations between the colonials and the Aboriginals remained relatively stable, and the bullyboys and bigots were by and large kept in check. It was only after he'd left Australia and other governors had taken his place that a culture of wanton disregard towards the Indigenous people became the norm, and massacre and theft grew commonplace.

BELOW: Governor Phillip still looks over downtown Sydney

His dream of a society that tolerated difference and sustained everyone died soon after he left Australia in 1792. Yet Phillip, of all the early representatives of Imperial Britain, had the most impact on the future of the little colony. That's why I've dedicated this chapter to him – even though it's only a brief one.

Arthur Phillip was a fascinating man who, rather like the villain in a whodunit, was doubly fascinating because he appeared to be so ordinary. Like Captain Cook, he was of humble origins. He was trained for the navy at a school for the sons of poor seamen, served as an apprentice on a squalid, grease-laden whaler, and joined the Royal Navy as a captain's servant. And yet this low-born and rather sickly man would eventually be given charge of an eleven-ship flotilla on a government-sponsored journey to the other side of the world.

It was noted very early in his career that Phillip was shrewd and talented; his rise through the navy's ranks bears witness to that fact. He fought in the Seven Years' War in Minorca and Cuba, and was seconded to the Portuguese navy when Portugal requested that the British lend them some capable officers to help them in their fight against the Spanish in 'the debatable lands' – contested territory at the mouth of the River Plate in South America. He also served as a British spy, journeying round the French ports to ascertain their 'naval force and stores in the arsenals'.

He had had little or no schooling, had been a sailor from the age of fifteen, and had no experience of the British penal system – but Lord Sydney

doesn't seem to have been concerned about these gaps in his CV. He wanted an officer to lead the First Fleet who would be robust and adaptable, someone capable not only of leading a complex naval operation and setting up a brand-new British colony from scratch, but also of administrating the largest open prison in the world. He couldn't have chosen anyone better than Phillip, whose combination of dry humour, reserve, efficiency, intellectual curiosity, commonsense and (by and large) level-headedness were the perfect qualifications for the job.

His personal life, though, is very revealing. It gives a clue as to the turmoil this reserved and dependable man seems to have undergone throughout much of his adult life. At the age of twenty-five he married Margaret Denison, a wealthy widow fifteen years older than him. He then took a sabbatical from the navy and ran her dairy in the New Forest, but six years later, for some mysterious

LEFT: Aboriginal by 'the Port Jackson Painter', a prolific First Fleet artist some maintain was Henry Brewer, c.1788–92

reason, their relationship broke down and, according to the official documents, they 'lately lived separate and apart'.

Then, in 1782, he became captain of a ship called the *Europe* and fell in with an unmarried man named Henry Brewer. They were very close, in fact so intimate that Phillip's American boson Edward Spain alleged 'they rode in the same boat . . . no doubt they had their own reasons for wishing to make the voyage together' – whatever that may mean!

Henry Brewer

Henry Brewer was a heavy drinker and decidedly unpopular among his contemporaries (apart from Governor Phillip).

According to his shipmate Edward Spain, he was the possessor of 'coarse harsh features, and contracted brow which bespoke him a man sour'd by disappointment; a forbidding countenance, always muttering to himself . . . and wearing . . . a blue hat of the coarsest cloth, a wool hat about three shillings a piece, cocked with three sixpenny nails, a tolerable waistcoat, a pair of cordurry breeches, purser's stockings and shoes, a purser shirt, none of the cleanest'.

But if one intimate adventure wasn't enough, at the island of St Helena the *Europe* picked up four British sailors and their women. Why they were allowed on board appears to have been a bit of a puzzle, although the bitchy Swain later wrote, 'Don't imagine that it was out of any partiality to any of them, except one . . . and had he given permission to her alone the reason would have been obvious to the officers and the ship's company.' The 'one' in question was a married woman named Deborah Brooks, who remained at Phillip's side for many years as his housekeeper and *amorata*. Indeed, both Henry Brewer (who became Phillip's clerk and, later, provost marshal of New South Wales) and Mrs Brooks joined the First Fleet and remained close to Phillip throughout his Sydney days.

By 1792, Phillip was a very sick man, exhausted by the effort of setting up a new colony, and constantly pleading with the British government to be allowed home. Eventually, permission was granted and he sailed back to England accompanied not only by Bennelong but also Mrs Brooks. By this time he was so ill it was thought he was about to die, but he confounded the pessimists by recovering and taking retirement with a Royal Naval pension of £500 per year. He then married Isabella Whitehead, the 45-year-old daughter of a wealthy merchant. What happened to Mrs Brooks isn't known.

Arthur Phillip was a man of honour, and although in many ways he was a progressive, he was an authoritarian rather than a democrat. He was, for instance, determined that the convicts in his charge shouldn't be seen as slaves, and that their rights, their health and their safety should be respected. Nevertheless, he viewed them as second-class citizens, morally and intellectually

incapable of providing the basis for a flourishing colony.

On the practical side, he left an indelible mark on the colony – by the time he retired from public life there were regular ships between Sydney and the outside world, flourishing crops of corn and wheat, and decent housing for both convicts and free settlers. But it is his philosophy that became so influential, and is still reflected in Australia's institutions today – a belief in the supremacy of law, the importance of community and the desirability of co-operation.

Arthur Phillip once said he hoped that when his time came, he would have done enough not only to satisfy his masters, but also to satisfy his own honour as an officer.

For all his faults, he can probably sleep easy.

LEFT: *The Pioneer*, a portrait of Arthur Phillip by H Macbeth-Raeburn, published in 1936
PREVIOUS PAGE: A view of Sydney Cove in 1794, attributed to convict Thomas Watling, but possibly painted in England from a drawing by Watling

1803–1877

A Dreadful and Awful Example to Others

There's a fancy restaurant on Pinchgut Island, in the middle of Sydney Harbour, where they serve fresh oysters with 'Francis Morgan dressing'. I recommend them – they're a savoury reminder of an unsavoury but very dignified man.

However much Governor Phillip may have wished to bring law and order to his new colony, crimes began to be committed almost as soon as the first settlers got off the boat. It soon became apparent that a system of punishment was going to be required to deal with the most serious offenders, but there weren't any fences or fortifications to lock up the evil-doers, and Phillip didn't seem to consider the construction of a prison stockade a priority. Instead, the worst offenders were banished in chains to the tiny island of Pinchgut, which was conveniently surrounded by shark-infested waters.

BELOW: The imposing Fort Denison, in Sydney Harbour, c.1885

Pinchgut

It was a little cone of sandstone, fourteen metres high, covered with bushes and stunted trees, which the local Eora people had called *Mat-te-wan-ye* and Phillip had christened Rock Island. It had been a popular site for them to swim, fish and generally hang out, but it was now transformed into a stark place of punishment.

There are two theories why the island became known as Pinchgut. In nautical terms, a gut is a shipping channel and the place where a channel narrows is called a pinch gut. But it may also have seemed an appropriate name because of the meagre rations doled out to those incarcerated there. Whatever its derivation, 'Pinchgut' was soon known not just as a place, but as a dire warning of the dreadful treatment meted out to those who committed crime in the new colony.

Not that the prospect of isolation, irons and chains, and semi-starvation were enough on their own to deter habitual criminals from their errant ways. Execution was soon added to this hideous cocktail.

Francis Morgan was brought to Pinchgut to be hung as a 'dreadful and awful example to others'. He was transported to the colony in 1793, having been caught wearing the watch of a Dublin man who'd recently been murdered. But three years later, on the north side of Sydney Harbour, he smashed the skull of another man, Simon Raven. This time he was found guilty of murder, and there was no reprieve.

He was taken to a gibbet erected on top of the island's promontory rock. It's said that, at the foot of the gallows, before the hangman placed the rope over his head, Morgan was asked if had any final words. He replied nonchalantly, 'Death is a morbid subject and I have no desire to confess

LEFT: Fort Denison today, site of a restaur ant with killer views

my sins . . . The only thing worth mentioning is the superb view of the harbour I have from up here. I'm sure there are no waters in the world that compare to it for beauty.'

After the hanging, Governor Hunter ordered Morgan's body to be tarred and hung from the gibbet post. It swung there for four years observing the superb views, before it finally disintegrated.

Walk to China

All colonies are built on dreams, and one of the most pervasive among the early convicts was that somewhere out in the wilds of Australia lay freedom. Many of them were convinced that Timor or perhaps New Guinea were a couple of days' hike away, or that a few hundred miles to the west was a mysterious 'white colony' where escapees would be offered sanctuary. Even free settlers came to believe these

myths, and eventually successive, frustrated governors sent expeditions in to the interior to disprove them.

But still the rumours persisted, particularly among the Irish convicts. This was not just because such men tended to have come from the countryside, where education for the poor was virtually nonexistent, but also because, once in Australia, their lives were made particularly miserable. Many of the Irish were dissidents rather than criminals, but the authorities viewed them as aggressive, insubordinate riff-raff, who were both stupid and threatening. They believed the only way to keep them in order was to brutalise them. A thousand lashes wasn't an uncommon punishment, and as many of them hadn't been issued with paperwork by the Irish government stating how long their transportation was to last, they were doomed to permanent banishment from their country and

Australia's Birth Certificate

The first person to sail round Van Diemen's Land was the explorer Matthew Flinders, who named the treacherous passage between the island and the mainland's southern coast Bass Strait, after his friend, the ship's surgeon and enthusiastic naturalist George Bass (the first European to describe my favourite Australian animal, the wombat).

In 1801 Flinders obtained the Admiralty's backing to chart the entire coastline of New Holland, and set out in the appropriately named HMS Investigator. He conducted a thorough survey of the continent's southern and eastern coasts, but by the time he reached the Gulf of Carpentaria in the north, his ship was in a dreadful state of disrepair and he had to abandon his scrupulous exploration. Nevertheless, he pressed on with the voyage and in 1803 hastily completed the first circumnavigation of the land that he described in a map he drafted as 'Australia', the first use of this appellation on any piece of cartography.

But on his journey home to England, his ship pulled into Mauritius, where he was arrested and detained by the French for six years. He finished the new map during this time and sent it to Sir Joseph Banks, who retained the Admiralty's preference for the term Terra Australis, despite Flinders arguing that 'Australia' was easier on the ear. Back in New South Wales, Governor Macquarie took up the cause and recommended Flinders' nomenclature be adopted, but it took until 1824 for the admiralty to officially christen the continent Australia.

The map, which has been called Australia's birth certificate, now resides in the UK Hydrographic Office in Somerset, but it can only viewed by appointment. Concerted efforts to have it returned to Australia in time for the bicentenary of Flinders death, in 2014, have so far been met with a polite but lofty refusal.

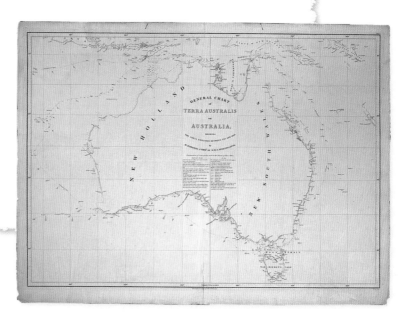

their loved ones. In this context, it's hardly surprising that they needed the consolation provided by stories of a Xanadu just around the corner.

One of the most bizarre notions to sweep through the colony was that China was separated from Australia by nothing more than a large river. It's easy now to scoff at such geographical ignorance, but at this time the centre of Australia was completely unexplored. Matthew Flinders didn't circumnavigate the continent until 1803, and up to that time no one knew for sure whether Australia was one great land mass, two separate islands, or a vast continent shaped like a Life Saver mint with a big ocean in the middle of it.

So the idea of walking overland to Peking or Hong Kong wasn't as irrational as it might seem. It was a practical attempt to make sense of a forbidding landscape, and it offered escapees the hope of freedom from their imperial masters.

On 1st November 1791, twenty men and a pregnant woman escaped from their labour camp in Parramatta in a bid to find freedom in China. They knew it must lie to the north of Sydney, but accidentally veered east and were soon hopelessly lost. The expedition swiftly turned from a shambles into a disaster. One man was speared to death by an Aboriginal, another died from heat and exhaustion, and within three days the party had accidentally split up, with little groups blundering haplessly around looking for each other. A large search party was sent out, and they eventually found the survivors hungry, exhausted and naked. The pregnant woman, Catherine Edwards, had been separated from the others. She was now closer to Sydney than she had been when she set out three days previously!

Once captured, the convicts were returned to Parramatta. But their dream hadn't died. As soon as they'd regained their strength, they ran away again. Whether or not they ever got to China no one knows.

Port Arthur

In 1803, Lieutenant John Bowen stuck a flag in the sand of Risdon Cove and declared Van Diemen's Land, or Tasmania as we now know it, the possession of King George of England.

It quickly became very useful to the prison authorities back in Sydney. As far as they were concerned, two types of convicts were emerging: those who could reform and those who couldn't, and the latter were a persistent problem. Sydney wasn't the appropriate place to house the growing number of recidivists – it was too easy for them to escape into the wilds of New South Wales. A penitentiary in Van Diemen's Land seemed a far more attractive idea. And so, in 1830, Port Arthur Penal Settlement was born. It was to be a penal settlement for the very worst offenders and the 'incorrigibles' or 'doubly damned', those who'd not only committed crimes before being transported to Australia, but had committed additional felonies once they'd arrived.

Its inaccessibility on the remote Tasman Peninsula made it the perfect location. Not only was it surrounded by icy waters full of

LEFT: Port Arthur today
ABOVE: Leg irons, chains, a ball and chain, a lash – the stuff of convict discipline, 1900
BELOW: The fearsome Dog Line on Eaglehawk Neck to prevent the escape of convicts, installed in 1832 and continued until the closure of Port Arthur in 1877

hungry sharks, but there was only one way out: across a narrow strip of land known as Eaglehawk Neck, which was illuminated by oil lamps and constantly guarded by soldiers and a line of eighteen savage dogs chained to posts.

When prisoners first arrived at Port Arthur, they were forced to perform long days of backbreaking, manual labour that was supposed to improve their character. If they worked hard and were well behaved, they could swiftly rise through the prison system and were trained in basic skills like carpentry, cooking or cleaning. But if they remained 'incorrigible' they were forced to continue with their gruelling hard slog, with the added indignity that they now had to wear leg irons. These monstrous manacles were welded together, so the prisoners were trapped in them twenty-four hours a day, and wore trousers with special buttons that allowed them to perform their ablutions without taking the irons off. They weren't just heavy, they were also extremely cumbersome, forcing those wearing them to shuffle slowly from place to place. The long lines of men which lugged freshly cut tree trunks around Port Arthur in this manner were known as centipede gangs. Accidents occurred – a 'centipede' could collapse like a line of dominoes if a man stumbled, and limbs would be crushed as the weight of the big trees crashed down on them.

The prison's policy was to deliberately overwork, underfeed and inadequately clothe the inmates, as punishment for their past misdeeds. This philosophy was explicitly

expressed by a governor of the colony, George Arthur, who stated that 'within the bounds of humanity, the offenders are to be subjected to the last degree of misery'.

The slightest breach of rules was met by physical punishment, often a flogging with a cat-o'-nine-tails.

One form of flogging involved tying prisoners to a metal triangle, a.k.a. 'the altar of discipline'. This was reserved for absconders, who when caught were tied to it to receive up to a hundred lashes, enough to reduce their backs to blood and pulp. If an absconder passed out, he was revived in a shallow bath of salt water, an agonising baptism that wasn't only implemented in order to allow the punishment to continue – the screams of the victim created a dramatic effect that made the event more vivid and memorable for those who were watching, to act as a deterrent. But just in case the fun went too far, a doctor stood by, who had the power to bring the grisly little procedure to a halt if any prisoner's life was in danger.

Once the punishment had been completed, those assembled were marched off to the strains of 'Praise the Lord', and the offenders were then given two days off work to recover. After that, they were put back in leg irons and many were assigned to work in the saltwater of Port Arthur's dockyard – another little dip to help them heal their wounds.

But this kind of theatrically brutal regime was becoming less popular, particularly among the fashionable new generation of prison reformers in London. In 1842, a new kind of

LEFT: From *The horrors of transportation* by Joseph Platt, c. 1849, depicting the author receiving 100 lashes

Flogging

The cat-o'-nine-tails was woven from nine thongs of leather, and each strip had nine knots tied along it, in order to catch the convict's flesh. Political prisoner John Frost described how a 'cat' was treated in order to make it more effective:

'[It] was made of the hardest whipcord, of an unusual size. The cord was put into salt water till it was saturated, it was then put into the sun to dry; by this process it became like a wire, the eighty-one knots cutting the flesh as if a saw had been used . . . The flogger using every means in his power to break the spirit of those who suffered . . .'

gaol had been built at Pentonville in London, whose regime was based on a very different vision of what a prison should be like. It involved constant observation and punishment, not of the body, but of the mind, in order to modify the prisoners' behaviour. In 1848, this radical exercise in social engineering was adopted at Port Arthur, where a new prison was built based on the model adopted at Pentonville and consequently was called the Model Prison.

To those on the receiving end, this new regime must initially have seemed a considerable improvement on the old one. Prisoners were regularly exercised, they were fed an adequate diet and the flogging stopped. But they were totally isolated, and no communication was allowed with either the wardens or their fellow prisoners. Matting was laid over the floor, not for comfort or warmth, but to block out the sound of anyone else's footfall. Warders wore felt slippers and used sign language to ensure the prisoners never heard them. The men were kept in solitary confinement for twenty-three hours a day, and when they were outside their cells they had to wear hoods so they couldn't communicate. They took exercise on their own in a small yard, and were fed through a hatch in their cell doors.

They had to obey dozens of rules and a rigid routine designed to train them in the virtues of order and discipline. Even in the little chapel, the pews were specially made in order to keep each member of the congregation isolated and alone. The only way the worshippers could communicate was by inserting their own words into the hymns, in the hope that the unseen prisoner in the next stall would hear them. This was solitary confinement at its most complete. Guantanamo Bay is a funfair compared to the mental cruelties inflicted at Port Arthur.

But if prisoners continued offending while they were locked in the Model Prison, how could their behaviour be scientifically modified? The answer was the punishment cell, which lay at the end of a long corridor behind four thick doors. The walls were a metre thick, it was completely devoid of light and soundproof, and locked inside it you could scream for days without being heard.

BELOW: The discrete pews of the Model Prison's chapel

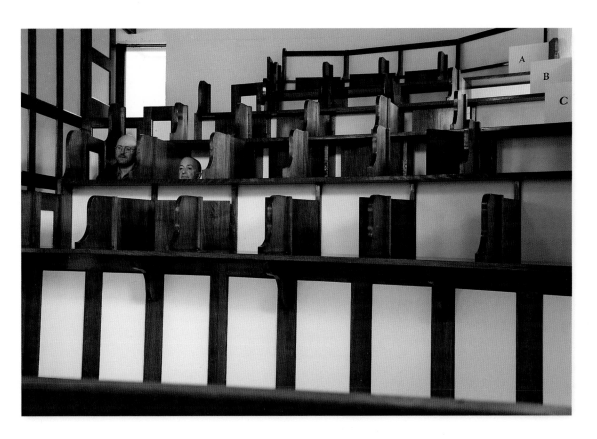

Solitary

I spent just over half an hour in the punishment cell during my visit to Port Arthur. For the first five minutes or so it was quite fun to be on my own in a little dark box. Then I gradually become aware of the sounds my body was making – my breathing, the rustles and cracks as I shifted from one foot to the other, the rumblings of my stomach – and after a while, even the blink of my eyelashes sounded like the crunch of a paper bag.

Then I began to retreat inside my own head. There was just me and my thoughts; the outside world seemed to have disappeared. In other circumstances this could have been the beginning of an illuminating meditation, but I was cold, uncomfortable and alone, and the experience didn't seem very transcendental at all.

My sense of time became totally distorted. When I was let out after thirty minutes I thought I'd only been inside for about ten. Whether I would have felt that same contraction of time after thirty days, though, I very much doubt.

Mad Billy

The Model Prison system caused far more problems than it ever cured, particularly psychological ones.

Billy Hunt arrived in Tasmania in 1825. He'd been found guilty of stealing a pocket handkerchief. Silk handkerchiefs had become all the rage in London and were worn temptingly dangled from gentlemen's pockets. So handkerchief theft became rife, and the law in its wisdom initiated a severe clampdown on the perpetrators of this heinous crime.

Billy was transported for fourteen years. Previously he'd been a chimney sweep, a seller of quack medicines and an actor. But there was a strange and sometimes glorious insanity about Billy. Shortly after his arrival, he committed several acts of violence in Hobart Town, and was incarcerated in an asylum for the insane. He got away, but was recaptured and ended up in Port Arthur. Once again he escaped, but this time he did so in a brilliant disguise. He dressed up in a kangaroo skin and hopped out of the prison grounds. It's said that two of the guards at Eaglehawk Neck were bored with their rations and were dreaming of kangaroo stew, and when they saw a big marsupial bounding its way to freedom, they raised their muskets to fire – at which the kangaroo stuck its hands in the air and yelled, 'Don't shoot, I'm only Billy Hunt!'

Poor Billy couldn't stay out of trouble. In 1834 he was sentenced to thirty days' solitary on bread and water for 'having in his possession a counterfeit shilling and endeavouring to traffic with the same'. In 1835 he was put in irons for three weeks for 'skulking in the rear of the military barracks without permission of his overseer, and other improper conduct'. In 1837 he received three months on the chain gang for 'sleeping under the same covering with George Meadowcroft'. (The charge was probably phrased in this way to save his life. Had he been found guilty of sodomy, he would have been hanged.) In 1839 he was given another month on the chain gang for 'disorderly conduct in the penitentiary and communicating with a hut not his own, contrary to orders'.

During the course of his time at Port Arthur, he received a grand total of 1800 days in leg-irons, 135 days in solitary confinement and 625 lashes.

Finally, his sentence came to an end, but sometime after 1844 this violent, imaginative and spirited soul was committed to the New Norfolk Asylum for the Insane and shortly afterwards disappeared from the records.

Closure

By the mid-1850s, it had become widely accepted that the kind of punishment inflicted at Port Arthur was not only cruel and futile but was also highly expensive, because so many of its recipients had to be further incarcerated in lunatic asylums at the end of their sentences.

There's an old church a little distance from the main complex at Port Arthur, subtly screened by imported English trees. It used to have thirteen spires and a sixty-foot steeple, on top of which was a giant cockerel. It was said that if ever this iron chicken fell to ground, the penal colony would close. In 1876,

a massive storm hit Port Arthur. Perhaps assisted by the ghosts of all the miserable souls who had passed through it, the steeple crashed to the ground, and the dislodged cockerel violently embedded itself in a tree. Port Arthur shut down the following year, and with it, one of the most dismal chapters in Australia's convict past.

Nowadays, Port Arthur is a museum and one of Tasmania's most popular tourist destinations. But in a tragic postscript to the litany of horrors it has witnessed over the past two centuries, in 1996 a 28-year-old man ran amok with a semi-automatic rifle in its café, gift shop and the surrounding grounds. Thirty-five people were killed and twenty-five injured. The gunman is now serving thirty-five life sentences plus 1035 years in Risdon Prison, outside Hobart.

Vinegar Hill

There was one group of convicts who terrified the little colonial administration – the Irish. They were considered desperate, dangerous and, what was worse, a profoundly destabilising influence on the young settlement.

In 1798, back in Ireland, there had been a fierce uprising against British rule, culminating in the notorious Battle of Vinegar Hill, in which 20 000 troops defeated an army of revolutionary United Irishmen, after which a field hospital was set alight, scores of Irish troops were burned to death, and hundreds of women and children were raped and slaughtered. Although the rebellion was crushed,

the British were reluctant to make martyrs of the revolutionaries, and many of them were transported to Australia.

So in 1800, Sydney and the surrounding area found itself filling up with Irish convicts who, unlike so many of their English counterparts, considered themselves not as poor disgraced unfortunates, but as heroic political prisoners. They were contemptuous of British authority, and once in Australia, they started organising a revolt.

A convict uprising was the colonial administration's worst nightmare. If Sydney's ruling class was overthrown, it would be at least ten months before news could be got to London and reinforcements arrive back in Australia. The administration used any means at its disposal to suppress the potential rebels – for instance, twenty-year-old Paddy Galvin 'was ordered to get three hundred lashes. He got one hundred on the back, and you could see his backbone between the shoulder blades. Then the doctor ordered him to get another hundred on his bottom. He got it, and then his haunches were in such a jelly that the doctor ordered him to be flogged on the calves of his legs. He got a hundred there and as much as a whimper he never gave. They asked him if he would tell where the pikes were hid. He said he did not know and would not tell. "You may as well hang me now," he said, "for you'll never get any music from me."' Such draconian behaviour only made matters worse, and Irish resentment grew.

During the hot month of February 1804, the plans for an uprising began

ABOVE: Waverley Cemetery, in the Sydney suburb of Bronte, where Major George Johnston lies surrounded by Irish patriots!

to accelerate. The leader was United Irishman Phillip Cunningham, a veteran of the original Vinegar Hill battle in Ireland. His strategy, if such it could be called, was to ignite the revolution northwest of Sydney at the relatively poorly guarded and remote settlement of Castle Hill, seize all the available weapons and march to Parramatta to link up with more convicts. From there a band of 1000 convicts or more would head for Sydney and commandeer enough ships to sail to freedom.

On 4th March a house was set alight on the government farm at Castle Hill, the signal that the revolt had begun. The Castle Hill mob then marched down to Parramatta, but the message never got through to the Parramatta rebels because the messenger turned informant and told the authorities what was about to happen. So Cunningham

decided to head north again to join up with a third group of convicts who were waiting for them at the Hawkesbury River.

Word of the uprising swiftly reached Sydney, martial law was declared and in the dead of night Major George Johnston, of the New South Wales Corps, and a contingent of twenty-nine soldiers, headed in the direction of the rebels. Even though they were weighed down by their heavy red coats and were hauling muskets, they arrived in super-fast time. Terror spurred them on – this was the greatest threat the colony had ever faced. At eleven o'clock the next morning, they confronted the rebels at a place that became known by the name of the original bloody confrontation in Ireland – Vinegar Hill.

A stand-off ensued. The rebels demanded 'death or liberty', and a ship

In Loving Memory of all who Dared and Suffered for Ireland in 1798

LEFT: Waverley Cemetery — also home to the world's largest memorial to the Irish Vinegar Hill Rebellion of 1798
PREVIOUS PAGE: Chatting to Historical Investigator Lynette Ramsay Silver about the Irish rebels of 1804

to take them home. Major Johnston said he wanted to parley, and the Irishmen were naive enough to believe he was willing to negotiate. Despite everything they'd undergone, they still believed in the notion of British military honour.

Had he been confronted by enemies of his own class and culture, Johnston may well have been as good as his word. But as far as he was concerned, the rowdy peasants who confronted him were to be managed in the most appropriate way – honour was not a relevant factor. He pulled a pistol from his sash and put it to a rebel's head. Immediately, one of his troopers did the same to Phillip Cunningham.

Johnston then gave the order to fire. Nine Irishmen were instantly killed and several others were wounded. The rest attempted to give as good as they got, but after about fifteen minutes Cunningham was run through by a sword and fell to the ground. The rebels thought he was dead and, leaderless and

demoralised, ran off in all directions. Cunningham survived, but not for long. The following day, 6th March, he was hanged from the staircase of the Government Store.

Major Johnston had successfully quashed Australia's first-ever rebellion. The bodies of the rebel leaders were left dangling among the trees from which they had been hanged – a gruesome warning to everyone of what the words 'Death or Liberty' really meant.

No one could have predicted that, four years later, there would be another rebellion, and this time Major Johnston and the New South Wales Corps would be the ones leading it.

1790–1835

By God, You
Shan't Keep It!

The Most Botched Government
Privatisation Ever

The First Fleet was by common consent well organised, with particular
attention given to the welfare of the convicts, but the Second Fleet was
the complete opposite.

　　Almost as soon as Phillip's first ships had set sail for Australia,
pressure mounted on the Westminster politicians to send out more.
Typhus and 'congestive disease' were rife in Britain's prisons and a
lethally cold winter beckoned. There was pressure, too, from gaolers
the length and breadth of the country. They complained they had
been promised that once Phillip's ships had departed, more prisoners
would be moved from their overcrowded gaols into the hulks, but

BELOW: Standing among the
direct descendants of King
George III's sheep, which
Macarthur brought to the
huge estate granted to him
by Lord Camden

the authorities had reneged on this undertaking.

By now, Lord Sydney had resigned, and his successor, William Grenville, felt obliged to respond to the lobbying with which he was being bombarded. He was a liberal man, a passionate campaigner for Catholic emancipation and an end to slavery, but inexplicably he gave the contract to transport the next batch of convicts to the largest slave transportation company in Britain: Camden, Calvert & King. In what has been described as the most botched government privatisation ever (and there would be pretty stiff competition for such an award, if it existed), the British government paid the company seventeen pounds, seven shillings and sixpence for each convict on board, but held no money back to guarantee their safe delivery to Australia. Consequently, the more convicts who died on route, the easier and more profitable it was for Camden, Calvert & King.

Three transport ships were commissioned to house the male convicts: the *Neptune*, the *Scarborough* and the *Surprize*. There were two storeships, HMS *Guardian* and *Justinian*, and the *Lady Juliana*, which was to transport 245 women convicts, and which soon gained a reputation as a floating brothel ('every man on board took a wife from among the convicts').

There was a host of characters on board the ships who would have a considerable impact on the new colony, none more so than the pugnacious and deeply unpleasant John Macarthur, a 23-year-old lieutenant in the newly formed New South Wales Corps.

Like so many of the early settlers, he wasn't born to rank or status. His father, a Scottish draper and 'seller of slops', had managed to scrape enough money together to buy his son an army commission – a sacrifice which would, of course, ensure that the young man had to move a considerable distance from the family home.

New South Wales Corps

Cook named the entire east coast region of Australia 'New South Wales' – including the parts we now call Queensland and Victoria. Soon the terms 'New Holland', 'Botany Bay' and 'New South Wales' became interchangeable, at least in the minds of the British public.

The War Office decided the First Fleet marines should gradually be replaced. A new unit of 100 privates and NCOs plus officers (including Macarthur) was sent over on the Second Fleet. This was the beginning of the New South Wales Corps (ironically referred to as the 'Botany Bay Rangers').

Francis Grose (who administered the colony till Hunter was appointed governor) made a dreadful error when he allowed Corps officers to sell liquor. Soon they'd cornered the whole market. As Tom Keneally says: 'The colonial love affair with dram drinking had been set going.'

It's not often that history provides us with a villain of the storybook variety; life's too complicated for such simplifications. But occasionally

RIGHT: John Macarthur,
artist unknown, c.1850s

someone appears on the scene who is so black-hearted that the epithet seems justified. Such a man was John Macarthur, who, though he transformed an entire continent, was a baddy – a real dyed-in-the-wool one at that.

Even before the Fleet departed, Macarthur was making trouble. He decided that he and his long-suffering wife Elizabeth deserved better quarters than the ones they'd been allotted on the *Neptune*. Captain Tom Gilbert refused to upgrade them, so Macarthur challenged him to a duel. Gilbert's shot missed, and Macarthur's went through Gilbert's coat. Honour should thus have been satisfied, but the vindictive Macarthur wasn't the kind of man to let an argument drop once he'd started it, and with the assistance of his crony Captain Nepean, brother of Lord

Tattoos

Maybe in an attempt to assert their individuality in these dreadful conditions, many convicts got themselves tattooed.

Simon Gilbert, a groom convicted of stealing a bridle, had the words 'Man in Irons' tattooed on one arm.

Eleanor Swift wore the words 'Patrick Flynn I Love to the Heart' on hers.

A girl called Elizabeth Stephen had the name of her boyfriend tattooed on an unspecified place that was visible only to her doctor!

Sydney's undersecretary, he managed to get Gilbert removed from his post. This had dreadful ramifications for all those on board, because Gilbert's replacement was the notorious Donald Trail, a callous and self-interested ex-slaver.

The primary motivation of Trail, and many of the other officers of the Fleet, was to make as much money for themselves as possible on the voyage, and so they busied themselves loading privately purchased goods onto the ships in order to sell them to the settlers once they reached Australia. To ensure there was sufficient deck-space for their consumer products, they threw the convicts' sea-chests overboard. This was more than just wicked selfishness, it was a death sentence. It ensured that the only clothes available to the convicts were their rudimentary uniforms, which provided no protection whatsoever from the icy blasts that would assault them over the many months ahead.

Convicts were chained two together, often for the entire voyage. During storms they were up to their waists in water; catarrh and congestive disorders were rife. The only toilets were big tubs that tipped over in the high seas. They received so little food that if a fellow convict died, his companions would keep quiet about it in order to obtain a few more rations, until finally the stink from the dead body would become so bad that the desperate ruse was exposed.

The journey was hard, long and dangerous. HMS *Guardian* hit an iceberg, and most of those who took to the lifeboats were never seen again. Those who stayed on board fothered the ship as Cook's men had done, and managed to limp into Cape Town.

The other ships avoided complete disaster, although their convict occupants were often on the receiving end of systematic abuse, both physical and sexual. This is epitomised by the image of the *Lady Juliana* leaving the Cape Verde Islands accompanied by a swarm of 'Yankee slavers', whose sailors rowed across to the prison ship to feast on the carnal pickings available there.

Finally, the battered ships sailed into Sydney Cove. The shocked settlers could smell them a hundred metres off. The dead were dragged off the decks and thrown into the harbour; the ill were carried ashore in their own excrement. For nights it would have been impossible to get to sleep because of the din of the wild dogs that were fighting and howling in a sandy pit close to the Tank Stream, where the bodies had been thrown.

Immediately upon landing, the ships' officers, led by Trail, set up booths full of sorely needed goods that they proceeded to sell at astronomically inflated prices, but there was little Phillip could do about it. He had no authority to punish Trail and the other profiteers; all he could do was to condemn them in despatches. The British government was so embarrassed by the episode that the whole affair was simply hushed up.

And did the politicians learn from their mistake? It would appear not. When the job of setting up a third fleet was put out to tender, the lucky winners were . . . Camden, Calvert & King.

A Very Lucky Man

The Macarthur family had had an eventful voyage. John had argued with almost everybody, including his erstwhile friend Captain Nepean, and he, his wife, child and servant had consequently been transferred to the *Scarborough*. (The desire of those on board the *Neptune* to get rid of the Macarthurs as swiftly as possible is vividly demonstrated by the fact that they executed the transfer in mid-voyage during high seas!)

At Cape Town, John had caught a fever that subsequently swept through the ship, and he was only beginning to be able to walk again on their arrival in Sydney. Nevertheless, he immediately launched ambitious plans to make money, both as an importer and a landowner.

Phillip was opposed to such profiteering. He thought that too much private trading would undermine the collective spirit he had nurtured in the colony, and that given the nature of private enterprise, the first goods to be traded would inevitably be alcoholic. In his opinion, this would cause considerable problems both for the settlers and for the Indigenous people – and in this he was particularly prescient. But a new profiteering culture was developing in the colony, and there was little that the gentle-minded utopians of the First Fleet could do to prevent its encroachment.

Though still an army officer, Macarthur, like so many small-town wheeler-dealers the world over, swiftly got himself a job in local government. He was appointed Regimental Paymaster and Inspector of Public Works, roles which gave him ample scope to make money on the side. Indeed, he rapidly became one of Sydney's most powerful figures.

When Governor Phillip retired, he was replaced by his colleague John Hunter, who initially formed a convenient bond of friendship with Macarthur. But this cosy relationship swiftly turned sour when Hunter tried to restrain the financial activities of Macarthur's New South Wales Corps, an army unit that was now the most powerful trading bloc in the colony.

Not only Macarthur's ire, but that of the entire Corps, now fell on the hapless Hunter. They treated him with barely disguised disrespect and his authority was fatally undermined. He sought solace in the bush, where he spent his time collecting animal specimens to ship home to Joseph Banks. Eventually, in 1799, his tenure was terminated and he was called back to London, but was ever-after consumed with guilt that he had failed to curb Macarthur and his disruptive, money-grabbing shenanigans.

Another First Fleet officer, Phillip Gidley King, had been eager to take over from the ineffectual Hunter, and as soon as he was appointed governor, King began to attack Macarthur's powerbase. He overturned a sentence of one year's imprisonment that had been handed down to a soldier convicted of assaulting Macarthur, closed the shop and smashed the barrels of a 'purveyor of spirituous liquors' who was one of Macarthur's men, and attempted to set up a government store in competition with the Corps where settlers could buy goods without having to pay an exorbitant mark-up to the military.

Macarthur saw all this as a terrible slight and organised a social boycott of King, persuading prominent members of the colony, and virtually all the officers of the New South Wales Corps, to refuse to attend the Governor's functions.

But Macarthur's superior, Colonel Paterson, was a close friend of Governor and Mrs King, and refused to cooperate in the boycott, so now it was his turn to feel the full force of Macarthur's rage. Macarthur obtained and disclosed a letter that put Paterson's wife in a bad light, knowing that the colonel would be forced to defend her honour (duels were officially illegal, but had been such a time-honoured practice among the gentry that courts rarely convicted).

Macarthur and Paterson's 'High Noon' moment took place at 1 p.m. on Monday, 14 September 1801. Ever lucky, Macarthur won the toss. Their seconds measured out twelve steps and the principals took their places facing each other. Paterson stood with his arm down, side-on to his opponent to minimise the chance of being hit. But hit he was, in the right shoulder. He couldn't hold his pistol any longer and dropped it, so Macarthur walked away unscathed. The ball couldn't be extracted from Paterson's shoulder and for a time the doctors didn't know if he would live or die. He survived, but was greatly weakened and prematurely aged by the injury.

Governor King was furious about the duel and ordered that Macarthur should be arrested, but then had second thoughts and, in order to defuse the situation, appointed him commandant of Norfolk Island, 1600 kilometres away in the Pacific. Macarthur refused to accept the appointment, saying it was a punishment, and that if he was to be punished he should first be tried by his fellow officers. King knew this would be a pointless exercise as all the officers were in Macarthur's pocket, so he sent him to England to stand trial.

However, this trip didn't bring about the fall of Macarthur, as the governor had hoped. Instead, it turned out to be the most incredible stroke of good fortune of his life. Not only that, it changed the destiny of Australia.

Macarthur had a series of the most amazing lucky breaks. The governor had written a 'very bulky' despatch denouncing him, which was sent to

ABOVE: Historian Stephen Gapps explains Macarthur's duel with Colonel Paterson by way of demonstration

England on Macarthur's ship, but it disappeared during the voyage, never to be seen again (whether the wily lieutenant was complicit in the disappearance no one knows). In addition, the chief witness against him, Captain Mackeller, who had been Paterson's second in the duel, boarded a whaler to travel to England to give evidence, but his ship went down with all hands. So when Macarthur got to England, his court martial was dismissed due to lack of evidence. He was now a free man.

A couple of years before the duel, he had bought a handful of Merino sheep – from the first of the breed imported to Australia from Cape Town. Ever the salesman, he had brought some small samples of wool from his sheep to England, and he now used his time waving them around and telling everyone that Australia could become the great provider of Britain's wool. This was music to the ears of British policymakers. At that time there was a serious wool shortage in Britain, as its usual source – Spain – had been disrupted by the Napoleonic Wars.

One of the most influential politicians on the receiving end of Macarthur's sales pitch was Lord Camden, the British Colonial Secretary, who was so impressed by his gift of the gab that he arranged for Macarthur to be given a major land grant in New South Wales on which to raise sheep.

But the best of all Macarthur's slices of good fortune was that, on the boat over, he'd met the son of the Prince of Wales' doctor. This may not sound a particularly significant piece of networking, but he managed to use this connection to take a look at the King's Merino sheep, the finest wool producers in England and perfectly suited to Australian conditions. It was four years before Macarthur returned to Australia, but when he finally stepped onto the return boat to New South Wales as a private citizen, he was not alone – he brought with him a small flock of royal sheep.

Back in Sydney, with the King's Merinos, the land grant and a letter to the governor stating that he was entitled to thirty-four convicts to be his shepherds, Macarthur caused severe consternation by insisting on claiming 'Cowpastures', prime grazing land by

BELOW: A plan of Camden Estate, 1847

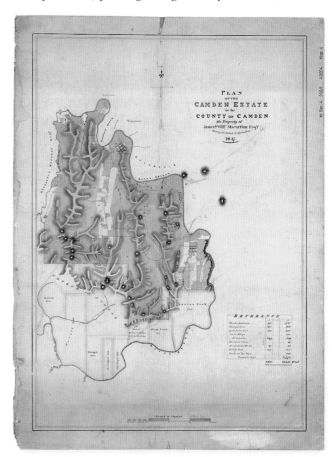

RIGHT: Camden Park
House, by Conrad
Martens, 1843

the Nepean River and formally the possession of the governor. In typical Macarthur style, a tug-of-war now took place between him and successive governors over the amount of land he was due, but eventually some sort of agreement was reached and he started to farm his vast new estate, which he named Camden Park in tribute to his patron back in England.

Wool was the perfect export cargo for Australia. It wouldn't perish on the long sea voyage to the British market, it was light enough for ships to carry in great quantity and was a very valuable asset. Macarthur was already rich; now the money cascaded in.

Bligh's Second Mutiny

When Phillip Gidley King, now a shadow of the man who had initially craved the governorship so much, followed his predecessor on the long voyage home, Macarthur found that in the colony's next governor he had a new enemy: William Bligh, an honest, bold, daring and pig-headed man who had gained notoriety thanks to the famous 1789 mutiny on the *Bounty*.

Captain Bligh's crew had accused him of being tyrannical; he accused them of being lazy and ill-disciplined. Matters came to a head when they refused to sail the *Bounty* out of Tahiti after becoming besotted by the seductive local women, and instead cast Bligh and his supporters into a longboat. Incredibly, Bligh managed to navigate it successfully across open seas for forty-seven days until they reached Timor.

A tough governor of New South Wales was needed to replace King, and Bligh's reputation as a strict disciplinarian qualified him perfectly for the job. He had the backing of Sir Joseph Banks and was specifically charged with cracking down on Sydney's recalcitrant soldiers. As more and more convicts poured in to the colony, its rulers felt increasingly vulnerable. They knew they had to rely on the army, but the Corps was now a major problem. Its soldiers weren't the cream of Britain's red coats – they were a bunch of ruffians recruited from Britain's poor and unemployed. They were only too happy to take advantage of the powerful situation they found themselves in, and did so with the help of a substance they were all too familiar with.

They cornered the market in what they called 'rum', a catch-all word for any kind of strong liquor. And as there was very little coinage in the colony, convicts and settlers alike used it not simply to get pie-eyed, but as a bona fide currency. Everybody traded in it. Indeed, the wages for the construction of many of Sydney's most famous landmarks were paid in rum. It was offered on 'wanted'

posters as the reward for catching bushrangers; there was even a rumour that a man had sold his wife for four gallons of the stuff.

At another place, and in another time, the problem of the Corps' profiteering might have been solved by a bit of behind-the-scenes arm-twisting, or one of the other forms of gentle bullying the political class deploys at such moments. But there was a fly – or rather, two flies – in the ointment: two powerful, aggressive egomaniacs, both determined to have their own way.

John Macarthur had been instrumental in ensuring that the Corps obtained a monopoly of the rum trade, and he'd profited enormously from it. The Corps was currently being led by Major Johnston, the same major who had quashed the Vinegar Hill Rebellion a few years previously. Though now a civilian, Macarthur still had close ties to Johnston and the

RIGHT: Australia's first political cartoon, showing Bligh being hauled from beneath his bed. One of the arresting officers displayed it in his house just days after the arrest

rest of his old Corps comrades, and it was central to his plans that the colony should continue to trade in rum.

Governor Bligh, though, recognised that the rum currency was debilitating to the people of the colony while propping up the power of an unofficial military elite, and so he released a proclamation prohibiting the use of rum 'as payment for grain, animal food, labour, wearing apparel, or any other commodity whatever'.

Macarthur was beside himself with rage, but Bligh continually provoked him. Indeed, at their first meeting he told Macarthur he didn't care for his business and was planning to revoke the jewel of his empire – his precious 5000-acre land grant. With characteristic bluntness, he added, 'You have got 5000 acres of land in the finest situation in the country, but by God, you shan't keep it!'

Matters quickly came to a head in December 1807, when the vessel

Parramatta, which Macarthur co-owned, returned to Sydney after a convict hidden on board had escaped in the Pacific Islands. Bligh fined Macarthur the substantial sum of £900 for failing to prevent the escape of a convict by sea. Macarthur refused to pay and was dragged into a court presided over by Judge Atkins and six members of the New South Wales Corps. Macarthur loudly proclaimed Atkins unfit to sit in judgement over him because Atkins owed him money and was his enemy. The judge rejected this, but Macarthur was supported by the six officers, who refused to swear Atkins in. The court was adjourned and Macarthur was released on bail.

The next day, 26th January 1808, was by coincidence the twentieth anniversary of the founding of the colony. Bligh had Macarthur re-arrested and imprisoned, and demanded the six New South Wales Corps officers appear before him.

But Major Johnston had other ideas. Having quelled a revolt at Vinegar Hill, he was now about to lead one.

Johnston rode to the barracks and ordered the release of Macarthur, to the cheers of the Corps. Macarthur promptly drafted a petition calling for Johnston to arrest Bligh and take charge of the colony. At 6.30 p.m., the Corps, with full band and colours and joined by 200 civilians, marched from their barracks to Government House to make the arrest. It was later stated that the soldiers found Governor Bligh hiding under a bed, in craven terror, and they had to drag him out.

But it's highly unlikely that Bligh sought refuge beneath his bedposts. For all his faults, cowardice was not amongst them. If anything, he was over-confident, and his personal courage made him rash and all too ready to engage in argument and conflict. Other witnesses said that he realised resistance was futile, ordered his horses to be saddled (possibly so he could ride to Hawkesbury to rally his supporters) and went upstairs to dress in his uniform. He then called for his sword and, while waiting on the stairs, was surprised by soldiers with fixed bayonets. They took him to the drawing room, which Bligh later said was 'crowded with soldiers under arms, many of whom appeared to be intoxicated'.

The arrest of Bligh meant that the New South Wales Corps had bloodlessly overthrown the Crown's representative in the colony – to this day, the only overthrow of a government staged on Australian soil.

Major Johnston spent two years as temporary administrator of New South Wales. He was later court-martialled in Britain but was given a surprisingly lenient sentence and returned to New South Wales, where he became a respected gentleman farmer.

Captain Bligh and his daughter lived under house arrest for a year, and eventually returned to England. Bligh was awarded a backdated promotion to rear admiral, but having been in the thick of two mutinies, he was never given another important post. Nevertheless, by all accounts he went on to live a happy life in the bosom of his family.

As for John Macarthur, he was exiled to England for a few years, but eventually returned to Australia after agreeing to refrain from participating in public affairs. With his sheep-breeding and other agricultural pursuits, he became the wealthiest man in Australia, but the darkness that had always been such a major part of his character eventually came to the fore. In 1832 he was declared a lunatic. He was cared for by his loving and long-suffering wife Elizabeth, but now in his rantings he accused her of promiscuity and infidelity. He died 'in unrelieved torments' at Camden Park in 1834.

Australia is now the largest wool producer on the planet. It's a commodity that not only made a poor, lowly, hot-tempered lieutenant the Murdoch of his day, but in time it also turned the fledgling colony into an economically robust nation, whose wealth and good fortune 'rode on the sheep's back'.

In Which I Discover a Long-Lost Ancestor

For a long time, it was thought that transported convicts were a dangerous underclass, born and bred to a life of crime. But in fact many of them were ordinary working-class men and women, often first offenders, convicted of minor offences like petty theft or receiving stolen goods. These weren't thugs and gang members, but labourers, small traders or servants, and they weren't afraid of a bit of hard graft.

Belgenny Farm is about an hour and a half's drive out of Sydney,

BELOW: Belgenny Farm, today an agricultural history centre

Hell on Earth?

Not every convict's life was hell on Earth. Their work could be back-breaking, particularly if they were on a government work gang, but the majority were able to make reasonable, if pretty Spartan, lives for themselves. The image of the emaciated wretch devoid of all hope is a bit of a cliché. It confuses convict-settlers with those who were punished for further offences committed after they'd arrived.

and was the headquarters of the once-mighty Camden Park estate owned by John Macarthur. Given his greedy and vindictive nature, you might expect the conditions in which his workforce lived to have been brutally inhumane. But nothing could be further from the truth. While exiled in England, he'd studied agriculture and viticulture, and when he returned, forbidden from taking part in public affairs, he turned his attention to his estates.

Set in rolling pastures reminiscent of England's South Downs, Belgenny comprised a charming cottage, a creamery, a slaughterhouse, a blacksmith's shop and a beautiful, well-appointed garden that contains the oldest oak tree in Australia, planted from an acorn by Macarthur. A little way off were clusters of two-roomed cottages in which the convicts lived. They were of sturdy if basic construction, and up to fourteen people lived in each one. But while the living space was less than generous, they were dry and weatherproof, with magnificent views over the surrounding countryside.

In the early 1800s, around seventy-five people lived at Belgenny, working as shepherds, farm labourers, ploughmen, wool sorters, gardeners and the like. But not all were convicts. There were 'ticket-of-leave men' (those in the later part of their sentence who were allowed to seek a wage from their employers), ex-convicts, free men and women who had been born in the colony, and even one fortunate who had received an absolute pardon. It seems that life here must have been fairly amenable if many of those who were able to leave chose not to do so. Indeed, convicts worked fewer hours in the penal colony than their contemporaries did back in England – a five-and-a-half-day week, sunrise to sunset in summer, and 8 a.m. to sunset in winter.

I spent a balmy summer's day at Belgenny researching convict life, and while browsing through a local history book that listed the convicts who had worked there, I spotted the name William J Parrott. I was immediately intrigued. My grandfather's name was Horace Parrott, and it's an odd and fairly unusual surname. Not only that,

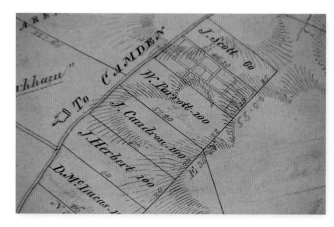

but Horace's father was called William Parrott, his father was Thomas William Parrott, and there had been several other William Parrotts in the family prior to that, although our family research had petered out long before the time of the first Australian convicts.

Could this William be related to me? Was he my great-great-great-great-great-grand-uncle, maybe? Mine is a typical London working-class family. For at least a couple of centuries they hadn't moved around much. Virtually all of them had lived in the same square mile around Shoreditch.

Without telling him of my suspicions, I asked a local historian if he had any idea where William Parrott had originally come from. 'Shoreditch,' he said without hesitation, and suddenly I was on a quest to discover my convict roots.

I didn't have much to go on. 'Convict arriv Albermarle 21/8 1791' the book said. 'Shoemaker. Received land grant Narellan 1810.' So at least it was clear he'd eventually been relieved of his convict's chains.

I drove to nearby Narellan looking for the plot in which my putative relative had settled. It wasn't difficult to find. I was confronted by a vista of rich, rolling grassland, beautifully manicured and watered. It was a golf course . . . my family golf course . . . a golf course that is probably rightfully mine!

A couple of days later I delved into the documents at the State Library in Sydney to pursue my newly discovered relative. The researchers couldn't have been more helpful. They found me the Belgenny Farm daybook, and a reference to what was certainly the same man. 'Parrott – shoemaker' it said, and listed various bills he had paid while still a convict, including

'Twelve gallons of wine at fifteen shillings a gallon'. So there are some habits that run in my family.

They showed me old maps of the area, from which it was clear that my great-great-great-grand-uncle's land became quite valuable. It was a big piece of prime property, and the new village of Narellan butted right up to it – a very pleasant spot in an increasingly prosperous village.

But what got me really excited was a copy of the Old Bailey documents recording his original conviction. He had been twenty-one years old when he was charged with breaking and entering, and stealing a quantity of silverware, the property of Samuel Brookes of Primrose Street, Bishopsgate (which is walking distance from Shoreditch, so he hadn't travelled far). He stole two silver salt-shakers, one spoon, eleven teaspoons, one pot of milk, two tablespoons, a cotton gown and a silver milk pot. In other words, he was convicted of stealing a tea set . . . total value about three quid. And yet he was sentenced to death. What a travesty of justice! What a blot on my family name! (Fortunately though, his sentence was commuted to transportation for life, and that's how he ended up at Belgenny Farm.)

Eventually, the big city beckoned, and William left Narellan and spent his final years in the the fast-expanding town of Parramatta, only twenty kilometres from Sydney. There's even a rudimentary map that indicates where he was buried. I spent about half an hour blundering about in the long grass and stubbly bushes, checking

BELOW: Touring my ancestral homelands

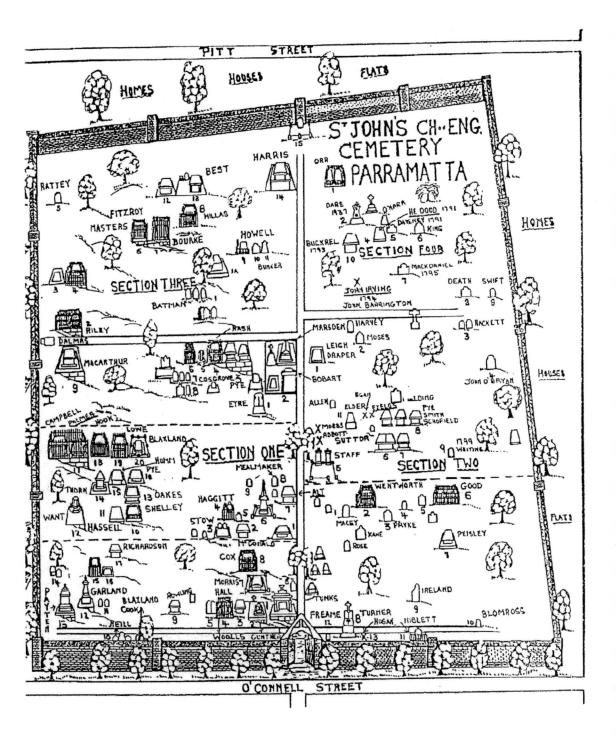

ABOVE: St John's Cemetery. Instructions directed me to Section 1, Row N, Grave 9, with this inscription: To the Memory of William Parrott, Who Departed this Life, June the 20th 1824, Aged 56

the headstones, trying to find Uncle William's grave. But either the map was inaccurate or his headstone had been removed and all tangible evidence of his death was lost.

Then it occurred to me that maybe there was no headstone. Perhaps what I was looking for was one of the worn slabs under my feet, half-hidden in the grass. After that, it didn't take me long to find it. It was crumbling badly and half the words were illegible. But it definitely said: 'William Parrott . . . departed this life . . . 1824 . . .'

I wasn't able to discover whether William had married or not, but there is a reference to a woman he lived with called Mary Smith. I don't know if

Mary was still around when he died, but I like to think someone must have cared about him because he was given a proper burial in a marked grave.

I'm glad I found the stone. Of course, I don't know if he really is a part of my family, but if he isn't, I'll happily adopt him.

1831–1861

Each Day the Journey
Became More Difficult

Australia is an island of some 7.6 million square kilometres. By the
1820s, Europeans had barely scratched round the edges, leaving the
vast interior and its riches wide open for exploration by whoever was
brave or greedy enough to accept the challenge. Tight along the east
coast, a huge chain of rugged mountains, the Great Dividing Range,
seemed impenetrable to the early colonists. The Blue Mountains of
New South Wales presented a vast sandstone labyrinth that went on
forever. The tantalising question was, what filled the vast distances on
the other side? Could there be rich farming lands or a giant inland sea,
or was it simply uninhabitable desert? Indeed, it turned out that away
from the green-fringed coast, much of the continent is searing desert
and harsh scrubland. The men who pioneered the exploration of this
unforgiving territory were unified not so much by their heroic nature,

BELOW: Crossing
the mighty Blue
Mountains, in New
South Wales

their bravery or even their navigational prowess, but by the fact that there was a tiny bit of all of them that was barking mad.

Most of us only know about the exploits of a handful of them, the ones who reached their goals or failed spectacularly. But there were hundreds who risked their lives this way and whose exploits are unrecorded – mostly forgotten government surveyors or stockmen on horseback who pushed a little further into the interior than anyone else. The result was that the country became accessible to sheep, cattle and the people who worked with them, and that transformed Australia.

Thomas Mitchell

One of Australia's most celebrated explorers, Thomas Livingstone Mitchell, wasn't just mad, he was bloody furious. He was constantly arguing with the authorities, he never obeyed orders and he left the department he was supposed to be running in complete chaos. He also had the unique honour of being the last man in Australia to challenge someone to a duel, and although he only managed to shoot a hole in his opponent's hat, on other occasions he demonstrated lethal capabilities.

Mitchell was born in Scotland four years after the Sydney colony had been established, and as a young man he joined the army, where he learned the art of surveying by mapping the various battlefields in the Peninsular War, in which the British were fighting Napoleon's army.

When the war was over, there was little for the young major to do in England, so he and his young family emigrated to Australia where he had been recommended for a job in the Survey Department. Within two years he had been appointed surveyor-general of New South

ABOVE: Sir Thomas Livingstone Mitchell,
artist unknown, c.1830s

Wales, a very important post that was extremely difficult for him to fulfil to the satisfaction of his employers. So much land was being discovered and allotted to potential farmers that if measurements were miscalculated, delays and disputes would break out over the boundaries, and development plans would grind to a halt. But surveying instruments were scarce and many of the surveyors were incompetent. Few of the senior figures in the colony understood the immensity of the technical problems involved in attempting to survey such vast areas with a degree of accuracy, so the department was continually under attack – and Mitchell was not a man to take criticism lightly.

His first major expedition in 1831 was to look for a river to the north-west of Sydney, which an escaped convict alleged he had seen. But Mitchell's path became blocked by Aboriginals, two of his party were killed and he was forced to turn back.

Four years later, after a succession of running battles with his superiors, he mounted his second expedition, following the Darling River for 500 kilometres, trying to find its mouth. But again disaster struck. Richard Cunningham, a botanist with the party, wandered off, and despite a long search, was never found, although later it was learned he had been killed by Aboriginals. Mitchell didn't consider himself an enemy of the Aboriginal people, but he loathed the Darling 'natives'. He described them as 'implacably hostile and shamelessly dishonest'. There was a shootout in which several of them died, and once

again Mitchell decided to return home. The information gleaned from this expedition was slight. More of the River Darling had been charted, but still no one knew its course or where it entered the sea.

Mitchell was a strangely contradictory person. Although blood was spilled on both these early explorations (some people even referred to the killings as 'massacres'), he was an intelligent man who respected Aboriginal culture, brought up two Aboriginal children – Ballendella and Dicky – as part of his family, and invented a boomerang propeller for steam ships, inspired by the bent throwing stick with which Aboriginals brought down their prey. Perhaps his attitude towards the 'natives' of the Darling owed more to his cranky and aggressive nature, than to any deep-seated bigotry.

His third expedition made his reputation. Once again he had been ordered to follow the Darling down to the sea, or if he discovered that it flowed into the River Murray, to go upstream along the Murray and investigate the previously unexplored territory in that direction. He found the junction of the two rivers – a major step forward in the colonists' understanding of the geography of south-eastern Australia – but bumped into a gang of Aboriginals who he was convinced were his old enemies from his previous forays into the area. Fearing this expedition was about to be scuppered too, he ambushed them. Seven Aboriginals were killed and the rest fled.

This time, though, Mitchell didn't immediately return home. Instead, he continued his journey, although once again he failed to complete a full exploration of the Darling, going instead up the Murray. It was a fortuitous decision; he discovered country far more fertile than any he'd ever seen in New South Wales, and so compellingly beautiful that he christened it 'Australia Felix' (we now know it as the State of Victoria).

A major problem for Mitchell was measuring the distances involved. On a long journey like this he couldn't use the cumbersome lengths of chain which nineteenth-century surveyors usually relied on. Instead, in one pocket he carried copious amounts of dried beans. As he rode, he counted his horse's steps. One – two – three – four . . . When he reached a hundred, he moved a bean from one pocket to another. Then he'd start counting from one again. He reckoned his horse took 950 steps per mile. So a hundred beans would represent a journey of approximately ten and a half miles. Not quite as accurate as GPS, but he became known as Australia's greatest surveyor, so his system must have worked tolerably well.

After swinging south-west, he rowed down the Glenelg River and eventually arrived at the southern coast, in Portland Bay, about 350 kilometres west of what is now Melbourne.

'I turned to observe the face of Tommy Come-last, one of my followers, who being native from the interior had never before seen the sea. I could not discover in the face of this young savage, even on his first view of the ocean, any expression of surprise . . . I was more astonished when he soon after came to tell me of the fresh tracks of cattle that he had found on the shore and then the shoe marks of white men . . . Proceeding round the bay with the intention of examining the head of an inlet and continuing along shore as far as Cape Bridgewater, I was struck with the resemblances to houses that some supposed grey rocks under the grassy cliffs presented; and while I directed my glass towards them, my servant Brown said he saw a brig at anchor, a fact of which I was soon convinced, and also that the grey rocks were in reality wooden houses.'

– THOMAS MITCHELL

He was exploring what he believed to be uncharted wilderness hundreds of miles away from the nearest white man, but had instead stumbled on a thriving, well-provisioned community of English farmers, as neat, tidy and prosperous as any settlement in the heart of New South Wales. How on earth had it got there?

The Henty Brothers

The Hentys were a wealthy family of bankers and landowners from Sussex. In the wake of the Napoleonic Wars, British farming went into recession and the family was given permission by the British government to settle on land in Western Australia. But there was a dearth of productive land there, so they moved on to Van

Meeting of Major Mitchell and Edward Henty. Portland Bay. 1836.

Diemen's Land, which proved equally unprofitable. Two young Henty brothers, Edward and Francis, now began looking across Bass Strait at the enormous tracts of unclaimed land on the other side of the water. Eventually, they sailed across in their family ship, the *Thistle*, with some livestock and labourers, and without asking permission from the British or the New South Wales authorities, created a large farming estate at Portland Bay on the mainland's southern coast, travelling back to the Tasmanian port of Launceston whenever they became short of provisions.

In August 1835, Edward Henty was returning home from work, when a labourer rushed up to him in a state of panic. He told his master that they were about to be attacked by bushrangers, and sure enough, when Henty arrived at his farmhouse it had been barricaded against attack and the family gun had been loaded and primed. The family's worst fears were confirmed when Major Mitchell's party arrived.

'The appearance of the major and his band of five with emu feathers in their caps as well as a red tail feather of the black cockatoo, blue and red serge shirts very much tattered, patched and worn, and certainly very fierce and formidable looking, will go far to excuse the error made in confounding them with bushrangers, and our desire to protect life from property.'

– EDWARD HENTY

Mitchell's first night at Portland Bay seems to have been agonisingly embarrassing. At first he wouldn't even shake the brothers' hands or allow them to take his coat, and it was only after they'd softened him up with food, gin and a bed for the night that he began to treat them as anything other than riff-raff – a bit rich, given the state he was in after so long in the saddle.

After three days, the explorers left, much cheered by fresh provisions and copious amounts of alcohol. But Mitchell rewarded the Hentys' hospitality by reporting them to the governor, who had been totally unaware of their existence and was appalled that they'd settled in Portland Bay without his permission. He promptly sent them a stiff letter and a tax bill for tens of thousands of pounds.

Opposite is a copy of a nineteenth-century print called *Meeting of Major Mitchell and Edward Henty, Portland Bay, 1836*. I love the absurd romanticism of this picture. Mitchell looks so neat and tidy. It's as though he'd spent two hours with a make-up artist before he rode.

Despite his successes, Mitchell never became popular with the colonial administration, although he was a hero amongst the ordinary colonists. This wasn't just because of his discoveries, but also because of his passionately held belief that the recently discovered territories should be available to small settlers, not just big landowners.

Eventually, in 1855, Governor Sir William Denison, launched an enquiry into the Survey Department, although Mitchell believed this was simply a ruse in order to secure his dismissal. He was probably right, although he never had a chance to read its damning verdict. Before it was published he caught a chill while surveying a line of road in difficult country. He developed pneumonia and died.

Horrocks and His Camel

John Ainsworth Horrocks was a handsome, powerfully built man. He arrived in Australia at the age of twenty-one with one family servant, a blacksmith, a shepherd, four rams and a church bell. He didn't have any land, so he explored the deserts of South Australia, looking for somewhere to raise his sheep and grow some vines.

In 1846 he put together an expedition to explore the area around Lake Torrens, and had the novel idea that desert travel would be more efficient if he used desert animals. So he bought a camel (which could carry 160 kilos of gear through waterless country), an innovation that was later taken up by many other explorers.

Some camels belie their reputation and are relatively sweet-tempered, but Horrocks' camel 'Harry' was a monster. He bit the tent-keeper, a man called Garlic, leaving him with two gashes on his forehead and another on his cheek, picked up a goat by the

Bushrangers

Bushranger – n. An Australian brigand living in the bush (OED)

Irish convict Bold Jack Donohoe dressed in fancy clothes, was a shameless flirt and became a folk hero because he thumbed his nose at the authorities. Eventually, he was betrayed by one of his gang in exchange for a £100 reward, and a trooper shot him through the forehead. Within days, souvenir clay pipes were on sale in the streets – with a little bullet hole in the bowl from which the smoke leaked out.

Mad Dan Morgan does indeed seem to have been a bit psychotic. He was arrested for holding up a travelling salesman and was sentenced to twelve years' hard labour. He was released after six, but began a campaign of retribution against the society that had incarcerated him. He committed senseless acts of murder and violence, but became popular because the authorities couldn't catch him. He held the occupants of Peechelba Station hostage, and ordered the farmer's wife to play the piano while he regaled the other captives with stories of his life, and how he'd been blamed for things he hadn't done. When he finally stepped outside, he was shot by a single bullet in the back. As he fell, he cried, 'Why didn't you challenge me first, and give me a chance?'

BELOW: A Dan Morgan engraving, published in *Illustrated Melbourne Post*, 1865

Morgan Sticking Up the Navvies, Burning their Tents, and Shooting the Chinaman.—[SEE PAGE 11.]

scruff of its neck and tried to eat it, and bit a hole in the flour bag, leaving a trail of white powder and destroying valuable supplies.

Then, while they were out in the bush, Horrocks spotted a little bird some way off, which he thought would go well in the expedition's stuffed-bird collection. But as he was loading his gun, Harry lurched forward, the gun went off and the bullet went straight through the explorer's hand, taking off several of his fingers, before passing through his cheek and knocking out his teeth.

He died of gangrene twenty-three days later, but prior to his demise gave an order that the camel should be shot. It took two bullets to kill Harry – but only after he'd managed to take a bite out of a stockman's head.

Burke and Wills

The only Australian explorers I was even vaguely aware of were Burke and Wills (although I tended to get them confused with the Irish body-snatchers Burke and Hare!). I knew there had been clashes of personality on their expedition and that they'd both ended up dead. But I'd never realised how dark and complex their story was, slowly unrolling like a Greek tragedy towards its inevitable conclusion.

In 1860, the Royal Society of Victoria proposed an expedition to cross the continent from south to north, which the government agreed to fund. Victoria had only been a separate colony with its own government for nine years, and as its population and affluence had increased, so had its rivalry with the other Australian colonies. A transcontinental exploration wouldn't just offer the opportunity to document the mysterious interior, it would also be a chance for Victoria to

ABOVE: *The Start of the Burke and Wills Exploring Expedition from Royal Park, Melbourne, August 20, 1860,* by William Strutt, 1861

display some of its newfound wealth to the rest of Australia and beyond.

Several seasoned explorers were sceptical about the project and failed to put their names forward. One man, though, was desperate to lead the expedition. His name was Robert O'Hara Burke; he was thirty-nine years old, and by no means favourite for the post. He was a policeman with no obvious bush skills (and, it transpired, no obvious leadership skills), and no experience of exploration. But he was a Victorian, which appealed to local sentiment, he had been an officer in the Austrian army, which seemed to count for something, and he was highly motivated, with an overwhelming desire to break out of the straitjacket of middle-class social conformity and become celebrated as the man he felt himself to be.

With no other suitable candidate in front of them, the Expedition Committee voted by ten votes to five to give Burke the post of leader, and preparations were made for the hazardous journey ahead. The list of goods they took with them is long, comprehensive and absurdly reminiscent of the lyrics of a Gilbert and Sullivan opera.

80 pairs of camels' shoes
6 tonnes of firewood
Dandruff brushes
Assorted nipples
1 American tub
Conical balls
Blankets for Asiatics
Kangaroo thongs
1 Enema syringe
A Chinese gong

While some of these articles aren't quite as ridiculous as they might seem – dandruff brushes were used to brush the sand from the camels, and kangaroo thongs were whips made out of kangaroo hide – it does seem strange that those who compiled the list thought a large dinner gong was a necessity in the outback, and that one enema syringe was sufficient between nineteen men.

They set off on 20th August 1860 from Royal Park, Melbourne, watched by 15 000 cheering spectators. The nineteen men in the party included four Indian sepoys, three Germans and an American. They all wore special uniforms for the event, with the exception of the gaunt and bearded Burke. Trailing behind them were twenty-three horses, six wagons and twenty-six camels specially imported from India. Burke had rejected an offer

to have the equipment transported by ship to Adelaide, then up the Murray and Darling rivers to meet him later. The impracticality of that decision was vividly demonstrated when the lead wagon broke down before it had even left Royal Park.

At the end of the first day, they had travelled only seven miles. That night, Burke galloped back to Melbourne to ask a seventeen-year-old young woman with whom he was infatuated to marry him. There is no record of whether she accepted or not.

On the second day, two more of the wagons broke down.

A month in, Burke decided to rethink his transport arrangements. He ditched the carts and loaded all the provisions onto the camels. This meant most of his men would have to go on foot for the entire journey.

After six weeks, he discarded the

sixty gallons of rum that they had been using as a tonic for the exhausted camels. His second-in-command, George Landells, who was responsible for their upkeep, was outraged by this decision. Shortly afterwards, another row broke out between them over the best way to get the camels across a river, and Landells resigned from the expedition. He was followed by the expedition surgeon, Dr Hermann Beckler. It was then that the surveyor and navigator William John Wills was promoted to second-in-command.

Three weeks later, on 12th October, they reached the tiny settlement of Menindee, which consisted of little more than a pub, a store and half a dozen people. This was the last outpost from which they'd be able to obtain provisions or support. Beyond Menindee they were on their own. It was here that Burke decided to split his team in two. The previous July,

the South Australian government had offered a huge reward of £2000 (over three $300000 in today's money) for the first successful south–north crossing of the continental west, and the experienced explorer John McDouall Stuart was already somewhere in the outback, presumably trying to find a viable route north. Burke was frustrated by his own slow progress, and was deeply concerned that all his efforts would be upstaged if Stuart or anyone else was successful. So he took seven men, including Wills, and pushed on to Cooper's Creek, a small group of ponds that were at the furthest edge of land previously explored by Europeans. Partway there, he sent a co-opted Menindee man named William Wright back to Menindee to guide the rest of the team to Cooper's Creek in their own time, and set up a supply depot there for the long journey back to Victoria.

LEFT: *Pioneer party leaving Cooper's Creek,* by Samuel Thomas Gill, c.1861–80

Once at Cooper's Creek, it may have been wiser for Burke to remain there until the autumn, to avoid further travel through the hot Australian summer. Nevertheless, on 16th December he split his team again, leaving a party behind in charge of the depot, and making a dash north with Wills, John King, Charles Gray, six camels, a horse and enough food to last three months.

On 9th February 1861, the Burke and Wills group reached the Little Bynoe River, just below the northern coast's mighty Gulf of Carpentaria, their ultimate goal. But they were thwarted yet again. Their way was barred by a sea of salty mudflats and mangrove swamps. Burke and Wills attempted to wade through the morass in the baking heat, but travel was unbearably slow, and neither the camels nor the horse could move through the mud. They soon ran out of water, and only managed to advance fifteen miles before the combination of circumstances defeated them.

They decided to turn back, even though they were tantalisingly close to the sea. By this time the four men were desperately short of supplies. They had food for five weeks, but it would take ten to get back to Cooper's Creek.

They were forced to shoot some of their camels and their horse, and jettisoned much of their equipment. Gray fell ill, but the others thought he was faking, and when he was caught stealing their porridge, Burke attacked him (although reports differ as to whether he simply slapped the unfortunate man or beat him up). Gray died of dysentery on 16th April. The exhausted little party arrived back at Cooper's Creek on 21st April, only to find that the rest of their team had abandoned camp.

Burke had asked them to wait for him at their depot for three months. They had in fact waited four, but their own lives were increasingly threatened. They were running out of supplies and were beginning to feel the effects of scurvy. In case Burke should return, they buried some of their precious

ABOVE: *Arrival of Burke, Wills and King at the deserted camp at Cooper's Creek, Sunday evening, 21st April 1861*, by John Longstaff, 1907

food and left it under a coolibah tree (now known as the 'Dig Tree') with a message and date carved on the trunk. They had left on the morning of the twenty-first.

It was that evening that Burke and Wills returned – they had missed their comrades by nine hours. They were so sick they knew they had no hope of catching up with them, and decided to rest and recuperate, and eat the cache of buried food, before setting off again. They wrote a letter explaining that they were heading for the appropriately named Mount Hopeless, the nearest settlement in South Australia, a hundred and fifty miles away. They buried it under the Dig Tree, but made a mistake that was to prove fatal. They didn't change the mark on the tree or alter the date. They'd left a message, but

no indication that such a message existed.

It may seem that the decision of the depot team to leave in order to ensure their own survival was at best unwise, and at worse, a little callous. But they didn't believe they had abandoned their leader. The other party, under the leadership of William Wright, were due to return to Cooper's Creek from Menindee with more supplies. Had Wright been able to deliver them to Cooper's Creek in time, the situation would have been retrieved and Burke would have returned to Melbourne in triumph. But Wright had terrible problems of his own. The expedition had run out of money (£11 500 had already been spent on it), so he wasn't able to purchase enough pack animals. And each day the journey became more difficult: the heat was overwhelming, he became desperately short of water and his team were harassed by a group of Aboriginal warriors. All this slowed him down dramatically. Then three of his party died of malnutrition.

Nevertheless, while attempting to locate Burke's tracks, he had virtually the only piece of good luck this benighted expedition experienced. He came across the depot party on their way back from Cooper's Creek. The two groups immediately joined forces and returned to the Creek with their refurbished supplies.

When they arrived at the Dig Tree, Burke, Wills and King had left again, and there was no sign that they'd been there. It didn't occur to Wright and the others to dig for the buried supplies to check whether they'd been eaten or not, as there were no further instructions on the tree. Convinced Burke hadn't returned, they reasoned that if he was still alive, he must have returned home by another route, so they headed back to Menindee.

Meanwhile, Burke's team were in dire straits. Their last two camels had died, they were exhausted and so were their supplies. There was no way they could cross the mighty Strzelecki Desert, which lay ahead of them. They were forced to return yet again to Cooper's Creek. The local Aboriginals gave them fish to eat and nardoo, the seeds of a water plant that could be ground into flour to make pancakes. But even that turned out to be an error. Unless nardoo is properly prepared in the Aboriginal way, it breaks down the body's vitamin B. The more the men ate to stem their hunger, the sicker they got.

The last few weeks of their lives are vividly documented in the dignified and understated journal that Wills wrote at the time:

'Mr Burke and King are preparing to go up the Creek in search of the blacks. They will leave me some nardoo, wood and water with which I must do the best I can until they return . . . I feel myself if anything rather better but I cannot say stronger. The nardoo is beginning to agree better with me; but without some change I see little chance for any of us. They have both shown great hesitation with regard to leaving me, and have repeatedly desired my candid opinion in the matter. I could only repeat, however, that I considered it our only chance, for I could not last long on the nardoo, even if a supply could be kept up.'

Burke died on the trek around 28th June. King buried his body and returned for Wills, but he too was dead. King, who had remained fitter than the other two, found the tribe of Yandruwandha Aboriginals, who gave him food and shelter.

On 15th September, a rescue team from Melbourne arrived at the Dig Tree, and a week later found King among the Yandruwandha. He was in a sick and emaciated state, but survived the arduous journey back to Melbourne. He died ten years later, aged thirty-one.

Posthumously, Burke found the celebrity he had once craved when, eighteen months later, his funeral at

Melbourne General Cemetery was watched by some 60 000 mourners.

Like Children in a Park

Although the sacrifices such men made were often colossal, soon the tasks they had set out to achieve were virtually completed. Vast tracts of land had been opened up, not only in New South Wales and Victoria, but in South Australia, Western Australia and in what would soon become Queensland. But of course, this land wasn't empty – people had been living on it since long before the construction of the Egyptian pyramids.

A nagging problem arose for the colonisers – how could they take land if it belonged to someone else? The solution was the application of a legal formula which stated that it didn't belong to anyone else – the land was deemed 'terra nullius', meaning that it was owned by nobody. Lawyers argued that in order for land to *belong* to someone, they had to do more than just live on it; they had to cultivate it and transform it from its original state. If they didn't, they were simply nomads wandering across it, like children strolling through a public park.

In 1835, the Governor of New South Wales, General Sir Richard Bourke, had proclaimed that Indigenous Australians – the Aboriginals – didn't own any part of Australia, so they

BELOW: Violent clashes belied *terra nullius,* as illustrated by Samuel Calvert, 1867

AUSTRALIAN ABORIGINES. — WAR.

couldn't buy or sell land unless it had been specially given to them by the King of England. White people, on the other hand, were given free rein to take part in land deals, and had the law's protection if they wanted to do so. But as more settlers took ownership of this land that 'belonged to no one', they increasingly came into contact and conflict with people who didn't know Latin and, even if they had, would have absolutely rejected the concept of *terra nullius*.

A cycle of violence erupted. Away from the eyes of the authorities, remote farms were established, the cattle and sheep on them were speared by Aboriginals, who then suffered merciless retribution.

The Aboriginals had been put in an impossible situation. They had held their territory since time immemorial. Yet strangers had now moved in, destroyed the habitat in which they hunted, and replaced the native animals with livestock that devoured the roots and vegetables that they'd always eaten. If they attempted to kill and eat the cows and sheep, they were chased off, and if they moved to another territory, they were attacked by the tribe who already lived there. Their only choice was death by starvation or death from the barrel of a gun. It's little wonder that so many chose the latter.

Like the battles that Pemulwuy's men had engaged in, these violent exchanges were often far more than simple skirmishes. An early Victorian settler called Edward Curr wrote that if ever there was a dispute between the white settlers and the Aboriginals,

war inevitably broke out and would last between six months and twelve years, depending on the nature of the territory.

But the colonists' response couldn't have been more chilling or brutally efficient. In Victoria a court clerk wrote the following about a mild crime committed by an Aboriginal bushman against some livestock:

'It was, of course, impossible to identify any black fellow concerned in the outrage, and therefore atonement must be made by the tribe.'

That tribe was the Kurnai. They were known to camp near a waterhole at Gammon Creek, where a posse of white men ambushed them, firing indiscriminately. When a ceasefire was finally called it is estimated that sixty men, women and children had been shot and thrown into the creek. It was a war in which only one side was armed.

James Carrot

A bushranger in Van Diemen's Land (Tasmania) called James Carrot murdered the husband of an Aboriginal woman he'd kidnapped, then forced her to wear the head of the dead man around her neck, as a warning that he was not to be trifled with.

Within a single generation the Aboriginals of Tasmania had been virtually wiped out.

GOVERNOR DAVEY'S
PROCLAMATION
THE ABORIGINES

LEFT: This Tasmanian noticeboard would have hung from a tree as a sign that the colonial administration was prepared to offer equality of justice to the local Aboriginals. Nevertheless, no white man was ever hung for killing a Tasmanian Aboriginal, and within a few decades most of the Indigenous population had been wiped out

Some of the darkest acts against the Aboriginals were perpetrated in isolated settlements on the islands between the mainland and Tasmania, and off the coast of South Australia. They were populated by seal hunters, whalers and occasional escaped convicts or colonial deserters who, out of sight of the colonies and their law officers, were a law unto themselves.

Not content with slaughtering whole populations of seals and rendering them virtually extinct, the sealers raided Aboriginal camps, stole the women and used them for labour and sex – some men had up to five slave 'wives'. These were not simply acts of brutality. The removal of women from their homes was one of the most effective ways of bringing local communities to their knees. It devastated the Aboriginal population.

The perpetrators of these atrocities weren't prosecuted, but as incidents of massacre increased, some colonists in the cities began to grow very uneasy.

Massacre at Myall Creek

On 10th June 1838, a posse of white men arrived at the Myall Creek cattle station. They claimed they were looking for some Aboriginals who they believed had been stealing cattle. The Aboriginals on the station were known to be peaceful, and they knew nothing of the crime. Nevertheless, the men tied them up in a great huddle – twenty-eight terrified men, women and children – and led them off into the bush. A station hand by the name of George Anderson protested, but he was

on his own; there was little he could do, although his intervention did save the life of one woman and a child.

The men wandered around with their captives for about an hour in an ineffectual fashion – clearly, they didn't know what to do with them. But something must have triggered a change in their attitude. Shots were heard, and all the Aboriginals were murdered. Most of the children were decapitated, the adults hacked to death, and all the bodies burned.

The next day the posse returned to Myall Creek, cooked themselves breakfast and boasted to Anderson about what they'd done.

After the station manager returned some days later, he travelled 250 kilometres to the nearest authorities to inform them of the massacre. Eventually, a report on the matter arrived on the desk of George Gipps, the Governor of New South Wales. A crusading journalist called Edward Smith Hall picked up the story and demanded that the perpetrators be tracked down. After having been further persuaded by the Attorney General, John Plunkett, that he should take action, Gipps initiated an investigation a month later.

In a way, it was remarkable that anything should have been done at all. Scores of similar atrocities had taken place prior to that throughout Australia without any court action being thought necessary. But times were changing. An educated elite was now establishing itself in the colony's new cities, who wanted no truck with such casual slaughter.

The following year a trial was held,

with eleven of the twelve suspects charged with murdering 'Daddy', an old man whose charred remains were among the most identifiable of the bodies at Myall Creek. The ringleader and only free settler, John Fleming, went into hiding and was never caught.

The suspects were represented in court by lawyers paid for by 'The Black Association', an organisation specially set up for the purpose of defending them by local landowners and stockmen. At the trial, the judge reminded the jury that there was no difference in law between killing a white man and a black man – nevertheless, they took just twenty minutes to find all eleven men not guilty. One of the jurors told a newspaper that he believed the men had participated in the massacre, but chillingly justified his actions by saying: 'I look on the blacks as a set of monkeys, and the sooner they are exterminated from the face of the earth, the better. I knew the men were guilty of murder but I would never see a white man hanged for killing a black.'

But now Gipps, Plunkett and Hall had the bit between their teeth, and before they could be released, seven of the eleven men were charged with the murder of one of the Myall Creek children. This time a jury found the men guilty of murder. On the morning of 18th December 1838, they were hanged. It was the first time in the frontier area that white men had been executed for killing Aboriginals.

Not that everyone agreed with the verdict. The *Sydney Morning Herald* declared: 'The whole gang of black animals are not worth the money the colonists will have to pay for printing the silly court documents on which we have already wasted too much time.'

A monument to the victims of the massacre was unveiled in the year 2000. It has since been vandalised, with the words 'Murder', 'Women' and 'Children' chiselled out of the memorial plaque in an attempt to make it illegible.

Rocking and Digging in All Directions

'This is a memorable day in the history of New South Wales. I shall be a baronet, you will be knighted, and my old horse will be stuffed and put in a glass case and sent to the British Museum!'

Thus spoke Edward Hargraves to his partner, John Lister. He'd just discovered alluvial gold. He didn't have much, not even enough to fill a tooth, but he knew that just one tiny piece meant there would be plenty more around.

I've searched the British Museum but haven't been able to find Hargraves' horse, and John Lister certainly wasn't knighted, nor was Hargraves made a baronet. But he did pocket £10 000, which the government had offered to the first person to discover gold in New South Wales, and he kept it all for himself. Lister got nothing, and Hargraves took early retirement from the goldfields and instead earned his living lecturing on the subject of how to find gold.

BELOW: The biggest gold nugget ever found – miners and their wives posing with the finders of the 'Welcome Stranger', Richard Oates, John Deason and his wife, 1869

The Meanness of Melbourne

Hargraves couldn't have dreamed what an impact his find would have on New South Wales. In 1852, just a year after his lucky strike, 850 000 ounces of the stuff was discovered in the state. That presented the neighbouring State of Victoria with a problem. There was an exodus of Victorians leaving their jobs and crossing the border in order to chase wealth beyond their wildest dreams.

So Victoria decided to offer a reward similar to the one that had worked so well for its neighbour. But Melbourne folk pride themselves on being much more level-headed than the flashy hucksters of Sydney, so they only offered £200 – just two per cent of Sydney's offer. And their meanness paid off – the incentive worked even more spectacularly than it had in New South Wales.

Gold had already been discovered in central Victoria the previous year, but the farmer who found it had kept quiet because he didn't want his sheep disturbed. The 200 quid swiftly changed his mind, though, and triggered a goldrush that would dwarf the one in New South Wales. Gold was found in Ballarat, then in Clunes, Warrandyte and Buninyong, followed by Castlemaine, Daylesford, Creswick, Maryborough, Bendigo, Heathcote, Mafeking and Ararat. The onslaught on Victoria's landscape was almost indescribable.

'The forest, whose echoes but a few months ago were awakened only by the rushing of a stream, the voice of the bell-bird, or the cry of the jay or laughing jackass, now reverberates to the sounds of human industry, wheeling, washing, rocking and digging in all directions.'

– JOHN SHERER

Initially, the journey to the Victorian goldfields from Melbourne, whether through Geelong off a steamer or directly west, was a slow cross-country effort with bullock carts, horses or wheelbarrows. Conditions were dire with no proper roads, and many prospectors had their belongings smashed or ruined and lost horses to the treacherous dusty paths in summer or the appalling bogs in winter. Food and water were at a premium, and bushrangers along the routes added further dangers.

And if the diggers comforted themselves with thoughts of making their fortunes in the bucolic setting of virgin countryside, they were in for a big disappointment when they arrived. Frenzied activity had reduced the diggings to a barren landscape, featuring little more than tents, pits and rivals. Melbourne's *Argus* newspaper described the scene that awaited new arrivals:

'The road which winds along the creek through the diggings is, from the constant traffic, ten times more dusty than even dusty Melbourne, and the heavy gusts of wind which pour through the gullies with great violence whirl it up in clouds, and scatter it far and near upon everything around. The newly erected tent does not, therefore, long retain its brilliant whiteness; a few blasts powder it effectually, and give it the same sombre, indescribable, dusty hue that distinguishes its neighbours, and soon take off every appearance of freshness.'

Central Victoria, and Ballarat in particular, became the nucleus of the richest alluvial goldfield the world had ever known. You couldn't throw a stone without it landing on a nugget – at least, that was the belief that fuelled the gold rush.

Gold fever gripped everyone. From respectable citizens . . .

'The whole town of Geelong is in hysterics, gentlemen foaming at the mouth, ladies fainting, children throwing somersets [i.e. somersaults] with excitement.'

. . . to the lowest of the low . . .

'All the ruffians and rogues from Melbourne and the scum of convicts from Van Diemen's Land.'

Law enforcers were seduced by its lure too. Eighty per cent of Victoria's police quit their jobs and headed for the goldfields. Towns around the state were deserted as people began to flood inland.

The discovery of gold had come hard on the heels of a major worldwide economic depression. All over the world there were poor but enterprising people who were attracted by the vision of adventure and riches beyond

TOP: The settlement of Mafeking in the Victorian goldfields, 1900
ABOVE: The gold brought hordes to Australia on ships from all over the world to Sandridge Railway Pier, Port Melbourne, c.1880

compare. The magnet of gold drew them to Australia in their droves. About one in every fifty citizens of Britain and Ireland migrated to New South Wales and Victoria at this time, as well as hordes of Europeans, North Americans and Chinese. In fact, there were more new arrivals around this time than the total number of convicts who'd landed in the colony over the previous seventy years! It took only two years for Victoria's population to grow from 77 000 to 540 000.

Initially at least, finding gold was a bit like shopping for sweets at a pick'n'mix counter. When Victoria's Governor La Trobe visited Ballarat a month after the first find there, he was introduced to a team of five men who'd dug up 136 ounces of gold one day and 120 ounces the next. The 'Welcome

Stranger', the largest gold nugget ever found, weighing in at over seventy kilos, was discovered lying just an inch underground in the root of a tree!

Predictably, this kind of instant wealth led to wild and crazy nights on the town, fuelled by booze and the belief that the gold would never run out. Like bankers who've just received their latest bonus, one successful miner dressed his horse in golden horseshoes, another bought up all the supplies of champagne he could find, filled a horse trough with it, and invited all and sundry to help him drink the lot.

Pubs and hotels were booming, theatres opened their doors, and exotic entertainment became a hot ticket. But no entertainer hit the headlines like Lola Montez.

BELOW: Cashing in the 'Welcome Stranger' nugget (replica)

Her Name Was Lola

Lola was an exotic Spanish dancer, although she wasn't actually Spanish and her name wasn't Lola. She was born Eliza Rosanna Gilbert in County Sligo, Ireland, and her father was an ensign in the Indian Army. He died of cholera when she was four years old and her mother, who was still only nineteen, married another army officer, Lieutenant Patrick Craigie, the following year.

Little Eliza grew to be a 'queer, wayward little Indian girl', and was sent back from India to Scotland to stay with her stepfather's parents. But her behaviour wasn't considered suitable by the dour citizens of Montrose – during a church service she surreptitiously decorated the wig of an old man in the pew in front of her with flowers, and is reported to have been seen running through the streets without any clothes on. In a hint of things to come, her art teacher described her as having 'excessive beauty, but the violence and obstinacy of her temper . . . caused . . . painful anxiety to her good aunt'.

At sixteen she eloped back to India with a Lieutenant James, but five years later they had separated and she returned to England, where she made her London debut as 'Lola Montez, the Spanish Dancer'. Unfortunately, she was recognised as Mrs James and a scandal broke, so she swiftly departed for the Continent. In Paris, she fell in with a sophisticated circle of writers and bohemians, had an affair with the composer and virtuoso pianist Franz Liszt (the Eric Clapton of his day), and it's said was intimate with Alexander

Dumas, the author of *The Three Musketeers*.

She was still only twenty-five when she arrived in Munich, where King Ludwig I of Bavaria fell under her spell. She was soon his mistress (there was a rumour that when they first met, he asked her in public if her breasts were real, and she responded by unbuttoning herself and revealing them in their full glory). She grew to be very influential at court, but she wasn't only bad-tempered and arrogant, she was also liberal-minded (which may not come as much of a surprise), and created a lot of enmity among the more conservative courtiers. Despite this hostility, Ludwig

Why Wasn't There a Gold Rush Sooner?

1823 – James McBrien discovers traces of gold in Fish River in New South Wales.

1839 – Explorer Paul de Strzelecki finds small amounts of gold in the Blue Mountains. Governor George Gipps requests that no mention is made of it in his reports.

1850 – William Campbell finds gold on his sheep run in Victoria.

1851 – Beginning of the Great Australian Gold Rush.

The discoveries before 1851 weren't very big. Gold was mainly found in isolated places, and the news didn't spread far.

With so many convicts in the colony, the authorities were nervous that there'd be violence if news of a discovery leaked out.

In the 1830s and '40s only a few people in the colony knew where to look for gold and how to find it.

Up until this time, all gold found in Australia belonged to the government. There wasn't much point prospecting for it if you had to hand it over when you found it!

made her a countess and gave her a large annuity. But by 1848, Europe was awash with revolutionary fervour and, partly because of his romance with Lola, Ludwig was forced to abdicate and she had to flee the country.

She went to Switzerland and waited for the King to join her, but he never did. So she moved to London where she became attracted to yet another man in a uniform, a cavalry officer named George Heald. They married, but unfortunately, under the terms of the divorce from her previous husband, it was illegal for her to do so while he was still alive. Consequently, she had to flee yet again, to avoid being charged with bigamy.

Lola and Heald spent time in France and Spain, but within two years her new marriage had collapsed. She moved on to San Francisco and remarried, this time to a Californian businessman, but again the marriage failed.

In August 1855, she arrived in Australia, having decided to resume her show-business career. But the respectable theatre audiences there were appalled by her act, which, according to Melbourne's *Argus*, was 'utterly subversive to all ideas of public morality'. The show lost money, and Lola moved on to the goldfields.

ABOVE: Despite the doubt expressed by the writer of the pencilled caption, it's now generally agreed this is a photograph of Lola, by C.D. Fredericks, c.1856

The miners had less rarefied tastes than the respectable burghers of Melbourne. In Castlemaine she played to a crowd of 400 diggers, including members of the local council who had adjourned their meeting in order to watch her famous 'Spider Dance', in which she traipsed about 'alluringly' while freeing herself from an infestation of small, black, decorated arachnids that dropped from her many petticoats. There was rapturous applause, and some say she was rewarded with a shower of gold nuggets from the appreciative diggers. Unfortunately, though, there was a smattering of heckling, and she broke the exotic spell she'd conjured up by losing her temper (a trait which seemed to bedevil her all her life) and giving the audience the sharp edge of her tongue.

Following this mixed reception, she moved on to Ballarat, where the review in the *Star* was glowing:

'The characteristic and fascinating Spider Dance has been performed by Madame Lola Montez with the utmost success throughout the United States of America and before all the Crowned heads of Europe. This dance, on which malice and envy have endeavoured to be fixed the stain of immorality, has been given in the other colonies to houses crammed from floor to ceiling with rank and fashion and beauty.'

But its rival, the *Ballarat Times*, panned her. Its review was a stinging condemnation not only of her performance but of her moral character, and Lola was so enraged she stormed into the office of its editor, Henry Seekamp, and chased him into the street, flailing his backside with a riding whip she'd recently won at a bazaar.

A year later she was back in America, but her glamour days were over. She embarked on a new career lecturing and writing books on women and beauty. She died, after contracting pneumonia, one month short of her forty-second birthday.

'There are many kinds of pimples, some of which partake almost of the nature of ulcers, which require medical treatment. But the small red pimple, which is most common, may be removed by applying the following twice a day:

Sulphur water 1 oz
Acetated liquor of ammonia 1 oz
Liquor of potassa 1 gr
White wine vinegar 2 oz
Distilled water 2 oz

These pimples are sometimes
cured by frequent washing in
warm water, and prolonged
friction with a coarse towel.
The cause of these pimples is
obstruction of the skin and
imperfect circulation.'

– *the art and secrets of beauty*,
BY LOLA MONTEZ

Monster Meetings

Life on the goldfields of Victoria
wasn't all golden horseshoes and spider
dances. It was hard work and you had
to pay the government for the privilege
of doing it.

Within months of the discovery of
gold, the authorities imposed a monthly
miner's licence. It must have seemed
reasonable in the early days when

gold was plentiful and easy to access.
The government sacrificed its right
of ownership to it, and in return the
diggers paid the state a small tax. The
majority of miners readily paid up. But
as the diggings became more difficult
to work, the amount of tax, and the
fact that it was imposed on both
successful and unsuccessful diggers
alike, became more contentious. The
manner in which the licences had to
be purchased, and the way in which
the system was enforced, aggravated
the situation. There were very few
places that issued the licences, and it
usually took hours, sometimes days, of
standing in line and dealing with rude,
harried clerks to renew them. During
inspections, there was no redress if a
licence had been lost or left in a tent,
and newly arrived diggers commonly
complained that they were arrested for
not having a licence before they'd even
set up camp.

Then, in December 1851, plans were
announced to double the licence fee
to three pounds. Many diggers were

well-educated; indeed, there was a much higher literacy rate on the goldfields than in the cities. Some had even been forced to flee their original homes because of their activities as political dissidents. These weren't the kind of people who would take harassment by the authorities lying down.

In response to this tax hike, an anonymous person who signed himself 'A Digger' posted a notice, calling for what he called a 'monster meeting' (a phrase inherited from the Monster Meetings of Ireland, at which the Fenian republicans would pour scorn on the 'monstrous' English).

The poster wasn't simply a whinge against high taxes, it was a red-blooded political analysis, criticising 'the tyrannical laws of the colonial legislature dominated by the conservative attitudes of the pastoral squattocracy'.

The words had their intended effect. On 15 December 1851, at four in the afternoon, more than 10 000 diggers gathered at Forest Creek in the Mount Alexander goldfields. There was a host of speakers (the Monster Meetings were nothing if not democratic), but one man, Laurence Potts, moved the crowd like no other. 'Will you be ridden over with an iron hand, to please the wishes of squatters or any other class?' he demanded. 'Will you tamely submit to have your hard earnings torn from your grasp, to enrich the pockets of the few? Or will you come forward like men and maintain your rights? Remember that union is strength, that though a single twig be bent and broken, a bundle of them tied together yields not nor breaks.' The language of revolution had made its way to Australia and found root in the soil of the goldfields.

The scale of the meeting and the resolve of its participants startled the colonial government. The plans to double the licence fee were shelved. But the authorities weren't going to back down with good grace. Soon afterwards, they introduced a law that any man found without his licence would be liable to a fifty-pound fine or six months' imprisonment.

The Wathaurong

Prior to the gold rush, the Ballarat region had been the territory of the Wathaurong people. But their land was laid waste by intensive mining. Within ten years all substantial tree cover had been lost. 'Every tree is fouled, every feature of nature is annihilated.' Native animals were wiped out too – kangaroo, emu, bandicoot, native rats, snakes and lizards, the whole gamut.

Gold had been of no importance to Aboriginal people, but now many of them joined the hordes of prospectors, and did so on financially equal terms with their European counterparts. This was the only period in colonial times when Aboriginals enjoyed independence from the authorities. Many proved successful diggers, and some amassed phenomenal wealth. There was also good money to be made from entertaining the miners, and from the sale of highly prized possum rugs.

But there was a terrible downside to all this potential wealth – health issues, food depletion, alcohol abuse. The Aboriginal population of the area decreased by 50% during the gold years.

Discontent continued to bubble. In 1853, signatures began to be collected for a petition. The diggers were no longer angry merely about the tax rise – the licences were now being used as instruments of intimidation, harassment and oppression. To recruit new police, Governor La Trobe increased police pay by fifty per cent, but was still forced to accept anyone who could be persuaded to wear the uniform. He assembled a motley collection of ex-convicts, ex-prison wardens, raw recruits and retired soldiers. These men were often brutal and corrupt, applied violence to get their own way, and used bribery and other scams to supplement their income.

By mid-1854, the State of Victoria was employing more than 1600 policemen, an even higher proportion of the population than in California during the Wild West days, and many of them were in plain clothes, working undercover to infiltrate diggers' groups. The goldfields well were on the way to becoming a police state. But in addition to the thuggery, the brutality and the corruption, there was a principle at stake. Though the diggers were being taxed, they had no say in the administration of their lives. Their slogan became 'taxation without representation is tyranny'.

Twenty-three thousand people signed the Bendigo goldfields petition, which was then sent hotfoot to Melbourne. Unfortunately, on the way, the coach containing the biggest batch of signatures was held up in a gold heist, and most of the names were lost. Only 7000 remained, and they were mounted on a thirty-metre-long piece of material fringed with silk that was presented to Governor La Trobe, who predictably rejected every single demand.

But the Monster Meeting and the petition were just the first gusts of a storm that was about to hit the goldfields, and the powder keg of discontent was set alight by a single episode.

Incident at the Eureka Hotel

In the wee hours of 7th October 1854, two Scottish diggers who had indulged in a night of heavy drinking, Peter Martin and James Scobie, ended up outside the Eureka Hotel, a seedy and notorious establishment adjacent to the Eureka goldfield. The landlord, James Bentley, wouldn't admit them, and insults were exchanged through the pub's shutters, including some indelicate allegations on the subject of Bentley's wife. The two sozzled Scots then staggered off down the Melbourne road, but were followed by Bentley and some of his henchmen, who violently attacked them. Martin managed to crawl away, but Scobie was hit over the head with a shovel and died almost immediately.

At the inquest Bentley was cleared of any involvement in the murder by the presiding magistrate, John Dewes, who was a friend of his and was even rumoured to be his business partner. The verdict outraged the Eureka miners, who saw it as yet another example of corruption in high places. A 5000-strong crowd gathered and burnt down the hotel. Three miners were arrested and charged with the pub's destruction, which provoked even more fury.

Britain had already lost one colony eighty years previously by deploying exactly the same draconian tactics.

The mood that led to the Boston Tea Party and the American Revolution was the same as that of the diggers, who demanded the release of the men charged with burning down the hotel. The authorities, in an attempt to regain control of the situation, re-arrested Bentley, and he was tried for murder and eventually sent to prison for manslaughter. But it was too little, too late.

Several Monster Meeetings followed, culminating in more than 10000 angry miners gathering at Bakery Hill on 11th November, where they formed the Ballarat Reform League. It committed itself to agitating for manhood suffrage, the abolition of the licence tax and the opening up of land for small farming settlements. It also advocated ceding from Britain if matters didn't improve. The *Ballarat Times*' Henry Seekamp wrote that the formation of the League was 'not more or less than the germ of Australian independence'.

The League wasn't merely an excuse to indulge in revolutionary rhetoric. On 29th November, the miners pledged to burn their licences, a direct challenge to the power of the State of Victoria. Up until now it had been the advocates of 'moral force' who had been in the ascendancy; now the diggers who supported direct action were holding sway.

But the police were in no mood to listen to incendiary talk, and later that same day they burst into the gravel pits of Eureka and arrested anyone without a licence. The mood grew nastier, and the resolve of the miners grew stronger.

The next day the diggers built a stockade at Eureka, under the command of Peter Lalor, an Irishman born into a family of political activists, with an Italian, Raffaello Carboni, as his lieutenant. Carts, pit props and fallen trees were piled high. Pikes and ammunition were brought in. Diggers scoured surrounding districts

ABOVE: Peter Lalor, by Ludwig Becker, 1856

for weapons. Five hundred men and women swore an oath on the blue and white Southern Cross flag, devised for the occasion and speedily sewn by miners' wives.

Carboni was an Italian nationalist in his mid-thirties. He'd served a short spell in prison because of his politics while training to be a priest in Rome, but left the church to work in a bank and became a member of the revolutionary Young Italy movement, under the leadership of General Garibaldi. He was injured, his cause was momentarily lost, and now, four years later, he found himself on the Victorian goldfields leading the call for reform or revolt, and made a speech the words of which are eerily familiar to us a hundred years later:

'I had a dream. A happy dream. I dreamed that we had met here together to render thanks unto our Father in heaven for a plentiful harvest . . . We must

meet as in old Europe . . . for the redress of grievances inflicted on us, not by Crown heads, but by blockheads, aristocratical incapables, who never did a day's work in their life.'

The diggers marched, two abreast, from Bakery Hill to Eureka, led by a Canadian flag-bearer carrying the Southern Cross. Among them were French, Germans and Swedes, as well as veterans from the American Revolution. This was an international brigade, and they wanted regime change and an Australian republic. Soon there were seven or eight hundred diggers inside the stockade. They were armed (Carboni encouraged them to grab any pole or metal shaft capable of 'piercing the tyrants' hearts') and ready for the next visit by the licence-fee collectors. In the quest for liberty they were prepared to pay their fees in blood. Indeed, the password to gain entrance to the stockade was 'Vinegar Hill', a reminder of two previous bloody insurrections.

But the army was ready for them. This revolt was the worst-kept secret in the colony. The soldiers were given rum for courage and they attacked the stockade in the dead of night, when many of the rebels were out in the surrounding countryside setting up outposts to prevent the surprise arrival of reinforcements.

The action was swift and the killing indiscriminate. A correspondent from the *Melbourne Morning Herald* was stopped 300 metres from the stockade and shot dead through the chest. A digger who had been shot in the legs was set on by three policemen; one knelt on him, another tried to strangle him, and the third went through his pockets. Dozens of diggers were killed; many were summarily executed. Carboni, who was easily recognisable by his shock of red hair, was beaten up, stripped of his clothes and thrown naked into gaol. The rebel leaders were arrested and faced the death penalty for high treason. Those, like Henry Seekamp, who had escaped were rounded up.

The government's very authority had been challenged by the uprising. It now wanted a quick, decisive trial, and was confident it had an unbeatable case. Police had infiltrated the public

meetings, the identities of the rebels were well known, and they had been armed, organised and mobilised for action.

To make absolutely sure the jury delivered a guilty verdict, this first man the Crown elected to try wasn't white, but an African American called John Joseph. The evidence was presented, the arguments were heard and the jury retired to consider its verdict. But then the most extraordinary thing happened. The jury returned a short time later and delivered a verdict of 'not guilty'. This so enraged the prosecutor, William Stawell, that he sought a month's leave of proceedings so he could put together another list of jurors. One hundred and seventy-eight were eventually found, but the next defendant was tried and the outcome was the same . . . and the next . . . and so on. They were all found not guilty. The jury may have known in their hearts that the men had led an insurrection, but they weren't prepared to let them be punished for it.

Finally, four months after his arrest, Carboni was put in the dock. The judge reminded the jury that the punishment for high treason was to be hung, drawn and quartered. 'Never mind the stench,' he was alleged to have said (at least according to Carboni). 'Each piece of the treacherous flesh must remain stuck up at the top of each gate of the town, there to dry in spite of occasional pecking of crows and vultures.'

The jury retired. Twenty minutes later they returned, and it was yet another 'not guilty' verdict.

In the same year as his acquittal,

ABOVE: *Eureka Stockade riot, Ballarat, 1854,* by J B Henderson, 1854

Carboni was elected to the Ballarat Local Court and was unopposed to represent Ballarat in the Legislative Council. The following year, Peter Lalor was elected to the Victorian Legislative Assembly.

The American writer Mark Twain called the Eureka rebellion 'the finest thing in Australasian history. It was a revolution – small in size, but great politically; it was a strike for liberty, a struggle for principle, a stand against injustice and oppression . . . It is another instance of a victory won by a lost battle.' And he was right. In the years that followed, the licence system was abolished, police numbers were cut and political representation was extended to the miners.

Australia is a rare nation. It wasn't born in blood. No uprising threw out its colonial masters. No revolution established a new government. A bunch of pike-bearing seditionists were not only acquitted of bearing arms against Her Majesty the Queen, but were shortly afterwards elected to the Queen's government.

And in true antipodean fashion, the nearest Australia ever came to a revolution began with a drunken punch-up outside a pub.

A Large-Brained, Self-Educated Titan

By the mid 1830s, transportation, which for over three decades had been the lifeblood of the Australian colonies, was falling out of fashion. Ordinary Australians resented the convicts because they were a pool of free labour which undermined their wages and jobs, the middle classes didn't like them because they lowered the tone of the neighbourhood, and the colonial governors found them hard to control and were frustrated that the British wouldn't pay their maintenance costs. On the other hand, there was a shortage of skilled workers. If transportation was banned, who would build the houses, roads and public buildings that a flourishing nineteenth-century colony required?

Nowadays, most Brits moan about the jetlag and the interminable flight, but two hundred years ago the journey to Australia took over six months and would have cost a year's wages. However bleak life

BELOW: Sir Henry Parkes at his desk in the Office of the Colonial Secretary, Sydney, 1891

might have been in Blighty, the cost of voyaging halfway round the world was a massive disincentive to all but the most adventurous and entrepreneurial.

An urgent solution was required, and in 1831 a plan was hatched. The colonial government would sell parcels of Crown land and use the proceeds to pay shipping companies to deliver healthy migrants from the UK to New South Wales – and the passengers would travel for free.

The shipping companies had suddenly been given a perfect way to make money. Their agents turned up at market places and public events throughout Great Britain, waxing lyrical about the opportunities that Australia offered. They convinced thousands of poor Britons to abandon everything and everyone they knew, and leave their homeland forever, in exchange for the dream of a new land filled with hope and promise, where the poor could become rich landowners and farmers.

The 'Bounty Immigration Scheme' was born, and by 1839 both Sydney and Melbourne were welcoming a wave of free migrants.

Henry the Tide Waiter

One man seduced by the promise of wealth and success was Henry Parkes, a Coventry boy and the youngest son of a poor tenant farmer who'd been kicked off his land due to debt. Henry hardly got any schooling, and from an early age worked on a rope-walk (a long, narrow building where hemp rope was twisted) for four pence a day, as well as 'breaking stones on the Queen's highway with hardly enough clothing to protect me from the cold'.

When he was old enough to be apprenticed, he was sent to Birmingham to work for a bone-and-ivory turner. He now began to educate himself in the library at the Birmingham Mechanics Institute, and joined the Chartists campaigning for a secret ballot and votes for all men. It was an exciting time for young working-class reformers. There were petitions to organise, marches through the streets, and crowded meetings with fiery orators.

When he was twenty-one he married Clarinda Varney, the daughter of the local butcher. The young couple regularly attended Carr's Lane

Shipping Rates

Once the emigrants had arrived safely in Australia and had been checked by a government doctor to ensure they were healthy, the shipping company received its bounty, which, at 1840 rates, was:

£19 for each unmarried female domestic, healthy and of child-bearing age;

£38 for each husband-and-wife team;

£5 for a child up to seven years old;

£10 for a child between seven and fifteen.

Independent Chapel, where the aging but remarkable Pastor James gave virtuoso two-hour sermons entirely from memory. Henry's twin passions, the Chapel and the Charter, were dominant influences for the rest of his life.

Eventually, he set up his own ivory- and bone-turning shop, but despite his emerging talents he was an incompetent businessman and couldn't make a go at it. So he and Clarinda moved to London, where they spent a miserable few months while Henry tried to find work. They lived in a single furnished room with a 'good-sized' wardrobe where, according to Henry, they kept their bread, cheese and coal. Their only water supply came from the River Thames, into which drained all of London's sewage and waste.

When winter came, it was bitterly cold. Henry still hadn't got a job, and although his tools had been sent down from Birmingham, he couldn't even afford to collect them from the delivery office. By December 1838, he and Clarinda couldn't stand their London life any longer. The Australian colonial propaganda boasted that mechanics in the colonies could earn a whopping forty or fifty shillings a week, so they applied to emigrate on a free passage, and after a two-month wait were accepted. Henry and the now pregnant Clarinda left England in March 1839.

Seventeen weeks later, they arrived in Sydney with a brand-new baby, born just two days before they landed. But their dream of a new life was immediately shattered by the stark reality of life in the colony. They had arrived in the dead of Sydney's winter, with only three pence in the world, and no job. In order to survive, they had to sell their belongings.

'I have been disappointed in all my expectations of Australia, except as to its wickedness; for it is far more wicked than I had conceived it possible for any place to be . . . For the encouragement of any at home who think of emigrating, I ought to add that I have not seen one single individual who came out with me on the *Strathfieldsaye* but most heartily wishes himself back home.'

– HENRY PARKES,
IN A LETTER HOME

But eventually Henry's luck changed. He got a job on the estate of one of the colony's richest settlers, Sir John Jamison, and although it was poorly paid, it led to him being hired by the New South Wales Customs Department on the recommendation of Sir John's son-in-law. He now had regular work as a tide waiter, searching merchant ships for contraband, and was able to pay off the debts he'd run up. At last his new life could begin, although it's doubtful if at that time anyone but Henry would have predicted that one day he'd become premier of New South Wales.

Tragedy at the Heads

While for Henry and Clarinda the journey to Australia had been arduous, for others it was tragic. Australia's vast coastline is a graveyard for over 6500 wrecked ships – that's one for every nine kilometres of coast. In the nineteenth century, sea travel to Australia was treacherous. European mariners sailed wooden ships that were tiny by today's standards. For power they relied on the wind catching their sails. To navigate they used the stars and sextants, and even their most up-to-date charts were often unreliable.

In August 1857, one hundred metres from the towering cliffs that guard the entrance to Sydney Harbour, one of Australia's worst maritime disasters took place, and it shook the youthful confidence of Australia to the marrow.

The good ship *Dunbar* was massive, the largest vessel ever built in Sunderland. With a hull and frames of British oak, a deck of East India teak, and a figurehead depicting a British Lion, she was a first-class ship.

The doomed vessel was reaching the end of an arduous eighty-one day journey from Plymouth when she was hit by one of Sydney's legendary southerly squalls. She arrived off Sydney Heads on the night of Thursday 20th August. It was a dismal evening. Heavy rain impaired vision, obscuring the sentinel cliffs at the entrance to Port Jackson. Captain Green had made a number of previous visits to Sydney and had even captained the *Dunbar* on a previous visit there. But this time he made a miscalculation that was to have disastrous consequences. He squared up for the run in, apparently believing they were approaching North Head.

When the shout 'breakers ahead!' was heard, the Captain, still believing they were north of the harbour entrance, ordered 'hard-a-port'. Instead of entering the safety of the harbour, the *Dunbar* drove smack onto the boulders at the foot of South Head. The impact brought down the top masts, mounting seas smashed the life boats to pieces, and the *Dunbar* tipped over in the stormy sea. It began to break up almost immediately.

One man, Able Seaman James Johnson, was hurled on to a rocky ledge. He scrambled higher and clung to his precarious hold for thirty-six hours until he was spotted from the cliff top. Eventually he was rescued by an Icelander, Antonia Wollier, who climbed down the rock face. Johnson was the sole survivor.

For days afterwards, Sydney's Harbour and beaches were littered with the detritus of death. Mutilated bodies, seventeen from the North Shore alone, clothes, shoes, ship's stores, barrels of dried fruit – each tide cast more evidence of the tragedy onto Sydney's beaches.

About 20000 people lined George Street for the funeral procession; banks and offices closed and church bells rang.

The disaster had a profound effect on the city. Everyone who lived there had either arrived by sea, or was descended from people who had arrived by sea. Captain Green was an able sailor in charge of a top-class vessel, and he'd been in waters with which he was familiar, just a few miles off the safest harbour in the world. Despite all the dazzling technological innovations that the nineteenth century had ushered in, it was clear that Australia was still isolated and vulnerable. While it still loved its Mother Country, it was going to have to look after its own.

LEFT: Sydney's South Head, where the *Dunbar* met its fate
PREVIOUS PAGE: A memorial inscription on the cliff above the wreck site: DUNBAR C.P. 25TH AUG 1857 RECUT BY E.S.E. 20 AUG 1906

Don't Come On Board – We Are Dying of Fever!

It's a wonder anyone arrived in Australia at all, because if shipwrecks didn't kill you, disease probably would. The story of the *Ticonderoga* may not be well known (she was named after a 1758 battle in Vermont, in which 15 000 British and American troops were defeated by 3500 Frenchmen), but the deadly chain of events on board is all too familiar.

A long, arduous journey was a fact of life for the thousands of hopeful migrants on their way to the new colony, as were storms at sea, cramped conditions, the stench and heat of hundreds of bodies crammed together, and inevitably sickness and even death. So when little Caroline Lamden died on board the *Ticonderoga* in 1852 from a fever (probably typhus), it would have come as no surprise.

There was no possibility of her body being kept on board until it reached her new homeland – she had to be

buried at sea. The grieving family, and other passengers and crew, would have gathered on the upper deck, while her body, sewn into sailcloth and weighted with iron bars or chains, was placed on a wooden board. The ship's bell would have tolled as the captain read the service. As he said the words 'we therefore commit her body to the sea', the board would have been tilted upwards, tipping Caroline into the ocean below. Then the ship would have sailed on, leaving no grave to visit, no memorial to the life lost.

Within two months, a full-blown typhus epidemic had broken out on board. The stench from so many victims was overwhelming and terrifying. By now an average of two or three people were dying every day, and medical supplies soon ran out. Many of the ill succumbed to the freezing conditions. During bad weather, sea burials had to be postponed, and the bodies were stored on deck. Sharks began to follow the ship, and grieving families watched in horror as the corpses of their loved ones were snatched away by the huge scavengers when they were tipped overboard. The crew began throwing the bodies of babies and children over the side in the dead of night, to save their parents the agony of seeing their young ones cast into the ocean.

When the ship finally saw land and entered Victoria's Port Phillip, ninety days after it had left Liverpool, it was in a hideous state. Inside the Heads, it was met by a pilot boat, whose captain wrote in his log:

> 'The large ship got into Port Phillip safely . . . She was crowded with passengers and they all called out in frightful yells, 'Don't come on board, as we are dying of fever!' I was informed they . . . had lost 102 on the passage. The ship had three decks and it was in the middle deck that the mortality took place . . .'

The ship's doctor, who was himself sick, reported that there were still 300 desperately ill passengers on board. The captain wasn't allowed to land in Melbourne, but instead put in at Port Nepean on a beach called Portsea, chosen because of its isolated but accessible position and good anchorage. A quarantine ground was marked out with yellow flags and white paint on the trees, and tents were erected using sails and spars from the ship. The government purchased two houses nearby that had been occupied

by lime-burners and converted them into hospitals.

It may have been a beautiful setting but seventy more people died there. The sick were laid out on the beach, and attendants swatted the flies away from them with clumps of twigs and attempted to shelter them from the fierce sun. Such conditions were far from ideal, but at least the patients were clean, and fresh food was brought to them from Melbourne. A ship called the *Lysander* sailed over from South Australia, and was outfitted as a hospital for the worst cases. Eventually, once the survivors had been restored to health, another ship arrived to take them on the short trip to Melbourne, although many were terrified to get on board, fearing they were about to be abandoned in some faraway destination.

More than one-fifth of all the passengers who had embarked at Liverpool were now dead. Eighty-six of the victims were children. One man, named Malcom McRae, lost, one after the other, his ten-year-old daughter, his two-year-old son, then his six-year-old son, and finally his wife.

Henry and the Toyshop Mob

Despite tragedies like these, Bounty Immigration was popular with emigrants and locals alike. Meanwhile, opposition to transportation reached fever pitch. Many settlers now saw themselves as 'Australians', rather than temporary visitors far away from their real homes on a little island in the North Sea. They resented Britain

dumping its poorest and most troubled people on them. A campaign was launched to draw attention to the acts of cruelty involved in the punishment of convicts, behaviour which was no longer deemed appropriate in this liberal-minded new colony.

The treatment of convicts was also an issue for the British establishment, although for them it wasn't the cruelty but the leniency that outraged them. Many thieves and scoundrels who had been transported returned not only with suntans but with thousands of pounds in their pockets. Where was the punishment in that? What kind of disincentive did it offer the criminal classes? But more importantly, transportation hadn't turned out to be the cheap way of disposing of undesirable elements that its supporters had promised. In the first four years of its operation, it had cost the British government a staggering £574 592. Those who had originally opposed the system on cost grounds had been proved absolutely right.

The Colonial Office was, by and large, persuaded by these arguments, and indeed it didn't have such a desperate need to send its felons to a foreign country now that prisons like Pentonville had increased the number of jail places available in the UK. Nevertheless, there were still so many petty thieves, malingerers and all-round bad hats congregating in the big cities that it was an option the British didn't want to abandon entirely. For a while they stopped sending convict ships to Sydney, but in 1848 Prime Minister Earl Grey sent out a transportation vessel called the *Hashemy*, which contained not just convicts but also well-behaved prisoners who the British had decided to 'exile' rather than transport. In other words, they weren't to be incarcerated once they landed but would be allowed to earn a wage or set up a business.

By this time Henry Parkes had quit his job in the Customs Department. He was an avid collector, and after a further dismal attempt to set up as an ivory-and-bone turner, he opened a shop in Hunter Street where he sold ornaments, whale's teeth, boxing gloves and toys. But his real interest lay in politics, particularly those of the radical type that he had enjoyed as a young man in Birmingham. He had made a number of friends among Sydney's intelligentsia, and in the room behind the shop they plotted and organised. The 'Toyshop Mob' became a political force to be reckoned with, and they even managed to get one of their number, a reforming lawyer called Robert Lowe, elected to the New South Wales Legislative Council.

Sydney's residents were outraged by the arrival of the *Hashemy*, and Parkes's parlour became one of the epicentres of the agitation. They thought the difference between 'exiles' and 'convicts' was semantic hair-splitting on the part of their imperial masters in London, who still wanted to foist English criminals on the young colony. Thousands of them demonstrated at Circular Quay. Parkes even hired an omnibus sporting a banner with the word 'Defiance' on it. A delegation, in which he and Robert Lowe were included, took their petition to Government House, where

the supercilious Sir Charles Fitzroy dismissed them, insisting that he was not going to be persuaded by a mob, that the *Hashemy* was going to offload its passengers as planned, and that was that.

But even though they lost the battle, the incident proved a great victory for the Toyshop Mob, because no more convict ships were ever sent to Sydney. And perhaps more important in the long run was the sea-change in Australian politics that this episode presaged. At a second mass meeting, Parkes spoke to the huge crowd from the top of his bus, and a motion was passed that: 'It is indispensable to the well-being of the colony . . . that its government should no longer be administered by the remote, ill-informed and irresponsible Colonial Office, but by ministers chosen from and responsible to the colonists themselves . . .'

Ordinary Australians were beginning to take control of their own destiny.

Bride Ships

It wasn't only men who took advantage of the Bounty Immigration Scheme. So many male convicts had been transported during the early years of the colony that Australia was now in dire need of more women. Men outnumbered women by as many as twenty to one in some outlying areas, and it wasn't only potential wives but domestic servants who were in short supply. The Colonial Office produced large posters that were put up in post offices specifically targeting potential women migrants. Priests and ministers told their female congregations it was their Christian duty to cross the sea, work hard and make new respectable lives in the outback, and it quickly became acceptable for both working-class and middle-class women to

AUSTRALIA.

GOVERNMENT EMIGRATION

TO

NEW SOUTH WALES

Farmers, Mechanics, Agricultural and other Labourers and Small Working Capitalists, MARRIED (with or without Children), NOT EXCEEDING 35 YEARS OF AGE; and

DOMESTIC SERVANTS,

NOT EXCEEDING 30 YEARS,

Are provided with Assisted Passages to

SYDNEY.

By the Agent-General for New South Wales.

Full Particulars and Forms of Application may be obtained from the Emigration Department, New South Wales Government Office, 5, Westminster Chambers, London, S.W.

RIGHT: Emigration poster, c.1883

An Idiot's Guide to Federation

1. Until 1901, Australia didn't exist – at least not as a nation. Mathew Flinders popularised the use of the word 'Australia' to describe the continent, and the British Admiralty adopted it in 1824. But all through the nineteenth century there was still no political entity of that name, just a loose collection of colonies dotted around the continent's enormous coastline.

2. For the first forty years after the First Fleet landed, there was only one such colony, New South Wales, which stretched from the northern tip of Australia all the way down to the far south, and included the big island known as Van Diemen's Land. (In fact, for some of this time New South Wales even included New Zealand, which was 2000 km away across the ocean!)

3. Then, in 1825, the people of Van Diemen's Land decided they wanted a colony of their own and established what we now know as Tasmania.

4. Meanwhile, over 3000 kilometres from Sydney on the west coast, there was a tiny little military outpost called the Swan River colony, which grew to become Perth. It too eventually wanted its own colony and so Western Australia was born.

5. South Australia was originally a settlement of free settlers around Adelaide. It achieved colonial status in 1836, but was much bigger than it is now, extending all the way up to continent's northern coast.

6. Then, as the north-eastern towns like Brisbane and Cairns grew, they began to flex their political muscles, and finally broke away from New South Wales, taking with them its top third, to create Queensland.

7. Melbourne started life as a tiny settlement founded by Sir John Batman, and was consequently called Batmania (what a pity they ever renamed it). With its fertile land, its wealth and massively increased population, not to mention its newfound confidence, it soon became the capital of a state named after Queen Victoria, which quickly grew to rival New South Wales.

8. Then, on New Year's Day, 1911, the top half of South Australia was removed and became the Northern Territory. The Australian Capital Territory was created out of a little part of New South Wales, with the nation's capital city, Canberra, being established there in 1913.

apply for tickets in order to obtain work in Australia as governesses, dairy maids, cheese-makers and domestic servants.

The journey was certainly gruelling, but it was eased slightly by the fact that on certain days the women were allowed to wash in a wooden tub wearing a shift, while modestly screened by awnings. In addition, books and sewing materials were donated by women's charities, so there were books to read, literacy classes and parlour games.

These were, by and large, intelligent and gutsy women who, while they would not be given the same opportunities as their male counterparts, would in time raise the next generation of politicians and opinion-formers. I don't think it's too farfetched to say that the character of these women can still be seen in the faces of Australian women today.

Henry, the Father of Federation

Once more educated women and men were settling in Australia, they began demanding to be governed not by lords, knights and the sons of rich landowners, but by people of their own class and background. It was within this context that Henry Parkes had such a dazzling political career. He was tall, with a striking face, a leonine head of hair and a dominating personality. He was also a talented if straightforward orator, who talked like an ordinary man living among ordinary people. The politician Alfred Deakin described him as 'a large-brained, self-educated Titan whose natural field was found in parliament and whose resources of character and intellect enabled him in his later years to overshadow all his contemporaries'.

During his 'Toyshop' years in the late 1840s and '50s, Parkes became a successful journalist – at one stage he was even a newspaper proprietor. But a recurrent theme throughout his life was his inability to sort out his business affairs, and he was forced to declare himself bankrupt after running up debts of nearly £50000.

Nevertheless, he was becoming a significant figure in the colony, both as an editor and as a politician. Eventually, in 1872, he became premier and seventeen years later – having presided over not one, not two . . . but five administrations – he might have been forgiven for retiring gracefully. But no – on 24th October 1889, at the Tenterfield School of Arts, he delivered a speech in support of a great Australian idea that could become a tangible reality, and, if it did, would change Australia forever. That idea was Federation, and Henry Parkes became known as its father.

Up to the beginning of twentieth century, New South Wales, Victoria, Tasmania, Western Australia, South Australia and Queensland were all separate British settlements, and they acted alone. Individually, they grew and prospered, but they didn't really get on with one another; in fact, they actively distrusted each other. They had different forms of government, different laws, different taxes, and you even needed to clear customs when you were travelling between them. The American writer Mark Twain said the colonies' convoluted tariff system was 'the most baffling and unaccountable marvel that Australasia can show'.

It seems obvious to us now that Darwin, Hobart, Sydney and the rest are much better off being one country,

but a hundred and fifty years ago a lot of people were very resistant to the idea. It wasn't until the 1860s that the notion of nationhood started to grow in the public consciousness. Newspapers began writing about 'Australia's' interests, and started getting excited about 'Australia's' sportsmen, especially when its cricket team beat the Brits.

But what really focussed minds on the subject of federation was fear. Britain wasn't the only empire colonising the world. Germany, France, Italy and even the Russians were on the move, and the South Pacific was an alternative prize. While all the different Australian states had their militias, they couldn't be mobilised to one area if, say, Sydney was attacked. If Australia was going to have a national army, it needed to be a nation.

So it was that at Tenterfield, New South Wales, Henry Parkes made a ringing call for a great national government for all Australia. The Tenterfield Oration, as it became known, set the ball rolling towards Australian Federation.

'The great question . . . is . . . whether the time has not now arisen for the creation on this Australian continent of an Australian Government . . . Australia has now a population of three and a half millions, and the American people numbered only between three and four millions when they formed the great commonwealth of the United States. The numbers are

Western Australia

Western Australia lagged behind the other colonies. It only achieved colonial status in the 1890s and had a tiny population. But then gold was discovered there. Soon Western Australia's gold production was second only to Johannesburg. Suddenly, federation with the other colonies didn't seem particularly attractive – why would they want to share their new-found wealth with everyone else? They became the last state to approve Federation, in 1900, then in 1906 their parliament voted to leave it again! But the rest of Australia ignored their decision, and they stayed in.

In the 1930s, Victoria and NSW were in the middle of a depression. WA didn't want to have to bail them out and voted to leave again by a huge majority. The Federation then appealed to the UK, who said 'No, you can't leave.' Once again, they didn't.

Economic conditions then got better, and the argument for leaving diminished. The Australian economy is in good shape now, but if there was a slump and Western Australia decided it didn't want to share its rich mining resources with its unemployed brothers and sisters in the other states, would the spectre of secession loom again?

about the same, and surely what the Americans have done by war, the Australians can bring about in peace.'

— HENRY PARKES, AT TENTERFIELD

Not that this speech galvanised the political class into moving particularly quickly. There followed ten years of horse-trading between the states (and with New Zealand, which finally decided it would be better off going its own way). The problem was that every state wanted to protect its own interests. Queensland threatened to pull out because a federal constitution would mean the end of its 'black labour system' (a virtual slave trade of South Sea Islanders). Western Australia was richer than the other

colonies and threatened to go it alone, and no state wanted the others dumping cheap goods on it and thus undermining its own industries.

In 1898, a referendum was held on the question of whether the states of Australia should join under one federal government. The ballot was open only to men over twenty-one, with the honourable exception of South Australia, where women could vote too. Though it received a majority support in each state, the referendum failed as the 'yes' vote in New South Wales didn't meet the specified level.

But the Federationists were not to be beaten, and there was a second referendum a year later. This time New South Wales, Victoria, South Australia, Queensland and Tasmania

delivered a resounding yes, and the following year Western Australia joined them.

Henry's Dream Comes True

The Commonwealth of Australia Constitution Act was passed by the UK parliament on 5th July and received the Royal Assent on 9th July 1900. The inauguration of the new 'Commonwealth of Australia' took place on New Year's Day, 1901, in Centennial Park in Sydney.

But the Father of Federation, Sir Henry Parkes, didn't live to see it. In his last few years he had faced personal tragedy. Yet again debt had overwhelmed him and he was forced to sell many of his personal possessions, including his valued collection of autographs. Clarinda died in 1888, and although Parkes married again a year later to Eleanor Dixon, this marriage was never recognised by his family. Then Eleanor died too, leaving Parkes with a young family and failing health. But even in his old age he was able to attract the ladies, and he married Julie Lynch, who nursed him till his death in April 1896, just short of his eighty-first birthday.

A Brief Diversion in Order to Consider Why the Australians Are So Damn Good at Sport

Sportsmen were representing Australia for a long time before Australia existed as a nation. In 1882 an Australian XI played an English XI at cricket. There had been England v Australia matches prior to that, but usually with more Australians on the field than Englishmen, because the English were reckoned to be their sporting superiors. But to the surprise and shock of virtually everyone, at this historic match at the Oval in Kennington, London, the Aussies beat the Poms by seven runs, and *The Sporting Times* published a satirical obituary:

RIGHT: From *The Sporting Times*, London, September 2nd 1882

In Affectionate Remembrance

OF

ENGLISH CRICKET,

WHICH DIED AT THE OVAL

ON

29th AUGUST, 1882,

Deeply lamented by a large circle of sorrowing friends and acquaintances.

R.I.P.

N.B.—*The body will be cremated and the ashes taken to Australia.*

ABOVE: Rupertswood, and perhaps the very fireplace that created the Ashes
LEFT: The manse's magnificent stained-glass window

billed platypus beneath it.

This stately pile was owned by Sir William Clarke, one of Australia's richest men, and the first Australian-born baronet. He met the England team travelling to Australia aboard the *Penshawur* in hope of restoring their pride a few months after the Oval match, and as he was president of the Melbourne Cricket Club it must have seemed entirely appropriate for Clarke to invite the team to Rupertswood for Christmas. They played a friendly match against the Rupertswood staff. Indeed, it was so friendly that no one kept score, although 'the servants were run off their feet retrieving the many fours and sixes'. But after the match some local ladies presented the English captain, the Honourable Ivo Bligh, with a little terracotta perfume bottle containing the ashes of a cricket bail, and amid polite laughter Lady Clarke announced at dinner that the two countries now had a trophy to play for.

The urn wasn't all that Ivo took away with him. The Clarkes had a music teacher called Florence Murphy, and he fell head over heels for her. But he was nobility and she was most certainly not. How could the knot be tied? Fortunately, the Clarkes were very fond of Florence, so Sir William interceded with Ivo's disapproving parents and in February 1884 confetti rained down on the happy couple. A lavish wedding reception was held at Rupertswood, and Florence, on the death of Ivo's father, became the Countess of Darnley.

Moving swiftly along from this tedious tale of love among the aristocracy, the question remains:

I had always thought that after this panegyric the bails and stumps were burned, put in some sort of pot, and every four years forever after England and Australia have wrestled for 'The Ashes'. But I was wrong.

The Ashes were invented at Rupertswood, a house in Victoria of some gothic grandeur, which was at one time so opulent it even had its own railway station. Today it still retains some delightfully eloquent touches, including a dazzling stained-glass window of a stag's head that would appear to have been looted from the manse on a Scottish laird if it wasn't for the cute little stained-glass duck-

LEFT: A replica of the prized urn

why are the Australians so good at sport? Obviously, the weather has got something to do with it. They have more months in which to practise than those of us from countries with colder climes. There's probably a bit more toughness in their genes, due to the fact that the country was forged by the blood and sweat of convicts, and then by the raw hands of hardy free settlers and gold diggers. But there's another reason.

In the early colonial period, working hours were extraordinarily long. It was common to slog away for twelve to sixteen hours a day. That old saying 'hard work never killed anyone' probably wasn't true.

Centuries previously, medieval monks had lived by the rule of eight hours work, eight hours prayer and meditation, and eight hours rest. But by the time of the industrial revolution all that had been long forgotten. Working conditions were unregulated, and the health, welfare and morale of working people suffered. In 1817, a five-day week was first proposed, with the slogan 'eight hours labour, eight hours recreation, eight hours rest', but to no avail.

By the mid-1800s the big Australian cities were in the middle of a building boom, and workers began to realise that they had some power in the marketplace because their skills were in demand. Of course, this was happening all over the world, but Australian workers weren't class-bound, they were articulate and independent, and they found their voice first.

It started with a group of stone-masons. They argued that, in the harsh

BELOW: England v Australia at the Sydney Cricket Ground, January 27th 1883

ABOVE: An Eight Hours Day Procession, May 1st 1895

Australian heat, eight hours was an appropriate amount of time to work each day. As a result of the Victorian gold rush, Melbourne was growing rapidly and some very impressive stone buildings were going up. But the goldfields were also a siren's call to workers with their promise of untold wealth, so there was a labour shortage in the cities. This was a good moment to threaten industrial action, because there was no pool of skilled men to bring into Melbourne at short notice in order to break a strike. So Melbourne's building trades confidently joined the stonemasons, the chorus of protest became a cacophony, and after two weeks of agitation their bosses capitulated. On 21st April 1856, the eight-hour day was won. Not every worker in the country benefited, of course. But it was the fillip the union movement needed.

So what does the eight-hour day have to do with sport? Well, it's about the things that nineteenth-century Australians valued in life. They worked hard, and as far as they were concerned, that earned them the right to the rewards of leisure time. Consequently, the workers threw themselves at the things they enjoyed the most. And for most of them, that meant sport.

But what amuses me most about the fight for the eight-hour day – the part that seems so truly, madly, deeply Australian – is that workers got a holiday to celebrate the advent of the eight-hour day. In other words, they got time off to celebrate getting time off!

What About the Coloured Alien and the Chow and the Hindoo?

As the twentieth century was born, so was Australia. In a mere one hundred years, Terra Australis had been transformed from a collection of tiny colonial outposts into a fully fledged nation, complete with its own flag, its own army, its own government and its own way of speaking English.

But now we must discuss two little words, 'white' and 'Australia'. This wonderful new country wasn't created for everybody. Whether you were on the right of the political spectrum or the left, if you were white you would almost certainly have been part of the general consensus that believed the rights of those with skins of any other colour should be severely curtailed.

BELOW: A Chinese fruit-and-vegetable hawker in Sydney, 1895

A speech by W G Spence, trade union leader and Labour MP (the party later 'modernised' the spelling to 'Labor' in 1912), is typical of the spirit of the times: 'If we keep the race pure, and build up a national character, we shall become a highly progressive people of whom the British government will be prouder the longer we live and the stronger we grow.'

Not that racial intolerance was a new phenomenon among the people of the southern continent. It had been inherent in the colonial psyche since the days when William Dampier had turned his nose up at the inhabitants of Australia for being even more miserable than the Hodmadods of Monomatapa. But once potential workers with differently coloured skins began to arrive in large numbers, it grew unchecked.

Swamped by a Savage Race

In 1848, following a change in the employment laws, shiploads of Chinese labourers sailed into Sydney. They'd been recruited in China, where they'd signed contracts detailing their pay and conditions, and in return had undertaken to work in Australia for at least five years.

Their arrival stirred deep feelings of insecurity among Australian workers, who felt threatened by the prospect of seeing their wages undercut by the 'Yellow Peril'. Even the politicians on the Committee on Immigration foresaw Australia being swamped by aliens. They reported that the 'boundless regions of the Australian continent capable of containing millions of our fellow subjects may thus be occupied by a semi-barbarous or even savage race'.

LEFT: A stage coach taking Chinese passengers to the Victorian goldfields, c.1860

The treatment of these workers was appalling. The *General Palmer*, for instance, transported 332 labourers from China, but by the time it arrived in Sydney, sixty-three were dead. Throughout the journey they'd been given no blankets or clothes, and the only toilets available to them were massive chains hanging over the stern, on which they had to climb so they could shit into the sea far below. Many, particularly the sick, had fallen to their deaths.

Things weren't much better when the workers arrived at their unknown destination, probably a sheep or cattle station out in the bush. They were paid a fraction of the white men's wage, and had to buy their supplies at inflated prices from the company store, where their purchases were chalked up against their wages. Consequently, they often

racked up enormous debts and were forced to continue working until the money was paid off – an impossibility which could keep them trapped in Australia for years after their contract had expired. Many tried to flee, but if they were captured, they were put in jail, fined and then returned to their place of work. Invariably, it was their masters who paid the fine, so the workers now found themselves even deeper in debt than they had been before they escaped.

The fear and anger provoked by a few thousand migrant workers was as nothing compared to the outrage of the white settlers a few years later, when 40000 Chinese made their way to the Australian goldfields. By and large, they kept to themselves and were hardworking and law-abiding, but from the moment they arrived in a gold town they'd be on the receiving end of acts of spite. They were shunned, their pigtails were pulled, and when they walked through the streets, their tools, which they carried on a long bamboo poles, were sent flying. The whites justified their animosity in a host of ways. Chinese diggers were said to muddy the water needed for washing gold; they sifted through old mining rubble which the Europeans thought belonged to them; they were characterised as obsessive gamblers ('it is singular, though painful, to observe how intensely the passions of play turn this effeminate race'); if a white woman married a Chinese, she was deemed an opium addict and a prostitute.

Another contributing factor to this intolerance was the Asian work ethic. In one year alone, Chinese immigrants shipped more than 200 000 ounces of gold back to Canton. Nothing stirs envy like hard work and success!

By 1855, there was a general terror that migrant workers would flood the country. This fear was unfounded – most returned to China within a few years (between 1852 and 1889, there were 40 721 Chinese arrivals and 36 049 departures). Nevertheless, the Victorian state government introduced a tax 'to make provision for certain immigrants'. This involved a ten-pound levy, payable by every ship's captain bringing Chinese workers into Victoria. In addition, he could only disembark one Chinese national for every ten tons of goods. This effectively slowed the arrival of the Chinese into Victoria by sea, so instead the ships dropped them off in Adelaide, from where they travelled the 650 kilometres to the Bendigo goldfields on foot!

The notion of keeping out non-whites began to be part and parcel of Australian culture. It's no coincidence that the very first piece of legislation passed by the new Federation in 1901 was the Immigration Restriction Act, which outlined an effective mechanism for creating a white Australia.

'There is no racial equality. These races are, in comparison with white races . . . unequal and inferior . . . the doctrine of the equality of man was never intended to apply to the equality of the English man and the China man.'

– SIR EDMUND 'TOBY' BARTON,
AUSTRALIA'S FIRST PRIME MINISTER

In the run-up to Federation, the colonial premiers had been very

Henry and the Chinese

Even Henry Parkes advocated racial discrimination. On 7th July 1854 in the Legislative Council of New South Wales, he stated that the introduction of coloured, inferior workers would have bad results. He said white Australians would find it degrading to have to work alongside them, whites from outside Australia wouldn't want to go and live there anymore, and the morals of society would be seriously endangered by the laxity and promiscuity of such people.

explicit about who should be allowed into the country from now on, virtually saying 'We're going to ban anyone who isn't white, pink or slightly grey in colour'. But the UK was very nervous that the wording would offend the millions of people in the British Empire whose skins didn't match up to that description. So the British colonial secretary leaned on them to find a way of excluding references to skin colour without negating the desired effect. The new Australian national government came up with the idea of a 'dictation test', introduced ostensibly in order to make sure all immigrants were literate. It gave immigration officials the power to ban anyone from entering if they failed the fifty-word test. But the dictation didn't have to be in English – the adjudicating official could use any European language he wanted.

So now a non-white who spoke perfectly good English could arrive in

White Australia

What about the coloured alien
And the Chow and the Hindoo,
Men of Queensland ask Australia
* What do you intend to do?*
Out from mill and shop and garden,
Hawkers, fossickers and cooks;
Wipe them once for all and ever,
From the Federal nation's books.

– THE WORKER *newspaper*

Australia, and could even have lived there for many years and be returning from a trip to their family in Peking or Calcutta, but if they failed a dictation test in Swedish, they wouldn't be allowed back in.

This may sound completely mad, and indeed it was. But it meant that, as invariably happens when laws are passed to exclude people for specific reasons, it became a device that the authorities used to keep out anyone they didn't like for any reason whatsoever.

The Stolen Generations

By the late 1800s, guerilla wars between the Aboriginals and the colonists were largely over. Cattle-spearing still took place, but police stations now covered large areas of the country, and major insurrection was a thing of the past.

The only 'problem' now appeared to be how to manage Aboriginal decline. Most whites thought Aboriginals lazy, feckless and stupid, and were convinced that they were well on their way to extinction.

This assumption seemed to be borne out by the population figures for the State of Victoria – prior to the gold rush there had been about 60 000 Aboriginals there; after it ended, this had been reduced to approximately 2000.

In the 1880s Aboriginal Protection Boards were established throughout most of Australia. Theoretically, they had an obligation to ensure the wellbeing of the Aboriginals, but they were at best autocratic, and at worst brutally inhuman.

A 'half-caste law' was implemented in Victoria (and later in Western Australia): all Aboriginals who had white ancestry and were under the age of 34 were removed from their families and transported – often hundreds of kilometres – to a government institution or Christian mission. All contact with their parents was severed.

The plan was to train the girls as domestic servants and the boys as labourers, to offer them the chance to lead 'proper' lives, leaving the elderly and the 'full-bloods' abandoned on reservations. Consequently, the old way of living would die out, the young would be integrated into white society, and Aboriginal culture (and indeed, the Aboriginals) would disappear. It failed. There are now approximately 30 000 Victorian Aboriginals.

Incredibly, this policy of taking children from their families continued around the country up to the 1970s, and hence many of the so-called 'Stolen Generations' live with its repercussions today. Aside from being cut off from their families and their culture, many suffered the additional horrors common in such institutions.

Unsurprisingly, this piece of history remains the subject of emotional debate, and some defend the practice as a well-meaning effort to provide a form of child protection.

RIGHT: Children at the United Aborigines Mission at Colebrook Home, Quorn, South Australia, c.1936

LEFT: Egon Kisch addressing a huge crowd in the Domain, Sydney, 1934

The Dangerous Loony

Egon Kisch was born into a wealthy Jewish family in Prague (then part of the Austro-Hungarian Empire). He fought in the Austrian Army in WWI, but the horror with which he was confronted turned him into a fiery radical. In 1918 he deserted, and later that year played a leading role in an abortive left-wing revolution in Vienna, following which he became a founding member of the Austrian Communist Party.

By 1934 he'd become a celebrated newspaper reporter, and was invited to Australia to speak at an anti-fascist conference. But the Australian government wasn't enthusiastic about welcoming a known revolutionary communist and journalist to its shores, and acting on a British tip-off he was prevented from disembarking at Fremantle. His ship, the *Strathaird*, then sailed on to Melbourne where the reception he was given by his

supporters was so intense that he attempted to take matters into his own hands by jumping off it onto the dock below. Unfortunately, he broke his leg in the process and was rushed back on board.

The *Strathaird* now continued on round the coast towards Sydney, during which time Kisch's case was heard in front of High Court judge Doc Evatt, who ruled that Kisch had been wrongly excluded from Australia and that he should consequently be released.

But the federal government had another card up its sleeve. It now ordered Kisch to take the dictation test. The authorities' problem, though, was that he was multilingual, and whichever European language test they chose, they couldn't be sure he'd fail it. Eventually, they hit on a plan that they were sure would outfox him. He was instructed to write the Lord's Prayer in Scottish Gaelic!

Ar n-athair a tha air nèamh:
gu naomhaichear d'ainm.
Thigeadh do rìoghachd. Dèantar
do thoil air an talamh, mar a
nithear air nèamh.
Tabhair dhuinn an ar fiachan,
amhuil mar a mhaitheas sinne
d'ar luchd-fiach.
Agus na leig am buaireadh sinn,
ach saor sinn o olc.
Oir is leatsa an rioghachd agus an
cumhachd agus a'ghòir gu siorruidh.
Amen

Kisch refused to participate in this charade, thus he was deemed to have failed and was once again sent back to his ship. By now though, public opinion had swung in his favour and his case returned to the courts. The hearing was farcical. When Kisch's lawyers challenged Constable Mackay, who had administered the test, to take it himself, he translated 'Lead us not into temptation, but deliver us from evil' as 'As well as we could benefit, and if we let her scatter free to the bad . . .' The judge found that Gaelic was not a European language within the meaning of the Act, and at last Kisch was allowed to enter the country.

His newly acquired notoriety guaranteed him huge crowds, and Kisch travelled around the country warning them about Hitler's regime, and how the Nazis intended to orchestrate a huge international war and build concentration camps – what a dangerous loony!

'I have had three adventurous months since I last saw you.

I know the Police Court, the Quarter Sessions Court, the High Court with one judge and the High Court with five judges. But whenever the court let me go I was arrested again. I have learnt to speak English better. Perhaps I do not speak King's English but it's Kisch English anyhow.'

— EGON KISCH, SPEAKING AT THE
DOMAIN, SYDNEY, 1934

Populate or Perish

Even though the dictation test had been publicly ridiculed, 'White Australia' remained the policy of successive governments until the end of World War II.

Employers were enthusiastic about this idea too. Much of Europe had been ravaged by the war and national economies were in pieces, but Australia was experiencing a boom, and if profits were to be made, more workers were required. 'Populate or Perish' became the nation's new slogan.

At first, this simply meant encouraging existing Australians to breed faster and for longer, but although they did their level best, their patriotic nocturnal activities didn't achieve the population boom that had been hoped for. So it was decided to dust off a scheme that had been used a hundred years previously – Bounty Immigration. Once again, assisted travel would be offered to potential immigrants with particular skills.

So how would 'Populate or Perish' fit in with the concept of 'White Australia'? Would the country end up with another wave of unemployed

Asians? The solution was to turn yet again to the white folk back in Europe. But it wasn't only the British who took up the offer this time. From 1952 major sources of migrants included Italy, the Netherlands, Germany and Yugoslavia. The definition of 'white' (i.e. British) was being subtly altered.

On arrival, the new immigrants were put into transit camps. Life there was bleak. They were issued with grey army blankets, a camp pass and a set of rules. The beds in their huts were divided by blankets hung on wire, offering virtually no privacy. Living conditions were generally poor, with the lack of cleanliness typified by the greasy water in which they often had to do their washing up. Water supplies were inadequate and were sometimes cut off, even in the heat of the day.

The mixture of cultures among the migrants caused arguments, particularly between people who had been enemies only a short time previously. The food tended to be cooked in dripping, which some migrants found nauseating. Nevertheless, for all its shortcomings this new wave of migration was a big success, assimilation took place relatively easily, and the change in the make-up of the Australian population soon became visible to everyone.

An added incentive to encourage the British to emigrate was the 'Ten-pound Poms' scheme, so called because adult migrants paid only ten pounds for the journey to Australia, and their kids came along for free. But this policy wasn't directed solely at families. Child migration was the official policy of both governments, as an attempt for a

LEFT: Migrants arriving at an Australian port, 1964

solution to the child poverty, neglect and homelessness that was endemic in Britain. From the Australian government's point of view, it also played a strategic role in increasing the number of little white citizens.

Between 1947 and 1964 nearly ten thousand children were sent on the long and lonely journey to Australia. UK parents were persuaded to hand their children over on the promise that they'd be given healthy lives in the fresh antipodean air, far away from the slums in which they'd been brought up. Children were also taken from British orphanages, only to end up in similar institutions in Australia, where they were often neglected and subjected to physical, psychological and sexual abuse.

An Aerogram from Ireland

Yvonne Radzevicius is sixty-eight years old. At the age of nine months she was sent to a Scottish orphanage, the product of an alcoholic mother and an absent father. At the age of ten she was told her parents were dead and that she was about to be shipped to Australia. She still remembers the train journey to London, with other children crying all around her, being shoved in a shed and kept in a pen, and the endlessly long boat journey.

Her new home at Nazareth House in Western Australia was a brutal, uncaring place. Discipline was harsh (she remembers being deliberately pushed through a glass window by a nun because she had accidentally pulled the veil off the sister's

headdress), and she was compelled to remain in the orphanage until she was seventeen and a half, when she was allowed to leave to train as a nurse. If she'd wanted to go into domestic service she could have left sooner.

Years later, when she was in her early thirties, an aerogram arrived for her from out of the blue. It was from her godmother in Ireland, who'd managed to get hold of her address after several requests for information had been turned down by Nazareth House. Her godmother was at last able to tell her that when Yvonne was little and had been informed by the authorities that her mum and dad were dead, they'd been lying. Both her parents, and her five brothers and sisters, were still alive.

In 1979, she returned to England and, in 1981, she found her mum in a nursing home in London. Finally, in 1990, she went to Ireland and was reunited with her extended family.

I spent a gloriously sunny afternoon talking to her on a headland overlooking Sydney Harbour. She lives in Perth now, and was remarkably positive about her life, but said that one of the worst aspects of her early experiences is that though they toughened her up, she's never learnt how to love properly. She's involved in the Child Migrant Network and says she's one of the lucky ones. She was never subjected to paedophile rings and some of the other despicable experiences that sadly typified those institutions.

The last official child migrant party travelled to Australia in 1967, and the institutions to which the children had been sent began to close in the 1970s. But former child immigrants continue to live with the legacy of this tragically misguided policy.

1914–1942

Here is a Man Whose Death Will Lighten Your Heart

Incident in Port Phillip Bay

The first shot fired in anger at the beginning of World War I wasn't heard in Germany or on the fields of Flanders; it echoed round Port Phillip Bay less than eighty miles from Melbourne!

As August 1914 approached, the whole world waited for the announcement from Europe that hostilities were about to commence. The German steamer SS *Pfalz* was moored at Melbourne, and its captain was eager to get his ship out of Australian waters as quickly as possible before she was detained as a hostile vessel. Short of fuel, he suffered a nervous wait for enough coal to be delivered and loaded. Finally, at dawn on 5th August, the *Pfalz* set off through Port Phillip Bay. Once she'd passed through the heads she would be in open water, after which it would be full speed ahead until she reached

BELOW: The *Boorara*, née the SS *Pfalz*, which attracted the first shot of WWI, in Port Phillip Bay, Victoria

LEFT: One of the big guns of Fort Nepean, c.1943

the safety of South America.

But when the harbour master saw that the *Pfalz* was on the move, he instructed the Examination Service Vessel SS *Alvina* to try to stall her departure, in case word came through that war had been declared. Until he received that confirmation, he couldn't detain the German ship unreasonably, so after much stalling the *Alvina*'s inspection party had to let the *Pfalz* go on its way, at which point a party of German consular officials, who had been keeping an extremely low profile below decks, came out of hiding and began a rowdy celebration.

But as the *Alvina* headed off again, the message that the harbour master had been waiting for came through: the war had begun two and a half hours previously. He immediately dispatched an order – 'Stop the *Pfalz*, or sink her' – but the German ship ignored the signals to heave to. So Richard Veale, a young naval officer

on board the *Alvina*, ran up the H (for hostile) flag, signalling to the nearby garrison artillery that a warning should be fired across the *Pfalz*'s bows. This was followed by the first shot of World War I, fired from a six-inch mark VII gun from the battery at Fort Nepean. History had been made!

An Australian naval pilot bearing the heroic name Captain Robinson was on the bridge of the *Pfalz* guiding her out of the bay. He immediately telegraphed down to the engine room to instruct the ship to turn round and head back to port. But the German captain, realising that his escape was about to be thwarted, countermanded the order and telegraphed 'full ahead'. There followed a tussle on the bridge between the two captains, until Captain Robinson managed to persuade his German counterpart that if he didn't stop immediately, the next shot would go right through his ship.

So the *Pfalz* went back to

Melbourne, the crestfallen diplomats and crew were interned, and the ship was refitted and renamed HMT *Boorara*. For the next few years she was used as an Australian troopship. *Boorara* made it all the way through the war, though she was rammed by a French cruiser and twice torpedoed in the English Channel. As for Richard Veale, the young sailor who ran up the flag to fire . . . we haven't heard the last of him by a long chalk.

N'oublions Jamais (Let Us Never Forget)

It's hard now to comprehend why Australia should have thrown so many of its young men into a war that was taking place 10 000 miles away. But 'Mum' was under threat, and young

Australia was prepared to run to her aid. In 1915, tens of thousands of Australian and New Zealand soldiers (the ANZACs) were thrown into a disastrous, prolonged attempt to open up a new front in Turkey. It was doomed to failure. The ANZACs were machine-gun fodder for the entrenched Turks.

The Western Front was equally grim. At the Battle of Fromelles in 1916, 2000 Australians were killed in a single night, with a further 3500 injured. In the following six weeks there were another 23 000 casualties. Sixty-five per cent of all the men deployed by the Australians in France were killed or injured, the highest percentage among all the Allies. One of the primary reasons why Australia had federated was so that the nation

BELOW: Australia soldiers embarking during WWI, location unknown, c.1915–18

could have its own armed forces. Within seventeen years of Henry Parkes' dream becoming a reality, 60 000 members of those forces had been sacrificed in the 'war to end all wars'. And every single one of those casualties had been a volunteer.

A Simple Solution

By 1918, the war was over, and even though the loss of life had been terrible, the fighting had ultimately been successful, and the fledgling nation had contributed to the defeat of the tyrants in Europe. Now there was another tyranny that demanded attention. Australia is a vast continent comprising small, isolated clusters of population with not much in between. If Australia was to be genuinely united as a nation, the tyranny of distance would have to be overcome.

In Europe or America you don't have to go very far to hit the next town, so language, custom and culture tend to be intimately connected. In Australia you could drive for a day and not see a single human being. Sydney to Brisbane is 1000 kilometres. Melbourne to Perth is 3500 kilometres. In the nineteenth century you had to travel from settlement to settlement by sea, and it could take weeks to get from one port to the next. Western Australia, Queensland, Tasmania, South Australia, Victoria and New South Wales might as well have been different countries. And in a lot of ways, they acted like they were.

They may now have had a national flag, but how were they going to forge a national identity? The answer seemed obvious. Australia had to do what every other developing country had done – build a national railway network to link the population centres. An apparently simple solution,

but one that would prove almost impossible to realise.

It might have been sensible if all the interested parties had sat down and said, 'Gentlemen, let's agree to make all our rail lines the same width apart, so we'll be able to move people and cattle and armies efficiently across our great emerging country.' But they didn't.

In the 1850s, the three major Australian colonies had all wanted brand-new railways. Victoria and New South Wales both decided to build broad-gauge railways, but at the last minute New South Wales employed a British engineer who opted for the English standard gauge instead. Queensland was a massive state but didn't have a big population, so it couldn't afford to splash out so much cash on transportation and chose instead to invest in the world's first narrow-gauge track, which wasn't just cheaper but helped the little

Queensland trains go round bends and up and down hills more easily. To make the situation even more complicated, South Australia opted for a combination of narrow and broad gauge.

So when the mainline systems of the four colonies finally met in the 1880s, they didn't join up. Even in 1917, nearly twenty years after Federation, any passenger who wanted to travel from Brisbane to Perth had to change trains six times.

It was nearly a hundred years after the first railways had been laid down before the national government decided on a uniform standard gauge, and it wasn't until 2004, thirty-five years after man had managed to travel to the moon (without changing spacecraft), before the Adelaide to Darwin standard-gauge railway was finally completed.

Wire From an Old Piano

While the process of building a country-wide railway system was proceeding about as quickly as continental drift, nationhood took off in leaps and bounds, largely due to twentieth-century technologies like the aeroplane.

In the 1890s, an explorer and inventor called Lawrence Hargrave, based in the picturesque village of Stanwell Park, near Wollongong, started experimenting with box kites in order to attempt controlled, manned flight. He managed to link four kites together, fixed a little seat to them, and lifted himself sixteen feet into the air. He never achieved powered flight, but his contribution was an important one, because by demonstrating to a sceptical public that it might be possible to build safe and stable flying machines, he attracted popular support for an all-Australian aeroplane.

Hargrave was a principled man and, because he believed that knowledge should be shared by everyone, he never patented his designs. Consequently, over in the United States the Wright brothers were able to plunder his ideas, although they never admitted it.

'If there be one man more than any other who deserves to succeed in flying, that man is Mr Lawrence Hargrave of Sydney.'
— OCTAVE CHANUTE,
AVIATION PIONEER, 1893

It was another American who received the plaudits for becoming the first man to fly an aeroplane in the antipodes. The famous escapologist

LEFT: Lawrence Hargrave with some of his flying machines, c.1865–1915

ABOVE: Lawrence Hargrave (left) was visited by American inventor and scientist Alexander Graham Bell, at his home in Woollahra Point, Sydney, 1910

Hargrave

In 1889, Lawrence Hargrave revolutionised engine technology by inventing the 'radial rotary engine'. As early as 1892 he'd voiced his opposition to the idea of the 'connection of the flying machine with dynamite missiles'. Nevertheless, the radial rotary engine was extensively used in military aircraft.

He insisted that his working models should be placed somewhere where they'd accessible to the public. The only museum to agree was the Deutsches Technological Museum in Munich. Nearly all his models were destroyed by the Allied aerial bombardment of Germany in World War II.

Harry Houdini was touring the country's major theatres, and in order to drum up full houses took part in several promotional stunts, including leaping into Melbourne's Yarra River shackled by chains, plummeting to the bottom, freeing himself and swimming to the surface, much to the delight of the 20 000-strong crowd. On 21st March 1910, at 7 a.m. near Diggers Rest in Victoria, he surpassed even this piece of derring-do by keeping his Voisin biplane in the air for seven minutes and thirty-seven seconds in the presence of thirty signed witnesses – the first authenticated powered flight in Australia.

A few months after Houdini's piece of showmanship, the first successful all-Australian flight took place. The plane was built and piloted by John Duigan. It took him a year to assemble it, and he used wood, wire from an old piano, steel bands used for baling wool, and a four-cylinder, twenty-five horsepower engine. He then flew it a death-defying twenty-three feet!

This tiny distance may seem a little pathetic, but what Duigan did was remarkable. The plane was jam-packed with his own inventions, because he had virtually no technical information to work with. Not only that, but he'd never flown an aircraft before or even seen one.

But it was the Australian Flying Corps, founded in 1912, that paved the way for future generations of aviators. By the end of World War I, there were four squadrons of Australian pilots. Inspired by their experience, Australia now entered an age of heroic flyers

In the Shit

Such a funny day – we went to see a re-enactment of the first-ever recorded flight by an Australia on Australian soil (made by the Duigan brothers on 16ᵗʰ July 1910 in Victoria, by six nice old blokes who enjoy making replicas of ancient planes. The pilot was even older and lives out in the bush, miles away from anywhere. He was wearing an old-fashioned brown leather flying hat, which made his head look like a little nut, and a pair of huge flying goggles – a gnome riding on a butterfly!

The plane began to move and we all had to run alongside it to make sure the wings didn't scrape the ground. Finally one wheel lifted off – it was really exciting because it had never actually flown before, and the old blokes weren't sure that it could. Then a big gust of wind blew up and knocked it off-course. It was now heading straight for a little truck. But it missed, bounced along for a bit . . . and crashed into a great big pile of cow shit!

We all raced up to make sure the pilot was all right. He clambered out of his plane, staggered up to us and said: 'I've been in and out of the poo for years, but this is the first time that poo has saved my life.'

(not all of whom were men – there were a number of celebrated aviatrixes, including Nancy Bird Walton, the 'Angel of the Outback', who ran the first aerial baby clinic).

In 1920, two former AFC officers, Hudson Fysh and Paul McGinness, established the Queensland and Northern Territory Aerial Service, or QANTAS as it quickly became known. Soon there were flying mail services, overseas flying boats, and the legendary Flying Doctor Service. Distance was no longer a tyranny, it was just a fact of life.

Another Incident in Port Phillip Bay

The first Australian shot fired in anger at the beginning of the World War II wasn't heard in Germany or on the fields of Flanders; it echoed round Port Phillip Bay, about eighty kilometres from Melbourne . . .

No, you're not experiencing déjà vu – it's true! The Second World War got started in the same Australian waters as the First – well, at least Australia's involvement in it did. And even more extraordinarily, the order to fire was given by the same person, and the shot was fired from the same gun!

On 4th September 1939, a small Australian coastal trader called the *Woniora* was sailing through the Heads into Port Phillip Bay. She was ordered to heave-to for inspection to make sure she hadn't been captured by an enemy crew intent on attacking Melbourne. Richard Veale, who had given the signal to fire while on board

the *Alvina* at the start of World War I, was now chief of Port Phillip's Naval Examination Service. Years later he wrote about the World War II incident:

'Guided by my experience of the careless attitude of masters of local trading vessels towards the Naval Examination Service early in the 1914–18 war, I decided to administer a salutary lesson to such people, as soon as possible, in World War II. Therefore I directed the Battery Commander at Fort Nepean to fire a shot across *Woniora*'s bows . . . The publicity given to the firing ensured that all merchant vessels would comply with the Naval Examination Service requirements at every Australian port.'

This may not have been the most heroic incident of World War II, or even as exciting as brave Captain Robinson's death-defying wrestling match on board the *Pfalz*, but at least it ensured that from now on small merchant coasters would treat the Naval Examination Service with a bit more respect!

For the next two and a half years, this was not only the first Australian shot of World War II, it was also the only one fired in anger on Australian soil. As in World War I, the war was being played out on the other side of the world. But once again, Australian troops were present in great numbers, in Libya, Greece, Crete, Syria and Lebanon; and once again, it was in defence of 'Mum'. Great Britain was at war, so Australia had to be too – it may have been the middle of the twentieth century, but old-style nineteenth-century colonial attitudes towards secrurity still dominated Australian politics.

Think of Yourself as an Avenger

The moment this mindset began to alter can be pinned to a single incident, in 1942. Close neighbour Singapore, a crucial piece in the jigsaw of the British Empire, was regarded as the 'Gibraltar of the Far East', an island fortress packed with artillery. Australians could sleep at night confident that this strategically located outpost would protect them from being overrun by the aggressive might of Japan.

But this proved to be a complete fantasy. There may have been 90 000 Allied soldiers protecting Singapore, but many were inexperienced; the Japanese had only 65 000 men, but they were battle-hardened. Their onslaught caught the British napping. The Allies had been expecting an invasion by sea; indeed, virtually all Singapore's much-lauded defences faced seawards. But the Japanese attacked from the opposite direction, through the jungles and mangrove swamps of the Malay Peninsula.

They advanced with incredible speed – many stole bicycles rather than moving on foot. British troops had been told that they were poor fighters, but the reality was they fought with an unequalled savagery. Within days the Allies were in full flight – those injured were killed where they lay; those who

RIGHT: Australian troops leaving Port Melbourne, 16th November 1940 for overseas service

surrendered were shot. Some captured Australian troops were covered in petrol and incinerated. An instruction given to the Japanese soldiers read: 'When you encounter the enemy after landing, think of yourself as an avenger coming face to face at last with his father's murderer. Here is a man whose death will lighten your heart.'

On 8th February they attacked Fortress Singapore itself, murdering the patients at the Alexander Military Hospital as they did so. Despite the ferocity of the attack, Singapore might have been saved, but the Allies hadn't committed enough troops to its defence because they were reserving some for an expected onslaught along the entire coastline. That attack never came though, and on 15th February Singapore fell. The Japanese took 100000 prisoners, including 1500 Australians. It was an abject humiliation for the Allies, and one of the worst defeats in British military history. But

most significantly for Australia, it demonstrated that 'Mum' was no longer able to come to Australia's rescue when she was under threat.

Over Here

Australia was now completely vulnerable to Japanese attack, and when it came, it was from the air. Darwin was hit hard – in fact more bombs were dropped on it than on Pearl Harbour. Ten per cent of the population (243 people) were killed. But the bombardment didn't stop there. Broome was next, then Wyndham, Derby, Port Hedland in Western Australia, and Townsville in Queensland. The Japanese were an irresistible force, and only Australia's vastness protected it from an all-out invasion.

It's hard to believe that the iconic Bondi Beach was once covered in barbed wire, anti-tank traps and all the

LEFT: A Japanese midget submarine being raised from Sydney Harbour after being rammed and sunk in 1942

RIGHT: The Japanese advance on Singapore, through the Malay Peninsula, 1942

RIGHT: Bomb damage to oil tanks in Darwin

ABOVE: The Australian
War Memorial, Canberra

other paraphernalia needed to prevent a sea landing, but even the people of Sydney felt vulnerable. Everyone did their bit, including the Bondi Surf Club. In its minutes of December 1941, it resolved 'to purchase a wooden shovel and a rake for use in event of an air raid'. A couple of months later, though, they would be needing more than a couple of garden utensils to ward off the attack.

As if to prove that they could strike anywhere at any time, on 31st May 1942 two Japanese mini-subs entered the harbours of Sydney and Newcastle. One torpedoed a converted ferry, killing twenty-one sailors, and the other shelled Rose Bay, Woollahra and Bellevue Hill. Australians were shaken to the core. The enemy wasn't 'over there' anymore, it was right here. With Britain embroiled in its own fight for survival, Australia realised it would have to look for new allies. It was the beginning of the end of a very special relationship.

1940 – 2007

The Liberace
of the Law

A Nationalist Larrikin

Herbert Evatt was scarily clever. He'd won a sackful of academic
awards and medals, as well as acquiring three degrees from Sydney
University, all with first-class honours. It's little wonder everyone
called him 'Doc'. He was also a very principled man and dedicated
his life to championing the poor, the vulnerable and the excluded.
Eventually, he became so well respected that he was made president of
the United Nations, the kind of position to which previous generations
of Australians would never have dreamt of aspiring. And yet Doc Evatt
is hardly mentioned nowadays, and a lot of younger Australians haven't

BELOW: Herbert Evatt signs
the UN Charter at a ceremony
in San Francisco, 1945

even heard of him. I think that's a real pity.

It may seem surprising that such a towering figure isn't remembered with the same affection and pride as Roosevelt, Churchill or Mandela. But there was another side to Evatt; he generated huge amounts of anger and resentment, particularly in the Labor Party (of which he was an active member throughout his entire adult life). Some people thought he was an evil and treacherous monster, and the Murdoch press, always an acute judge of political competence and integrity, accused him of 'nationalist larrikinism' (a 'larrikin' being a young hooligan). He certainly had an enormous ego and could be demanding, hectoring and inconsiderate, but he was a master of detail, and worked day and night – even on his honeymoon.

After leaving university, he made such a name for himself as a lawyer that by the age of thirty-six he had been appointed the youngest-ever judge of the Australian High Court (it was he who heard Egon Kisch's appeal, making the celebrated ruling that eventually allowed the communist Kisch to stay in Australia – see page 184).

By the time World War II broke out, Evatt had become a well-established, rather paunchy public figure. But instead of basking in his success, he threw himself into full-time politics, and in particular into the war effort.

He certainly ruffled a lot of feathers. Australia still tended to be treated as a second-class nation by the big powers, but he managed to persuade them to give him all the planes the country needed. The Americans detested him, but he got them to accept that the voice of the world's smaller countries should be heard in the newly created United Nations. And while previously Virtually all Australian diplomacy had been handled by the UK, Evatt realised that in order for Australia to protect herself from any more attacks from Asia, it would need to make itself strong and independent, and so he negotiated a pact with New Zealand to help defend the Pacific – the first time two British dominions had ever signed a major agreement without consulting Mother England!

BELOW: Doc Evatt at the UN, 1949

But his biggest achievement came in 1948. He had already been a key player in setting up the United Nations, but now he was elected president of its General Assembly. Suddenly, an Australian was leading negotiations on behalf of the nations of the world, speaking up for small- and middle-ranking states, and presiding over the adoption of the Universal Declaration of Human Rights. Australia, in the person of Doc Evatt, was now a major player on the world stage – not bad, given that the country was less than fifty years old.

In his later years, Evatt returned to politics and became Labor Party leader. On his good days he still championed liberty and the little guy, but he became increasingly unpopular, so much so that the battle between his supporters and his detractors helped fuel a devastating split in the party a year after he lost the 1954 federal election.

He may have not have been the greatest team leader, and I'm not sure you'd have trusted him much in the cut-throat world of party politics, but Evatt was a visionary and a libertarian, and Australia was transformed by his contribution to its political life.

I Did But See Her Passing By

Throughout the 1950s, Australia had two important relationships – one was with its rich, flashy, confident new lover America, and the other was with its Mum, dowdy old respectable Britain. But however desperate it was to consummate relations with the US,

ABOVE: Prime Minister Robert Menzies with Queen Elizabeth II at an official function during her first visit to Australia in 1954

it wasn't prepared to cut the umbilical cord with Mother.

In 1954, Elizabeth II became the first British monarch to set foot on Australian soil (although, more properly, I should say that she became the first 'Queen of Australia' to set foot on Australian soil, because that's what she was then and remains today). Millions of Australians were bowled over by her.

Back home in England, watching my mum and dad's ten-inch black-and-white television set, I knew she had been a big hit, even though I was only eight years old at the time. I clearly remember besotted Australian crowds waving hundreds of tiny Union Jacks at her. Love was on display, even though the way it was expressed could sometimes be a bit creepy. When she returned in 1963, Prime Minister Robert Menzies recalled her visit with the words of the seventeenth-century poet Thomas Ford: 'I did but see her passing by, and yet I love her till I die.' There was only one love in Australia's life, and there always would be . . . or so I thought.

But the nation became equally loved-up when the president of the United States hit its shores a few years later, in 1966. The Vietnam War was escalating, and Lyndon B Johnson needed help. He drove around in his motorcade, waving and smiling, and said what a great buddy Australia was – it was a shameless piece of spin, and Australia lapped it up. Three quarters of a million people lined the streets of Melbourne. Close to a million turned out in Sydney.

Buoyed by his rhetoric, Australia went 'All the way with LBJ', as quipped by short-lived Prime Minister Harold Holt, into what became the longest major conflict in Australian history.

Johnson's Bitch

The bloody civil war in Vietnam that had been going since 1955 – between North Vietnam, under the leadership of wily old communist revolutionary Ho Chi Minh, and the puppet South Vietnamese government, supported by the US – provided the first real test of Australia's blossoming relationship with the Americans. By the 1960s, South Vietnam was in big trouble. More and more communists were managing to infiltrate their way into its territory, and the army was losing control of the countryside. The South Vietnamese president pleaded with the Americans for additional help, but the US didn't want to appear to be behaving like a big, bad imperialist empire poking its nose into other people's business for its own ends (even if that's exactly what it was doing). It desperately needed the involvement of some of the region's other countries

LEFT: An anti-war protest rally during the visit of South Vietnamese Prime Minister Ky to Sydney, 21st January 1967

Harold Holt
Kisses Ass

Abridged transcript of Australian Prime Minister Harold Holt's telephone conversation with President Lyndon B Johnson on 7ᵗʰ November 1966:

HOLT: *Is that you, Lyndon?*

LBJ: *Glad to hear you.*

HOLT: *I've got some film of you, film of the tour done by our information people, which I'll be sending over. I also want to send you the film we made about our boys in Vietnam, and the Fox Movietone people tell me they've got a film they can let me have if you'd like to see it and I'll get that, too.*

LBJ: *Oh, I wish you would. I'd enjoy it very much.*

HOLT: *All the backwash since the visit has been very good.*

LBJ: *Good. Well, I . . .*

HOLT: *. . . I've recorded the policy speech for the election and I don't think you'll find anything in there that will disappoint you. We're full steam ahead.*

LBJ: *I know there's not anything you and Australia's going to do that disappoints anybody because you're our kind of folks and we got to stay close together and get this job done. We're going to do it.*

HOLT: *Anyhow, congratulations on the tour as a whole. I think it went wonderfully well. It focused attention just where you wanted it focused and you put us all on the alert that the job has to be done.*

LBJ: *Well, we're very pleased with it . . .*

HOLT: *. . . Best wishes to Mrs Johnson. Young Christopher's got your picture hanging up now in the bedroom. It's an inspiration to him . . . I won't bother you again on a telephone call unless it's really of sufficient importance . . .*

LBJ: *Well, it's never a bother. It's always a great pleasure. You just pick up that phone anytime you've raised enough money to do it and we'll do likewise.*

HOLT: *(chuckling) All right . . . Good man, Look after yourself.*

LBJ: *Take care, Harold.*

HOLT: *Bye, bye.*

to give it credibility. That's why LBJ came to Australia – to ensure America was going to get the level of support it needed.

The Australians had already deployed a handful of military advisors in Vietnam, a policy strongly supported by the majority of the public (a 1966 poll found that sixty-four per cent of Australians were in favour of the war effort). But although a lot of people thought the close relationship between Holt and Johnson showed there was a strong and meaningful alliance between their two countries, there were some siren voices who believed that in modern parlance, Holt had become Johnson's 'bitch'. They argued that Holt was being seduced and pressured by his American counterpart in order to make sure Australia increased the number of troops it was prepared to commit.

Certainly, the handful of advisors soon become a two-battalion-strong Australian taskforce, but as the years rolled on and the casualties grew heavier, opposition at home grew, and Vietnam became the most contentious issue in Australian politics since World War I.

The Liberace of the Law

The early 1970s were a fine time to be a young, urban Australian. Amid the ever-growing anti-war demonstrations, the country was beginning to evolve its own unique counterculture. Artists and thinkers like Germaine Greer, Richard Neville, Michael Leunig, Clive James, Barry Humphries and Tom Keneally were attracting widespread attention; the Sydney Opera House was taking shape on the site where Bennelong had lived nearly 200 years previously; Sydney man Patrick White had just been awarded the Nobel Prize 'for an epic and psychological narrative art, which has introduced a new continent to literature'; and most significantly, the old political order – as epitomised by John Gorton (who had succeeded Holt after he mysteriously disappeared on a Victorian beach) and his Liberal Party (which had dominated Australian politics since the end of World War II) – was collapsing amid dithering and fratricidal combat.

It was in this context that two future prime ministers rose to prominence. In many ways they were very similar: they were both lawyers, both republicans, and both had a passion for culture which far exceeded that of most Australian politicians. In other circumstances they might well have been friends. But instead they became bitter enemies.

Gough Whitlam, the Labor Party leader, was from a successful, suburban family and was the author of several books. As deputy leader of the opposition, he'd helped rebrand Labor as a party with which a wide section of society could identify, just as Tony Blair would do so successfully twenty-five years later in the UK. And, like Blair, Whitlam had charisma and a sense of humour, and seemed in every way a prime minister in waiting.

His nemesis was Malcolm Fraser, the rising star of the Liberal Party government. He had studied at Oxford, and though he was tough, he was a thoughtful man, much more of a visionary than most of his relatively undistinguished Liberal Party contemporaries.

Fraser showed his steel when he resigned his post as Defence Minister in 1970, after a dispute with his prime minister. He returned to the front bench after Whitlam led Labor to power two years later, then successfully challenged for the leadership after Whitlam's second victory in 1974. The stage was now set for a battle royal between Fraser and Whitlam, but as events turned out, one man stood between them, although no one could have guessed the part he was about to play in Whitlam's downfall.

John Kerr was the governor-general, the Queen's representative in Australia. This imperial title, once held by political titans like Arthur Phillip and William Bligh, was now largely honorary, and for the previous twenty-five years or so had been little more than a pat on the back for national figures on the verge of retirement. But Kerr took the role very seriously, so much so that when it was offered to him, he only agreed to accept it if he got a guarantee that he'd be able to stay in the post for ten years, and could represent Australia overseas as its head of state. Prior to his appointment, he'd been serving as attorney-general of New South Wales, and because of his dress sense and vanity had been known as 'the Liberace of the Law'. Whitlam plucked him from relative obscurity and gave him the governor-generalship because he thought Kerr would provide a safe pair of hands. It was an appointment Whitlam would live to bitterly regret.

The result of the 1972 election hadn't been a landslide, but it did give Labor control of the country's law-making House of Representatives after twenty-three years in the political wilderness. The upper house, the Senate, which acted as a break on the House of Representatives, remained in the hands of the Liberals (and their National Party allies).

Whitlam immediately set in motion a frenzy of reform: conscription was ended and Australian forces were extricated from Vietnam; the People's Republic of China was formally recognised; sports teams selected on racial grounds were banned (thus boycotting South Africa's hated apartheid regime); the Northern Territory and the Australian Capital Territory were both given Senate seats and their own elected councils; and the 'White Australia' policy was finally abandoned. A promise was made to all Australians that from now on there'd be no discrimination on grounds of race, colour or nationality, and – perhaps surprisingly for such a profound statement of change – the nation seemed quite relaxed about this.

If Whitlam's economic policies had been as successful as his social reforms, he might well have been in office for as long as Tony Blair. But whereas his English counterpart had the good fortune to preside over a rosy economy, Whitlam was scuppered by the 1973 Yom Kippur War in the Middle East, which led to the Arab nations cutting supplies of oil to the West and a crippling threefold rise in petrol prices. Whitlam was in big trouble. He wanted to carry on with his expansive and expensive reforms (including his massively costly 'Let's Buy Back the Farm' campaign to stop foreign investors from buying huge tracts of

Australia, extracting the minerals and taking them out of the country), but all the Western economies were now suffering, and Australia's was in meltdown.

After retaining power in the 1974 election, the government then made a colossal mistake. It attempted to borrow US$4 billion to develop Australian natural resources and energy projects, not from 'responsible' bankers, but from a Pakistani businessman called Tirath Khemlani, one of hundreds of so-called 'runners' based in the Middle East who peddled often phoney loans to large borrowers. Whether Khemlani could really have got hold of such a colossal amount of money, and how far the negotiations went, no one knows or is prepared to say, but confidence in Whitlam evaporated.

Fraser, having seized leadership of the Opposition, now went for the jugular. He couldn't control the lower house but he could stop Whitlam's laws being ratified in the upper one, and when the Supply Bill (which stipulated the amount of money the government was allowed to spend) went to the Senate, Fraser and his colleagues stopped it dead in its tracks. Within weeks, Whitlam would run out of money with which to govern the country.

This was the moment when it would have been appropriate for the governor-general to intervene by knocking both men's heads together, in a subtle and diplomatic way so they didn't notice the pain. But he chose not to do so. Instead, on 11th November 1975, after some

desultory negotiations, and without prior warning, he called Whitlam to Government House and handed him a letter of dismissal. Whitlam was incensed. Malcolm Fraser, who had already been briefed by Kerr about what was going to happen and was waiting in another room, was then invited by the Kerr to form a new government. When the speaker of the House of Representatives attempted to remonstrate with the governor-general and tell him he had outstripped his authority, Kerr refused to see him.

Later that day the governor-general's proclamation was read out at Parliament House by a young secretary in a smart suit with microphones hovering in front of his face. It finished with the traditional words 'God Save the Queen', at which point Whitlam stepped in front of the microphones and added: 'Well may we say "God save the Queen", because nothing will save the governor-general. The proclamation you have just heard was countersigned "Malcolm Fraser", who will undoubtedly go down in Australian history . . . as Kerr's cur.'

Despite Whitlam's rancour, Fraser won the subsequent election and went on to hold the office of prime minister for the next seven years, although towards the end of his tenure he fell foul of his party, which had always thought him too progressive. Years later, he and Whitlam put aside their differences and campaigned together in support of an Australian republic.

But John Kerr never recovered from the acrimony generated by his fateful decision. For the rest of his term as governor-general he was beset by demonstrators and boycotted by Labor politicians. He'd always had a reputation for enjoying a tipple – cartoonists of the time used to caricature him with a bottle in his hand – but towards the end of his time in office, while presenting the 1977 Melbourne Cup, he appeared to be steaming drunk in full view of the public and the cameras. He was a broken man. Despite his original ambition to serve as governor-general for ten years, he resigned on health grounds even before his first term had been completed. He spent the last few years of his life in London, where, as journalist Phillip Knightley put it, 'he could be seen most days, usually the worse for wear, at one or other gentlemen's club'.

I remember 'the Dismissal' really well. It was on the front pages of all the UK newspapers and we looked on in fascination to see how it would play out. Surely the Australians wouldn't tolerate the Queen's representative sacking their elected government? Wouldn't this be the moment when Australia would take its destiny into its own hands and sever its constitutional ties with the UK? We waited with bated breath . . . and nothing happened!

There was certainly a tidal wave of outrage, but it was directed at Sir John Kerr, not at Elizabeth Windsor. And it's true there were a few stirrings of republican sentiment: in 1991, republicanism became the official policy of the Australian Labor Party; two years later, references to the Queen were removed from the Oath of Office, and instead naturalised Australians

LEFT: Sir John Kerr (right) takes a load off with former prime minister Robert Menzies, 1977

ABOVE: The fingerprints of British colonialism still abound in Australia

Australian, and how they felt about 'Mum'.

Many of us in England were gobsmacked when the result was announced – the Australian people had voted by fifty-five per cent to forty-five to keep Her Majesty as head of their household. Why didn't they decide to go it alone? Was it because the row over what sort of republic Australia should be muddied the waters? Was it because Australians truly wanted to remain nestled in the bosom of the UK? Or was it simply another example of the typical Australian 'she'll be right' attitude – 'If it ain't broke, don't fix it'?

Don't expect a Pom to answer that conundrum!

Out of the Shadows

In the second half of the twentieth century, Australia had been growing up as a country but, until the late 1960s, it had forgotten its elders – the people who had lived there for at least forty millennia. The Aboriginals were strangers in their own land, barely tolerated guests rather than citizens. Their land had been taken, their identity had been taken, even their children had been taken.

But, partly inspired by the example of black civil-rights campaigners in the US, activists among the Aboriginal community began raising their heads above the parapet. Charles Perkins and a coach-load of his fellow students went on a freedom ride through Aboriginal communities to draw attention to the sub-standard conditions in which so many Indigenous Australians

now swore an oath to 'Australia and its people'; laws were brought in which inhibited Australian institutions from having the word 'Royal' in their title, and the awarding of knighthoods was ended. Nevertheless, the Queen of England remained the Queen of Australia, and her appointee still held the magisterial office of govenor-general.

A quarter of a century after the Whitlam affair, though, the perfect opportunity arose to transform Australia's constitution. In 1999, a referendum was held on the question of whether the nation should finally split from Britain and become a republic. After 211 years of British occupation, it would be a true test of how Australians felt about being

were living. A Gurindji man named Vincent Lingiari led a walk-out of 200 Aboriginal stockmen from the British-owned Vesteys cattle station south of Darwin, protesting the appalling wages and conditions. They then established their own settlement and demanded the return of their tribal lands. They asked the United Nations to intervene on their behalf, but their claim was unsuccessful. Ultimately, though, it led to the Commonwealth Land Rights Act, which saw the Gurindji receive the freehold of 3250 square kilometres of their land.

In 1967, Australians went to the polls to consider changes to the Constitution that would address discrimination against Aboriginals. There were two articles in question. One stipulated that Aboriginals couldn't be included in the national census – and in that respect they were non-people. The other said that the federal government didn't have the

right to make special laws to deal specifically with Aboriginal welfare and advancement.

The referendum resulted in 90.8 per cent of Australians voting to right those wrongs. Some people think this was little more than a gesture, and it certainly didn't address all the issues confronted by Aboriginal Australia overnight, but it was a sign of the changing times.

More Aboriginal people than ever before were preparing to take their place in Australian society, and were only too happy to remind the rest of the nation when it was tardy in delivering on its promises. In 1972, on the night before Australia Day, young activists set up an 'Aboriginal Tent Embassy' outside Parliament House in Canberra. It's still there thirty years later, acting as a constant thorn in the side of those parliamentarians who might otherwise conveniently forget the issues that still beset the

native Australian population: poor life expectancy and health, high rates of imprisonment and deaths in custody, drug and alcohol dependence, high suicide rates, and of course, lack of representation in positions of authority.

Kicking and Screaming

Eddie Mabo was a young gardener from the Torres Strait Islands (situated between Cape York and Papua New Guinea), who worked at James Cook University in Townsville. One day in 1974, he was having lunch with some of the university's teaching staff, who were wryly amused at the way he talked about the island on which he'd been brought up as if it was his own. They tried to explain to him that this wasn't the case – it didn't belong to him or any other member of the Mabo family; it belonged to the occupant of Buckingham Palace! Eddie couldn't accept this – as far as he was concerned, his people had a right to their land and he was prepared to fight for it.

Consequently, Mabo became the focal point for a campaign which challenged the whole notion of *terra nullius* – that the land had belonged to no one when the colonials arrived. The case eventually went to the High Court but was thrown out, not because the arguments weren't convincing but because Eddie wasn't his father's natural son, and so, according to the law, had no right to inherit.

But five months after Eddie Mabo died in 1992, the High Court reversed its decision. From now on, Torres Strait Islanders would be able to make

LEFT: Eddie Mabo, whose name is now synonymous with Native Title

legal claims on their land. This was a milestone for native Australians. It blew the notion of *terra nullius* right out of the water, and offered Indigenous Australians the possibility of righting some of the wrongs that had been inflicted on them during the previous two centuries.

Of course, some conservatively minded politicians and their friends in the media were driven hysterical about this ruling. They said it would open the floodgates to Aboriginals trying to reclaim the whole of Australia, and terrified white citizens being dragged kicking and screaming from their suburban homes.

Up until the time of writing, this hasn't been the case! There have been many successful 'Native Title' claims made by Aboriginal groups across the nation, which award rights over what can and can't be done on tribal lands. But suburban Australians have remained undisturbed in their beds.

Sorry Seems to be the Hardest Word

For all their pious words, no Australian prime minister had been prepared to apologise to the Aboriginals for the cruelties of the past. In a sense this is understandable; nobody can be blamed for the sins of their forefathers, and anyway, the white population of Australia couldn't just pack up and leave . . . they'd have nowhere to go. But matters came to a head at the 2000 Sydney Olympics when there was a huge public protest by those who wanted an official apology to be made, particularly to the Stolen Generations of Aboriginals and Torres Strait Islanders who had been removed from their families and culture. Nevertheless, despite the groundswell of public opinion, the Liberal Party Prime Minister John Howard adamantly refused to say the 's-word'. To do so, he argued, would merely be empty rhetoric – and costly empty rhetoric at that, if irate Aboriginals started suing the government.

His fellow party member and former prime minister, the doughty Malcolm Fraser, now recast as a liberal statesman in more conservative times, disagreed:

'The attempt to separate "practical" from "symbolic" reconciliation seems to mean that the government will not acknowledge past wrongs, and will not accept any obligation to redress the effects of unjust treatment. But it is only possible

225

to share responsibility to answer
a problem once agreement has
been reached on each party's
responsibility for causing the
problem . . .'

– MALCOLM FRASER, PATRON OF
THE NATION SORRY DAY COMMITTEE,
PRESS RELEASE, 27TH APRIL 2005

The moment finally came in February
2008, when freshly sworn-in Labor
prime minister Kevin Rudd stood in
parliament and said the magic word.
At last, white Australia had publicly
recognised the terrible injustices it had
inflicted on its Aboriginal brothers
and sisters.

I interviewed the former PM and he
told me that he'd apologised not just
because it was his party's policy, but
because he passionately thought it was
the right thing to do.

Kevin Rudd: We'd been in the
wrong for a long, long, long time and it
was palpable, you could just feel it . . .
When I prepared the speech I had no
idea how it was going to go down –
lead balloon, or whatever – had no
idea that we'd actually be listened to
abroad. But I think when you try to
reflect honestly on what we've done,
there's no way you can justify stealing
generations of Aboriginal children,
taking them away from their parents.
It was just not humane.

TR: How long after you'd become
prime minister did you make that
statement?

KR: It was the first day of the
parliament. I thought it was important
to deal with the business early on.
It was a deeply emotional occasion
here, but I think it's added to healing

TOP: Crowds gather outside Parliament House to watch the Prime
Minister's historic 'Apology to the Stolen Generations', 2008
ABOVE: The former Prime Minister, Kevin Rudd, leads me through the
corridors of power

bonds. Certainly when I walk around
the place now and I meet Aboriginal
Australians they always give you a hug
and a cuddle, because there's something
fundamental about the extension of
basic human respect. And I think it's
made the country feel somewhat better
about itself. But that's the symbolism –
the substance is . . . closing the gap
further between the 'indidge' and 'non-
indidge' Australians. And that's still got
a long ways to go.

Rudd Tells Me Where To Go

WED 9.30 p.m. Melbourne
I may have lost my Kevin Rudd interview! It's really upsetting. You don't get an interview with an ex-PM every day. A Wikileaks story's broken that he told the Americans he'd support them if they attacked China. Huge furore. Shall I fly to Canberra and see if I can talk to him, or will it be a waste of time?

THURS 8.30 a.m. Canberra
What a media circus! I can't even get into the parliament building.

THURS 10.30 a.m. Canberra
Interview cancelled. Rudd can't get out. Maybe later?
I'll hang around for a bit. Return flight's at 6 p.m.

THURS 12.30 p.m. Canberra
Rudd can maybe reschedule for 5.30 p.m. I've changed my flight.

THURS 9 p.m. On flight to Melbourne. What a brilliant performer. He'd flown in from the Middle East this morning and looked a bit rough – he'd obviously shaved without a mirror. But he was relaxed, joked about the Wikileaks business and was incredibly candid. A fantastic interview. He talked candidly about politics but did the funny stuff too. I stopped him in mid-flow when he was going on about why the referendum had failed. 'Sorry, Kev,' I said, 'do you happen to know the Test score?' (We've been hammering the Aussies in Adelaide.) 'Bugger off!' he says, without losing his stride for a moment, then gets straight back to what he was saying. If there's one thing that separates politicians from us mere mortals, it's resilience.

The Splayd and Other Contributions to Making the World a Better Place

From the earliest days of European settlement the colonists were devising new bits and pieces to help them survive and prosper. Australia soon became a nation of 'bush mechanics'.

The Ute

'Could you please make a car that we can go to church in on Sunday and take the pigs to market in on Monday?' This was written by a Gippsland farmer's wife to Ford's managing director in 1932. Bank managers at the time were happy to lend money to farmers to buy a farm truck, but not a saloon car; hence the woman's plea! Thus, the utility vehicle (or 'ute') was born, with the front half of a sedan car and the rear end of a small lorry. It became a symbol of the nation, ideal for the needs of the small farmer . . . and the small farmer's wife.

The Splayd

Australian inventions are all about making life easier. The sweat of the convicts, the harshness of the environment and perhaps a little bit of Irish-influenced 'lateral thinking' have led to the attitude 'Bugger this, I'll fix it myself'. This is epitomised by the 'splayd' (a knife, fork and spoon all in one implement). Why lug three eating utensils around with you if you can make do with just one?

Vegemite

In the fine tradition of the very best inventions, the famous spread solves problems and meets needs. How can we get rid of our old brewers' yeast? What can we give the kids to spread on their toast? The English had their Marmite, and when an Australian came up with a similar product, he held a competition to choose its name and his daughter pulled 'Vegemite' out of a hat. But in an effort to grab more market share, the name was briefly changed to 'Parwill', an attempt at humour based on a tedious and tortuous piece of wordplay:

Q: Who might like a brown, syrupy, salty spread made from the sludge that coagulatesat the bottom of the barrel when you're brewing beer?

A: Ma-might, but Pa-will!!

Ho, ho, ho! How strange that they changed its name back to Vegemite.

It's a Beautiful Country. Really Cold. It's Right Near Switzerland.

So, 240 years after Cook landed, what is an Australian? Statistically, it's a 38-year-old woman living in either New South Wales or Victoria. She has 1.9 children and is married. She jogs or does some sort of routine exercise, and thinks she's in okay shape but may actually be a bit overweight. She works in a service industry and earns around $750 a week. She was born in Australia, but at least one of her parents or grandparents wasn't. She has sex 1.84 times a week, which she thinks isn't enough, and she'll probably die of heart disease.

BELOW: One of the golden beaches that epitomise Austria… er, *Australia*

But there's another answer to that question. Six and a half million people have migrated to Australia since the end of World War II. Nowadays they don't just come from Europe, but from every country in the world. In Australia's migrant Olympics, the UK is still in first place and neighbouring New Zealand in second, but just behind and coming up fast in bronze-medal position is China, followed by India, Italy, Vietnam, Philippines, South Africa, Malaysia and Germany.

Dress Him in Drag!

The Sydney suburb of Bankstown is named after Joseph Banks, but there are few other echoes of its early colonial antecedence. Nowadays it teems with Vietnamese tea shops and noodle bars, and it's where Anh Do was brought up.

Anh is in a similar line of business to me. He's a stand-up comic and television personality. He's confident, extroverted and totally at ease with the crowds who continually try to grab his hand and press him for a photo opportunity, as well as with the local shopkeepers who point at him and wave packets of sausages in his face. But like so many Australians throughout the country's stormy 223-year history, his cheerful demeanour and mateyness obscure a nightmare past.

He and his family escaped from South Vietnam in 1975 when Anh was two, after the communists had defeated the South Vietnamese army and its American allies. They left their village by canoe under cover of darkness and headed towards the sea.

Communist patrols were everywhere watching for escapees, so Anh's mum stuffed sticky rice into her children's mouths to stop them making a noise and giving the game away. Eventually, they reached the coast and boarded a battered old fishing boat, shook off a pursuing Vietcong patrol boat and escaped into international waters. The boat was overcrowded, the sun was fierce and there was very little drinking water. One young man became overcome by delirium, jumped into the sea and disappeared.

After a couple of days, the exhausted escapees saw a ship heading towards them. They thought they were about to be rescued, but as the

BELOW: Anh Do, a friendly face of modern Australia

About Bloody Time

1895 *South Australia becomes first parliament in the world to allow women to stand for election.*

1902 *Federal Australia grants women the right to vote and to seek election. (Right to vote had been also been established in South Australia in 1895, and in Western Australia in 1899.)*

1921 *Edith Cowan (left) is the first woman elected to any Australian parliament, in Western Australia.*

1943 *Forty-one years after being permitted to run, first women elected to Australia's federal parliament – Dorothy Tangney (Senate) and Enid Lyons (House of Representatives) – about bloody time!*

1990 *Carmen Lawrence becomes first female premier, in Western Australia.*

2002 *Marion Scrymgour (Northern Territory government) becomes the first female Indigenous minister in any Australian government.*

2008 *Australia appoints its first female governor-general, Quentin Bryce.*

2010 *Julia Gillard (below) becomes Australia's first female prime minister.*

vessel came nearer they realised it was full of pirates. They boarded the little fishing boat brandishing knives and guns, and stole everything of value, including the ship's engine. The huddle of refugees were now at the mercy of the sea, but at least they were still alive.

But then the same thing happened again. Another boat approached and the refugees cried out for help, but it was more pirates, who stripped them naked, looking for any small items the first pirates might have missed. They ripped the nappy off Anh's baby brother Khoa, and found a tiny piece of gold hidden in it. As a punishment for not handing it over, they dangled baby Khoa overboard and threatened to drown him. But eventually they relented and returned to their own boat, leaving the refugees with absolutely nothing – except that just before they sailed off, the youngest pirate threw a gallon container of water into the battered boat. This little act would save thirty-nine lives.

On the fifth day the castaways were picked up by a German boat, which took them to the Pulau Bidong refugee camp in Malaysia. Eventually, the Australian government offered to take them in. Anh's dad told the authorities he'd heard about Australia. 'It's a beautiful country,' he said. 'Friendly people, but really cold. It's right near Switzerland.' Anh told me this story with all the verve of a professional performer. At some moments it was hard to believe it wasn't simply part of his act.

When they finally arrived in Sydney, two smiling nuns gave them a big garbage bag stuffed with second-hand clothes, including two pairs of jeans. Anh's mum was in seventh heaven. The only time she'd ever seen jeans before had been on posters for cowboy movies. Now she had the wardrobe of a movie star. But something had been lost in translation. On the nun's list the children were described as a boy and a girl rather than two boys. So for the first few weeks in his newly adopted country, Anh's brother was forced to wear blouses and dresses.

Khoa is now as successful as his brother. He's a moviemaker and a recent recipient of the Young Australian of the Year award. 'It's because of that early experience,' Anh told me, winding up for the punch line like comedians the world over. 'If you want your baby son to become Young Australian of the Year – dress him in drag!'

But Anh's arrival in Australia had been a false dawn in its immigration history, I said. Things have never been as good since. I reminded him how, just before the 2001 federal election, Prime Minister John Howard had demonised refugees by falsely claiming that a boatful of Iraqis had thrown their children overboard in order to attract the attention of the Australian Navy. And that even today a lot of Australians, just like their ancestors at the time of the gold rush, regarded people like him as the 'Yellow Peril' – faceless hordes swamping Australia with their spring rolls, their chopsticks and their devious capacity for hard work. But Anh wasn't having any of it.

'Australia's a great country!' he retorted. 'What you're talking about isn't racism. Maybe we just need a bit more humanity, that's all. And anyway, things are better today.'

'But what about all those forms you have to fill in if you want to get into this country, with questions like "Which arm of government has the power to interpret and apply laws – Legislative, Executive or Judicial"? Or "What is the name of the proposal to make a law in parliament – The Royal Assent, Bill or debate"? Aren't they just a bureaucratic way of excluding non-Europeans who haven't got a sophisticated grasp of English?'

'Yes, that's true,' he conceded. 'If they want immigrants with the Aussie spirit, they ought to ask questions like: "It's raining, it's Saturday morning, do you mow the lawn or do you wait till tomorrow?"'

However much I probed him, I couldn't get him to say anything bad about Australians or the welcome they give to newcomers. Maybe that's just the kind of bloke he is.

Anh does less stand-up nowadays and much more corporate work. The big companies find the story of his rise from boat-person to successful citizen very motivating, and it's easier work than schlepping around the clubs night after night. He's even written an autobiography that topped the bestseller lists. He's got a wife, three kids and a golden career ahead of him. He's the epitome of the successful new Australian.

Oh, and I later discovered that the shopkeepers waved sausages at him because his face is on the pack. The sausage company is owned by his dad, and Anh has been doing a bit of promotional work for him on the side.

Stroppy Buggers

I'm almost ashamed to admit it, but after crossing the length and breadth of the continent listening to what Australians had to say, I've come to the conclusion that, by and large, transportation worked!

Of course, it didn't work for the convicts who died at sea or were flogged or hanged. It didn't work for the Aboriginals who were robbed of their land and massacred, and you could say it didn't work for much of the environment, which was stripped bare by generations of convicts' children.

But the convicts themselves were kept healthy and well fed, they were educated and given skills, and a lot of them were political dissidents, so although they may have been stroppy buggers, they were articulate and organised. They lived in a brand-new state created from scratch by caring men like Governor Phillip, who were big on justice, good government and the family, and their influence is still writ large in Australia today.

Add to that the commitment and toughness of the bounty immigrants, the resilience and drive of the women settlers, the work ethic of the Chinese diggers, the expertise of the Northern Europeans and the energy of the new waves of immigrants like Anh Do and his family, and you've got a pretty intoxicating ethnic cocktail – they're all part of the culture that's made Australia so special, so remarkable and unique . . . Oh, and yes, they're still stroppy buggers.

Bibliography

Tony Robinson's History of Australia is the result of lengthy conversations I had over the spring and summer of 2010 with some of Australia's finest historians. In particular, many thanks to Thomas Keneally, Tim Flannery and Professor Eric Willmott for their friendship and support, and for helping me develop an overview of Australian history. Thanks also to those below for sharing with me a lifetime's passion for their particular subjects. The insightful parts of this book are theirs, any errors are mine alone.

Captain Ross Mattson, Endeavour Replica; Dr Nigel Erskine, Curator, National Maritime Museum; Dr Wayne Johnson, archaeologist, Sydney Harbour Foreshore Authority; Jake Cassar, environmentalist; Rex Gilroy, author and adventurer; Steve Spillard, local historian; Cheryl Ward, PhD, RPA; Grace Karskens, historian, University of NSW; Alison Frommel, Education and Interpretation Officer, Sydney Harbour YHA; Binowee Bayles, Aboriginal Education Officer, Sydney Harbour Foreshore Authority; Jacqui Newling, Colonial Gastronomist, Historic Houses Trust, NSW; David Thompson, NSW National Parks and Wildlife Service; Lynette Ramsay Silver, historical investigator; Sean Fagan, Wadawurrung Aboriginal Corporation; Dr Liz Rushden, author and historian; Lyndall Ryan, Honorary Conjoint Professor, School of Humanities and Social Sciences, Faculty of Education & Arts, Ourimbah Campus, University of Newcastle; Dr Stephen Gapps, Australian National Maritime Museum; Shirani Aththas, Communication Officer, Australian National Maritime Museum; Hamish Maxwell-Stewart, Associate Professor University of Tasmania; Dr Ted Higginbotham, archaeologist; Paul Brunton, Senior Curator, Mitchell Library; Warren Brown, political cartoonist; Gren Silvester Henty, Henty descendant; Dave Phoenix, President of the Burke and Wills Historical Society; Dr Fred Cahir, University of Ballarat; Robyn Annear, author; Geoff Hocking, author; Kieran Hosty, Australian National Maritime Museum; Pauline Reid, Pre-Fab Houses, National Trust; Professor Marilyn Lake, President, Australian Historical Association; Joan Mitchell-Willis, dictation examiner, Scottish Gaelic Society of Victoria president; Yvonne Radzevicius, Child Migrant Network; Anh Do, entertainer and former refugee; Major Bernard (Bernie) Gaynor; Geoffrey Blainey AC, historian and author; Terry Egan, Duigan Project Chief and Instigator; Bruce Vickers, pilot and Chief Flying Instructor; Elizabeth Evatt, Evatt family member; James O'Loghlin, lawyer, TV presenter of The New Inventors; Kevin Rudd, Australian Foreign Minister and former PM.

Four books and one DVD have kept me focused while wrestling with Australia's history. The books are *Origins to Eureka* by Thomas Keneally, *The Colony* by Grace Karskens, *The Birth of Sydney* by Tim Flannery and the magisterial *Great Southern Land* by Frank Welsh. The DVD is *The First Australians*, directed by Rachel Perkins, which tells the continent's history from an Aboriginal perspective.

I also plundered the following books and websites on specific subjects.

CAPTAIN COOK

The Goat Who Sailed the World, Jackie French
www.anmm.gov.au/webdata/resources/pdfs/vessels/Endeavour.pdf
www.foundingdocs.gov.au/resources/transcripts/nsw1_doc_1768.pdf
(Cook's secret orders)
www.waterencyclopedia.com/Mi-Oc/Navigation-at-Sea-History-of.html

EARLY ARRIVALS

Guns, Germs and Steel, Jared Diamond

'Showdown in the Pacific: A Remote Response to European Power Struggles in the Pacific, Dawes Point Battery, Sydney, 1791-1925', Wayne Johnson, *Historical Archaeology*, 2003
Correspondence between Raymond Johnson, Egyptologist and author, and Dr Abou-Ghazi, Library of Egyptian Museum

EGYPTIANS

http://members.ozemail.com.au/~classblu/egypt/article.htm
www.mysteriousaustralia.com/egyptians_australia_mainpage.html

http://travel.webshots.com/photo/2870442180064923513dKBYxG?
    vhost=travel
http://heritage-key.com/blogs/ann/all-aboard-ancient-egyptian-
    ship-sails-legendary-land-punt
www.donsmaps.com/hoax.html
www.facebook.com/?ref=home#!/group.php?gid=364461693426
http://woywoynet.blogspot.com/2010/04/gosford-glyphs-2010-
    update.html

DAMPIER
A New Voyage Around the World, William Dampier, including
    introduction by Sir Albert Grey, 1927
'Dampier, William (1651–1715)', J Bach, *Australian Dictionary
    of Biography*, Volume 1, Melbourne University Press, 1966
Captain William Dampier, Buccaneer-Author, W H Bonner,
    Stanford, 1934
The Brethren of the Coast, P K Kemp and C Lloyd, London, 1960
William Dampier, Sea-Man Scientist, J C Shipman, Kansas, 1962
'William Dampier', L R Marchant, *Journal and Proceedings (Royal West-
    ern Australian Historical Society)*, vol 6, part 2, 1963
The Great American Barbecue and Grilling Manual, Smoky Hale, 2000,
    referenced in en.wikipedia.org/wiki/Barbecue
www.historyofaustraliaonline.com/William_Dampier.html
www.nndb.com/people/943/000096655/
www.sharkbay.org/default.aspx?WebPageID=181

FIRST FLEET CONDITIONS
The Fatal Shore, Robert Hughes
members.iinet.net.au/~perthdps/convicts/ships.html

JOSEPH BANKS
The Endeavour Journal of Joseph Banks, ed. Paul Brunton

LA PÉROUSE
Where Fate Beckons: The Life of Jean-Francois de la Perouse,
    John Dunmore
1788: Journals of Watkin Tench, ed. Tim Flannery

TANK STREAM
www.timeoutsydney.com.au/mediacontent/slideshow/tank-stream/
    tank-stream-tour/index.html)
www.cityofsydney.nsw.gov.au/waterexhibition/WaterSupplySewerage/
    TheTankStream.html
www.creativespirits.info/oznsw/sydney/sitescbd/tankstream.html
www.hht.net.au/__data/assets/pdf_file/0019/9145/
    Tank_Stream_1.pdf
The Tank Stream, Sydney Water (DVD)

THE ORGY
http://residentjudge.wordpress.com/2009/08/14/the-foundational-orgy/
www.thefreelibrary.com/Grace+Karskens,+The+Colony%3A+a+history+
    of+early+Sydney.-a0228508622
www.smh.com.au/news/entertainment/books/book-reviews/the-colony-
    a-history-of-early-sydney/2009/07/07/1246732326891.html

BRADLEY AND FOOD
1788: The Brutal Truth of the First Fleet, David Hill
Sydney Cove 1789–1790, John Cobley
Sydney's First Four Years, Watkin Tench
The First Fleet: A new beginning in an old land, John Nicholson, 1995

*Foodways Unfettered: Eighteenth-Century Food in the Sydney
    Settlement*, Jacqueline Anne Newling, 2007
The Sydney Gazette and New South Wales Advertiser
    (NSW: 1803–1842), Sunday 6 October 1805
A Voyage to New South Wales, William Bradley, c.1802
www.anmm.gov.au/site/page.cfm?u=1415&c=3164
www.anmm.gov.au/webdata/resources/files/
    Signals_84_pp10-15_TheCharlotteMedal.pdf
http://adbonline.anu.edu.au/biogs/A010134b.htm
www.acms.sl.nsw.gov.au/item/itemDetailPaged.aspx?itemID=412904
www.manly.nsw.gov.au/IgnitionSuite/uploads/docs/Hunter%20and%20
    Bradley%20survey.pdf
www.manly.nsw.gov.au/IgnitionSuite/uploads/docs/Capture%20of%20
    Bennelong%20in%20North%20Cove.pdf

ARABANOO AND PEMULWUY
Pemulwuy: The Rainbow Warrior, Eric Willmott
www.manly.nsw.gov.au/IgnitionSuite/uploads/docs/Capture%20of%20
    Arabanoo%20at%20Manly%20Cove.pdf

THE SPEARING OF PHILLIP
www.manly.nsw.gov.au/IgnitionSuite/uploads/docs/The%20Spear-
    ing%20of%20Governor%20Phillip%20at%20Collins%20Cove.pdf

EARLY SYDNEY ARCHAEOLOGY
A History of Sydney's Darling Harbour, Wayne Johnson and Roger Parris
Inside the Rocks: The Archaeology of a Neighbourhood, Grace Karskens
Painting the Rocks: The Loss of Old Sydney, Paul Ashton, Caroline
    Butler-Bowden, Anna Cosso, Wayne Johnson
Anchored in a Small Cove, Max Kelly
www.thebigdig.com.au/history/

PINCHGUT/FORT DENISON
www.sydneyarchitecture.com/ROC/QUA03.htm
http://aso.gov.au/titles/newsreels/australia-today-fort-denison-p/clip1/
www.smh.com.au/news/entertainment/good-living/restaurant-reviews/
    fort-denison-cafe-and- restaurant/2009/08/17/1250362024232.html

WALK TO CHINA
Tour to Hell: Convict Australia's Great Escape Myths, David Levell, 2008
The Sydney Gazette and New South Wales Advertiser,
    Sunday 26 June, 1803
http://newspapers.nla.gov.au/ndp/del/page/5720?zoomLevel=1
http://davidlevell.wordpress.com/tour-to-hell/chapters/
www.irishecho.com.au/tag/irish-vanguard
www.manly.nsw.gov.au/IgnitionSuite/uploads/docs/Convicts%20
    and%20Bushrangers(1).pdf
www.sl.nsw.gov.au/events/exhibitions/2006/ontherun/docs/captions.pdf

VINEGAR HILL REBELLION
The Battle of Vinegar Hill, Lynette Ramsay Silver
The 1804 Australian Rebellion and Battle of Vinegar Hill, Cameron Riley,
    Hawkesbury Historical Society, November 2003
www.hawkesburyhistory.org.au/articles/Battle_of_Vinegar.html
www.abc.net.au/tv/rewind/txt/s1209455.htm

SEAL HUNTER ATROCITIES
The Aboriginal Tasmanians, Lyndall Ryan
'The Cross Cultural Relationships Between the Sealers and the Tasma-
    nian Aboriginal Women at Bass Strait and Kangaroo Island in the

Early Nineteenth Century', *The Flinders University Online Journal of Interdisciplinary Conference Papers*, Kay Merry, Department of History, September 2003
www.theaustralian.com.au/news/arts/the-far-from-fatal-shore/story-e6frg8nf-1111115425471
www.themonthly.com.au/files/Quadrant_article_10_December_2003.pdf
www.historycooperative.org/journals/lab/85/ryan.html
www.smh.com.au/articles/2002/12/13/1039656215202.html
www.abc.net.au/schoolstv/australians/truganini.htm

PORT ARTHUR
Port Arthur's Separate Prison, published by Port Arthur Historic Sites
Caught In the Act, Phillip Hilton and Susan Hood
A Short History Guide to Port Arthur, 1830-77, Alex Graeme-Evans
Convict Records from State Library of Tasmania Archives
Charles Darwin in Hobart Town, published by The Royal Society of Tasmania
Tasmania travel guide, Lonely Planet
www.portarthur.org.au/index.aspx?base=1324

JOHN AINSWORTH HORROCKS
The Explorers, Tim Flannery
Horrocks family papers, PRG 966 (State Library of South Australia)
http://adbonline.anu.edu.au/biogs/AS10231b.htm

BURKE AND WILLS
The Dig Tree: The Story of Burke and Wills, Sarah Murgatroyd
Dig 3ft NW: The Legendary Journey of Burke & Wills, Sarah Murgatroyd
Where is Here?, Tim Flannery
www.burkeandwills.net.au/

MITCHELL
A People's History of Portland and District, 'The True History of the Hentys', J G Wiltshire
'Henty, Thomas (1775 – 1839)' *Australian Dictionary of Biography*, Volume 1, M Bassett
www.cultureandrecreation.gov.au/articles/greatdividingrange/
http://romareilly.tripod.com/mitchell/mitchell.htm
www.slv.vic.gov.au/ergo/the_hentys_at_portland_NEW

MACARTHUR
Man of Honour: John Macarthur, Michael Duffy, 2003
www.cultureandrecreation.gov.au/articles/macarthurs/
http://colsec.records.nsw.gov.au/indexes/colsec/m/f35c_maa-macg-03.htm
www.campbelltown.nsw.gov.au/default.asp?iNavCatId=1888&iSubCatId=2090
www.heritage.nsw.gov.au/07_subnav_01_2.cfm?itemid=5051536
http://elizabethfarm.wordpress.com/2007/03/05/duelling-pistols/
www.smh.com.au/articles/2003/01/24/1042911538043.html
www.brisbanetimes.com.au/news/queensland/piracy-duels-get-the-chop/2008/04/29/1209234808331.html

CAMDEN PARK
Convict Workers: Reinterpreting Australia's Past, Stephen Nicholas
Belgenny Farm, 1805-1835: The Early Years of the Macarthurs at Camden, Peter Mylrea, Camden Historical Society, 2007
Belgenny Farm, Peter Mylrea, 2000
The History of Studley Park, Ray Herbert
'Summary of Report on the Archaeological Excavation of the site of the 'Small Miserable Hut', Near Belgenny Farm, Elizabeth Macarthur Avenue, Camden, NSW', Ted Higginbotham, 2010
www.camdenhistory.org.au/Studley%20Park.pdf
www.records.nsw.gov.au/state-archives/resources-for/historians/convicts
www.environment.gov.au/heritage/places/national/hyde-park/information.html
www.hht.net.au/discover/highlights/guidebooks/hyde_park_barracks_museum_guidebook2
www.hht.net.au/discover/highlights/insites/convicts
www.sl.nsw.gov.au/discover_collections/history_nation/justice/convict/convict.html
www.oldbaileyonline.org/browse.jsp?ref=t17890708-34
www.belgennyfarm.com.au/about_belgenny

RUM REBELLION
Man of Honour: John Macarthur, Michael Duffy, 2003
The Rum Rebellion: Australian Rebellion, Cameron Macintosh, 2009
Letter to Elizabeth Macarthur, 1808 original manuscript, donated by Colonel J W Macarthur-Onslow and Miss R S Macarthur-Onslow, 1940, ML A 2898
www.sl.nsw.gov.au/events/exhibitions/2008/politicspower/docs/bligh_guide.pdf
www.smh.com.au/multimedia/2008/rumrebellion/main.html
www.sl.nsw.gov.au/about/media_centre/2008/Rum_rebellion_MRelease.pdf
www.australianstamp.com/coin-web/aust/earlyaus.htm#RumTradeAnchor

MYALL CREEK
Down Under, Bill Bryson
http://en.academic.ru/dic.nsf/enwiki/776918

GOLDRUSH
Nothing But Gold, Robyn Annear
Castlemaine: From Camp to City, Geoff Hocking
The Argus, September 21, 1851
www.sbs.com.au/gold/story.php?storyid=32
www.cultureandrecreation.gov.au/articles/goldrush/

MONSTER MEETING
www.egold.net.au/movies/democracy.htm
www.egold.net.au/biogs/EG00230b.htm

EUREKA
Eureka: from the official documents, ed. Ian MacFarlane, Public Records Office, Melbourne, 1995
The Rebel Chorus: Dissenting Voices in Australian History, Geoff Hocking
www.egold.net.au/biogs/EG00185b.htm
http://sheducationcom.ascetinteractive.biz/uploads//SovHill%20lawandorder%20notes%20ss1.pdf

LOLA MONTEZ
www.sl.nsw.gov.au/discover_collections/history_nation/gold/miners_life/montez/index.html

ABORIGINALS

Black Gold: A History of the Role of Aboriginal People on the Goldfields of Victoria, 1850–70, Dr David 'Fred' Cahir, School of Business, University of Ballarat

CHINESE

Our South Australian Past, Kathleen Bermingham
The Fourth of Eleven Tales of Robe, Kathleen Bermingham
www.prov.vic.gov.au/forgottenfaces/goldfields.asp

FEDERATION

Australia: A Social and Political History, Gordon Greenwood

BOUNTY IMMIGRANTS

Single & Free: Female Migration to Australia, 1833–1837, Elizabeth Rushen
http://libraries.hobsonsbay.vic.gov.au/Page/PagePrint.asp?Page_Id=249

THE DUNBAR

Dunbar, 1857: Disaster on Our Doorstep, Kieran Hosty
'Shipwreck that shook Sydney to the core', Steve Meacham, *Sydney Morning Herald*, 18 August 2007
'Melancholy Shipwreck: Loss of the Dunbar', *Sydney Morning Herald*, Wednesday 26 August 1857
'Shipping Column', *Sydney Morning Herald*, 29 September 1856
www.anmm.gov.au/site/page.cfm?u=1527
http://maritime.heritage.nsw.gov.au/public/documents/dunbar_cmp.pdf
www.maritime.nsw.gov.au/docs/wh/hornby_scroll.pdf

TICONDEROGA/QUARANTINE

Fever Beach, Mary Kruithof
Quarantined! The 1837 Lady Macnaghten Immigrants, Perry McIntyre and Liz Rushen
A Short History of the Nepean Peninsula, Richard Cotter
Pilot's Log, Captain Henry John Mollett Draper, Vol. 35 No. 1, issue 147
www.nepeanhistoricalsociety.asn.au/quarantine.html
www.parkweb.vic.gov.au/1park_display.cfm?park=281

HENRY PARKES

An emigrant's home letters, Henry Parkes, with preface and notes by Annie T Parkes
http://museumvictoria.com.au/journeys/life_at_sea.asp
http://museumvictoria.com.au/journeys/recording_1850_70s.asp
www.parlpapers.sl.nsw.gov.au/display.cfm?parl_id=15400

WHITE AUSTRALIA

Drawing the Global Colour Line: White Men's Countries and the International Campaign for Racial Equality, Marilyn Lake with Henry Reynolds
Creating a Nation, Marilyn Lake, with Patricia Grimshaw, Ann McGrath and Marian Quartly
Kisch in Australia: The Untold Story, Heidi Zogbaum
http://museumvictoria.com.au/journeys/immigration_restriction.asp
www.migrationheritage.nsw.gov.au/exhibition/objectsthroughtime/immigration-restriction-act/
www.immi.gov.au/media/fact-sheets/08abolition.htm
www.abc.net.au/100years/EP2_2.htm
www.hyperhistory.org/index.php?option=displaypage&Itemid=730&op=page

www.theage.com.au/news/Reviews/Kisch-in-Australia/2004/11/18/1100748127435.html?from=storyrhs

TRAINS

www.infrastructure.gov.au/transport/publications/files/history_of_road_and_rail.pdf
www.cultureandrecreation.gov.au/articles/railways/
www.infrastructure.gov.au/rail/trains/history.aspx
http://users.tpg.com.au/users/ipether/ausrhist.html
www.natrailmuseum.org.au/history.php
www.gobyrail.net/allaboard.html

FLIGHT

www.duiganreplica.org.au
http://museumvictoria.com.au/collections/items/405751/aeroplane-duigan-biplane-mia-mia-victoria-1910
www.ctie.monash.edu.au/hargrave/hargrave_bio_large_print.html

WORLD WAR I

Letter from Commander Veale to the Military Historical Society of Australia, 1983
www.firstworldwar.com/features/declarationsofwar.htm
www.parkweb.vic.gov.au/1park_display.cfm?park=281

WORLD WAR II

Letter from Commander Veale to the Naval Historian, Navy Office, 1975
www.awm.gov.au/atwar/ww2.asp

DOC EVATT

http://evatt.labor.net.au/publications/papers/211.html
http://evatt.labor.net.au/about_evatt/
www.toyandrailwaymuseum.com.au/leuralla-australia'sdrevat.html
www.lib.flinders.edu.au/resources/collection/special/evatt/evattbiog.html
www.toyandrailwaymuseum.com.au/leuralla-househistory.html
www.heritage.nsw.gov.au/07_subnav_01_2.cfm?itemid=1170133

INVENTIONS

www.whitehat.com.au/australia/Inventions/InventionsA.html
www.powerhousemuseum.com/exhibitions/success_innovation.php

8 X 8 X 8

www.rupertswood.com/5560850/rupertswood-mansion-cricket-the-ashes.htm
www.8hourday.org.au/history.asp
www.cricketweb.net/cricketbooks/6536.php

MULTICULTURAL OZ

The Happiest Refugee: A Memoir, Anh Do
'30 years ago today, the first Vietnamese boat people arrived', *The Age*, Farah Farouque, April 26 2006
www.citizenship.gov.au/_pdf/cit_chron_policy_law.pdf
www.citizenship.gov.au/learn/cit_test/_pdf/australian-citizenship-nov2009.pdf
www.citizenship.gov.au/learn/facts-and-stats/
www.citizenship.gov.au/_pdf/sep-2009.pdf
www.migrationheritage.nsw.gov.au/exhibitions/objectsthroughtime/objects/tudo/
www.anmm.gov.au/webdata/resources/pdfs/vessels/Tu_Do.pdf
www.awm.gov.au/atwar/vietnam.asp

Image sources

Except where noted below, photographs and video stills are courtesy of WTFN and Foxtel.

NATIONAL LIBRARY OF AUSTRALIA
PAGE 15: *The Bark, Earl of Pembroke, later Endeavour, leaving Whitby Harbour in 1768*, Thomas Luny **PAGE 26:** *Captain Cook taking possession of the Australian continent on behalf of the British crown, AD 1770, under the name of New South Wales*, Samuel Calvert **PAGE 28:** *An animal found on the coast of New Holland called kangaroo*, after a painting by George Stubbs, Rex Nan Kivell Collection **PAGE 28:** *Nouvelle-Hollande, Ile King, le wombat*, Choubard, Rex Nan Kivell Collection **PAGE 28:** *Nouvelle-Hollande, Nelle. Galles du Sud, ornithorinque...*, Choubard, Rex Nan Kivell Collection **PAGE 28:** Tasmanian devil picture card, W.D. & H.O. Wills, 19–? **PAGE 76:** Aborigines cooking and eating beached whales, Newcastle, New South Wales, Joseph Lycett, c.1817 **PAGE 84:** *Australian Aborigine*, Port Jackson Painter, Rex Nan Kivell Collection **PAGE 88:** *The pioneer, in 1788 Captain Arthur Phillip R.N. proceeded from Botany Bay to Port Jackson*, H. Macbeth-Raeburn **PAGE 92:** General chart of Terra Australis or Australia: showing the parts explored between 1798 and 1803, M. Flinders Commr of HMS Investigator **PAGE 128:** *Meeting of Major Mitchell and Edward Henty*, Portland Bay, 1836, J. Macfarlane from descriptions by C.R. Long **PAGE 161:** Sir Henry Parkes at his desk in the Office of the Colonial Secretary, Sydney, 1891 **PAGE 185:** Unidentified Chinese fruit and vegetable hawker with baskets of produce, from *Australian Reminiscences* **PAGE 225:** Walk for Reconciliation, Sydney Harbour Bridge, Corroboree 2000, Loui Seselja

STATE LIBRARY OF NSW
PAGE 67: One of the NSW Aborigines befriended by Governor Macquarie, 1810–21? **PAGE 96:** *Joseph Platt receives 100 lashes for running away*, artist unknown, woodcut, from *The horrors of transportation as related by Joseph Platt, who was transported for fourteen years! With an account of the hardships he endured, and his return to England*, Birmingham, c.1849 **PAGE 125:** Sir Thomas Livingstone Mitchell, c.1830s **PAGE 214:** Protest march and meeting addressed by Arthur Calwell during visit of Prime Minister Ky of South Vietnam to Admiralty House (Kirribilli), Anna Clements, C. J. Duff, Jack Hickson, Saturday, 21 January 1967

MITCHELL LIBRARY, STATE LIBRARY OF NSW
PAGE vi Map of the Southern Hemisphere showing the discoveries made in the Southern Ocean up to 1770, enclosed with a letter from Captain James Cook to the Earl of Sandwich, 6 February 1772 **PAGE 16:** James Cook – Papers, 1768-1773, together with associated papers, ca.1775, 1830, 1901 **PAGE 28:** Koala and young, 1803, J.W. Lewin **PAGE 40:** *Old Tank Stream Sydney*, J.B. Henderson, 1852 **PAGE 53:** *First interview with the Native Women at Port Jackson New South Wales*, William Bradley, *A Voyage to New South Wales*, 1802+ **PAGE 54:** *A Family of New South Wales*, engraved by William Blake after a painting by Philip Gidley King, 1793 **PAGE 57:** *Sydney Cove, Port Jackson 1788*, William Bradley, *A Voyage to New South Wales*, 1802+ **PAGE 62:** *Governor's House at Sydney, Port Jackson 1791*, William Bradley, *A Voyage to New South Wales*, 1802+ **PAGE 64:** Cnr. Cambridge and Harrington Street, under section of Essex Street **PAGE 68:** Australian Aboriginals pre 1806, attributed to George Charles Jenner and William Waterhouse **PAGE 69:** Banks Papers – Series 36a, Papers of Sir Jospeh Banks – charts and illustrations, ca 1790s, 1803 **PAGE 70:** *Taking of Colbee & Benalon. 25 Novr 1789*, William Bradley, *A Voyage to New South Wales*, 1802+ **PAGE 72:** Painting of Bennelong, Australian Aboriginals pre 1806, by William Waterhouse, c.1793 **PAGE 112:** Plan of the Camden Estate in the county of Camden, property of James & William Macarthur, Esq. showing the extent of agriculture, 1847 **PAGE 115:** The arrest of Governor Bligh, 1808 **PAGE132:** *The Start of the Burke and Wills Exploring Expedition from Royal Park, Melbourne, August 20, 1860*, William Strutt **PAGE 142:** *Governor Davey's Proclamation to the Aborigines, 1816*, c.1828–30 **PAGE 160:** *Eureka Stockade riot, Ballarat, 1854*, J.B. Henderson, 1854 **PAGE 165:** *Wreck of Dunbar South Head*, Dr Doyle's sketch book, John Thomas Doyle & Samuel Thomas Gill **PAGE 172:** Sir Henry Parkes, *Eminent citizens [of] New South Wales*, 1850–1900 **PAGE 192:** Huge crowd in the Domain to hear Communist Party speaker Egon Kisch, 18 November 1934 **PAGE 202:** Photographs and drawings of flying and other machines, c.1865–1915, Lawrence Hargrave

DIXSON LIBRARY, STATE LIBRARY OF NSW
PAGE 22: *Mr. Banks*, painted Benjamin West, engraved J. R. Smith **PAGE 86–87:** *A direct north general view of Sydney Cove, the chief British settlement in New South Wales as it appeared in 1794, being the 7th year from its establishment*, attributed to Thomas Watling, Dixson Galleries, c.1794 **PAGE 107:** *John Macarthur 1767–1834*, c.1850s **PAGE 113:** *Camden Park House*, Conrad Martens, Dixson Galleries **PAGE 136:** *Pioneer party leaving Cooper's Creek, Burke and Wills Expedition*, Samuel Thomas Gill, Dixson Galleries **PAGE 183:** England v Australia Cricket Match at the Sydney Cricket Ground, January 27 1883

STATE LIBRARY VICTORIA
PAGE 79: *Pimbloy [Pemulwuy] Native of New Holland in a canoe of that country*, S. J. Neele, 1804, Rare Books Collection **PAGE 94:** Dog Guard, Eaglehawk Neck, postcard c.1914–41 **PAGE 130:** Morgan Sticking up the Navvies, Burning their Tents, and Shooting the Chinaman, published in the *Illustrated Melbourne Post*, January 25 1865 **PAGE 140:** Australian Aborigines – War., published in the *Illustrated Melbourne Post*, Samuel Calvert, 27 May 1867 **PAGE 145:** Unearthing the Welcome Stranger Nugget, W. Parker, 1869 **PAGE 148:** Distant View of Mafeking, Victoria, W. Hale, 1900 **PAGE 152:** Lola Montez, C.D. Fredericks, 1856 **PAGE 158:** *Peter Lalor*, Ludwig Becker, 1856 **PAGE 184:** Section of the Eight Hours Day Procession showing columns of men marching behind banners, May 1, 1895 **PAGE 186:** Stage coach laden with luggage and many Chinese people en route to the goldfields, c.1860 **PAGE 197:** Boorara X Pfalz, Allan C. Green, c.1900–54 **PAGE 199:** Australian Soldiers Embarking, T.P. Bennett, c.1915–18 **PAGE 209:** Japanese advance on Singapore, through Malay Peninsula, c.1942

NATIONAL ARCHIVES OF AUSTRALIA
PAGE 207: Embarkation from Port Melbourne on 16 November **PAGE 212:** Dr H. V. Evatt at the United Nations, 1949 **PAGE 213:** Robert Menzies with Queen Elizabeth II on Australian tour, 1954 **PAGE 215:** Mr Harold Holt and President Lyndon Johnson, 1966 **PAGE 219:** Gough Whitlam greets the crowd gathering outside Parliament House on 11 November 1975 **PAGE 220:** Sir John Kerr with Sir Robert Menzies at his home, 1977

NATIONAL GALLERY OF AUSTRALIA
PAGE 222: Prime Minister Gough Whitlam pours soil into hand of Vincent Lingiari, Northern Territory, 1975, © Mervyn Bishop/Licensed by Viscopy

NATIONAL GALLERY OF VICTORIA
PAGE 138: *Arrival of Burke, Wills and King at the deserted camp at Cooper's Creek, Sunday evening, 21st April 1861*, oil on canvas, John Longstaff, Gilbee Bequest, 1907

KERRY STOKES COLLECTION
PAGE 1: *The landing of Dampier*, Norman Lindsay, c.1925

NATIONAL GEOGRAPHIC
PAGE 8: Sea Cucumber (*Bohadschia graeffei*) spawning, Great Barrier Reef

KEITH MCINNES PHOTOGRAPHY & TECHNICAL
PAGE 83: Statue of Arthur Phillip, Royal Botanic Gardens, Sydney

MUSEUM VICTORIA
PAGE 148: Sailing Ships Moored at Sandridge Railway Pier, Port Melbourne, Victoria, circa 1880

NATIONAL MARITIME MUSEUM (UK)
PAGE 17: Portrait of Cook, William Hodges, c.1775, © National Maritime Museum, Greenwich, UK. Acquired with the assistance of the © National Heritage Memorial Fund

AGENCE FRANCE-PRESSE
PAGE 33: Tall Ships parade, Australia Day, 2011

NZETC COLLECTIONS, VICTORIA UNIVERSITY OF WELLINGTON LIBRARY
PAGE 21: Black Stains on the Skin called Tattoo New Zealand, *The Endeavour Journal of Joseph Banks 1768–1771 [Volume Two]*

THE LIBRARY OF CONGRESS
PAGE 27: *Endeavour beached at Endeavour River for repairs after her grounding on the Great Barrier Reef in 1770*, Johann Fritzsch, published 1786

ART GALLERY OF BALLARAT
PAGE 157: The Eureka Flag, 1854

DREAMSTIME
PAGE 31: Captain Cook Monument in Cooktown, Queensland

UNITED NATIONS
PAGE 211: Herbert Evatt Signs the United Nations Charter, 26 June 1945, San Francisco

AUSTRALIAN WAR MEMORIAL
PAGE 198: A 6-inch gun of the Port Phillip Fixed Defences, Point Nepean, Victoria, 1943–4 **PAGE 208:** Japanese midget two-man submarine captured in Sydney Harbour, 1 June 1942 **PAGE 209:** Blazing buildings light up the night, after the bombing of Darwin by Japanese carrier borne aircraft on 19 February 1942

CITY OF SYDNEY ARCHIVES
PAGE 216: Sydney Opera House under construction, 5 March 1966

STATE RECORDS, NSW
PAGE 173: Emigration poster, c.1883

JOHN OXLEY LIBRARY, STATE LIBRARY OF QUEENSLAND
PAGE 191: Mapoon boys outside dormitory, Western Cape York, c.1910

STATE LIBRARY OF WESTERN AUSTRALIA
PAGE 194: Migrants arriving at Fremantle, 1953, Ship arriving at Fremantle 1940s, Naturalisation ceremony – swearing allegiance to the Queen, Woorooloo 1955

POWERHOUSE MUSEUM
PAGE 203: Hargraves and Graham Bell in Woollahra Point, 1910

NEWSPIX
PAGE 224: Eddie Mabo, News Ltd, Saturday 1 January 2000 **PAGE 231:** Julia Gillard, June 25, 2010

ARCHIVES OFFICE OF TASMANIA
PAGE 94: Relics of Convict Discipline, 1900

ST JOHN'S ANGLICAN CATHEDRAL
PAGE 121: St John's Cemetery Guide, Parramatta

SENATE RESOURCE CENTRE
PAGE 178: Opening of the First Parliament of the Commonwealth of Australia, 9 May 1901

THE BULLETIN
PAGE 187: *The Mongolian Octopus – his grip on Australia*, Phillip May, *The Bulletin*, 21 August 1886

THE PUNCH
PAGE 226: Crowds gather outside Parliament House for Sorry Day, Phil Hillyard

Index

Acknowledgements

Many thanks to Shaun Gilmartin, Daryl Talbot, Steve Oemcke, Ben Ulm and Lucy Cooke, for ensuring the success of this project and looking after me in Australia.

Thanks to Shayne Bailey, Lisa Bennett, Peter Coleman, Dave Collins, Sean Cousins, Bill Cox, Ben Crane, Anna George, Tracey Hastie, Terry Hopley, Jenna Matheson, Ben Nguyen, Christine Perkins and Mary Wagstaff, for their unswerving support.

Thanks also to Melissa Fletcher, Olwyn Jones, and Juvae Williams for putting the TV research together, Jenny Brown, Jane Manning, and Rowan McGillicuddy for their work on the scripts, to Ben Ball and everyone in the office at Penguin Australia, but particularly to my editor Michael Nolan for his help, advice and incisive notes, and, as always, to my agent Sarah Dalkin for her good counsel, affection and business acumen.

Finally, thanks to Alice Ford for her research and fact-checking, my PA Heli Mathias for typing the manuscript, additional research, proofing and advice, and to Louise Robinson for her secretarial work, love and support throughout the journey.

VIKING

Published by the Penguin Group
Penguin Group (Australia)
250 Camberwell Road, Camberwell, Victoria 3124, Australia
(a division of Pearson Australia Group Pty Ltd)
Penguin Group (USA) Inc.
375 Hudson Street, New York, New York 10014, USA
Penguin Group (Canada)
90 Eglinton Avenue East, Suite 700, Toronto, Canada ON M4P 2Y3
(a division of Pearson Penguin Canada Inc.)
Penguin Books Ltd
80 Strand, London WC2R 0RL England
Penguin Ireland
25 St Stephen's Green, Dublin 2, Ireland
(a division of Penguin Books Ltd)
Penguin Books India Pvt Ltd
11 Community Centre, Panchsheel Park, New Delhi – 110 017, India
Penguin Group (NZ)
67 Apollo Drive, Rosedale, North Shore 0632, New Zealand
(a division of Pearson New Zealand Ltd)
Penguin Books (South Africa) (Pty) Ltd
24 Sturdee Avenue, Rosebank, Johannesburg 2196, South Africa

Penguin Books Ltd, Registered Offices: 80 Strand, London WC2R 0RL, England

First published by Penguin Group (Australia), 2011

10 9 8 7 6 5 4 3 2 1

Text copyright © Tony Robinson 2011

The moral right of the author has been asserted

Cover and text design by Laura Thomas © Penguin Group (Australia)
Cover images: Sydney Opera House – Frank Chmura/Getty Images,
Map image – J. Archer/Getty Images
Typeset in Sabon by Post Pre-press Group, Brisbane, Queensland
Colour Reproduction by Splitting Image, Clayton, Victoria
Printed and bound in China by 1010 Printing International Ltd

National Library of Australia
Cataloguing-in-Publication data:

Robinson, Tony, 1946–
Tony Robinson's history of Australia / Tony Robinson.
9780670075843 (hbk.)
Includes bibliographical references and index.
Australia – History.

994

penguin.com.au